EN BREVE

THIRD EDITION

A Concise Review of Spanish Grammar

EN BREVE

THIRD EDITION

A Concise Review of Spanish Grammar

Seymour Resnick
QUEENS COLLEGE OF THE CITY UNIVERSITY OF NEW YORK

William Giuliano
QUEENS COLLEGE OF THE CITY UNIVERSITY OF NEW YORK

With the Collaboration of Phyllis M. Golding
QUEENS COLLEGE OF THE CITY UNIVERSITY OF NEW YORK

HOLT, RINEHART AND WINSTON
HARCOURT BRACE COLLEGE PUBLISHERS
Fort Worth   Philadelphia   San Diego   New York
Orlando   Austin   San Antonio
Toronto   Montreal   London   Sydney   Tokyo

Publisher: Ted Buchholz
Senior Acquisitions Editor: Jim Harmon
Developmental Editor: Marsha Hall
Foreign Language Project Editor: Lupe Garcia Ortiz
Senior Production Manager: Tad Gaither
Senior Art Director: Serena B. Manning
Illustrator: Faith DeLong
Text Designer: Rita Naughton
Compositor: P&M Typesetting, Inc.

Cover Image: Werner Forman Archive,
Museum of Archeology, Madrid /Art Resource, N.Y.

Address for Editorial Correspondence:
Harcourt Brace College Publishers, 301 Commerce Street, Suite 3700, Fort Worth,
TX 76102.

Address for Orders:
Harcourt Brace & Company, 6277 Sea Harbor Drive, Orlando, FL 32887.
1-800-782-4479, or 1-800-443-0001 (in Florida).

Printed in the United States of America

ISBN: 0-15-500748-3

Library of Congress Catalog Card Number: 93-77580

5 6 7 8 9 0 1 2 016 9 8 7 6 5 4 3

Contents

Preface

This third edition of EN BREVE preserves its basic purpose: to offer a clear, lively, concise, and practical review of grammar with varied functional exercises. By not including *extensive* reading and conversational material found in most other review texts, EN BREVE affords instructors the opportunity to select plays, stories, poetry, or conversational material of their own choice. We have clarified some grammar explanations and have revised many exercises to make them more communicative in order to stimulate greater student interest.

Although we prefer the grammatical sequence we have developed, there is enough flexibility for instructors to present certain lessons at an earlier point. As an example, some instructors may wish to present *para/por* or the subjunctive earlier. Much of the material in Lesson 12, e.g., numbers, telling time, days and dates can be presented at any time. Some instructors may wish to postpone or deemphasize certain topics of a more difficult nature.

Other features of EN BREVE are the following:

1. Each grammar section is immediately followed by one or two exercises which allow students to check their comprehension of the grammatical principle involved. Answers to these section exercises are supplied in Section A of the Appendix, so that self-study may be done effectively to save class time. We suggest that these exercises be assigned regularly and spot-checked occasionally to be sure that they are being done carefully. This guided study at home then makes the **Basic Class Exercises** (without answers) at the end of the lesson much easier for the student.

2. The numbers of the **Basic Class Exercises** correspond to the numbered grammar sections. Thus, a student who has difficulty with an exercise can quickly refer to the section involved and restudy it. These basic exercises give complete practice in the grammar of the lesson. Following the **Basic Class Exercises**, there is

an optional section called **Elective Exercises**. These exercises are not limited to one grammar principle as are the **Basic Class Exercises**. They are more comprehensive, usually involving several or all of the grammatical elements discussed in the lesson. Instructors may choose from these exercises the ones which best suit the needs of their class.

3. A review exercise based on the previous lesson is included at the end of each lesson. In addition, after Lessons 6 and 12, there are comprehensive review sections covering the preceding six lessons.

4. Verbs are given special attention in EN BREVE. Formation and use of tenses are treated systematically in the first eight lessons, the indicative in Lessons 1 to 5, and the subjunctive in Lessons 6 to 8. Other grammatical principles are also included in these lessons.

5. Each lesson contains a section on **Idioms and Word Study** with corresponding exercises to build vocabulary and to gain facility in the use of important idioms. In eight of these sections we have added a brief, practical conversational supplement.

6. In order to enliven the study of grammar, numerous proverbs and selections from many poems and songs have been used to illustrate grammatical points. These selections may also serve to introduce mini-culture capsules. The poets represented range from the Renaissance to the 20th century, and include some of the greatest names of Hispanic literature: the Marqués de Santillana, Jorge Manrique, Santa Teresa, Gil Vicente, Calderón, Góngora, Espronceda, Bécquer, Rosalía de Castro, García Lorca, Sor Juana, Martí, Darío, Nervo, Gabriela Mistral and others. Most of the poems and songs used here are popular favorites, known by heart by many speakers of Spanish. More complete versions of thirteen songs appear in Appendix C. (For convenient reference, we have indicated these selections with a dagger [†] in the body of the text.) It is suggested that the student memorize some of the poems, songs and proverbs, both for esthetic pleasure and as an aid in remembering vocabulary and grammatical constructions. We have chosen some of our favorite selections and hope that they will appeal to both instructor and student. Each instructor, of course, may have individual preferences to supplement or replace the selections used in this text.

7. We have also made brief adaptations of six works of literature for use in a variety of exercises:

Cervantes, the windmill episode in Chapter VIII of *Don Quijote*
Fernán Caballero, *La Gaviota*
Alarcón, *El libro talonario*

Pardo Bazán, *Primer amor*
José Hernández, *Martín Fierro*
López y Fuentes, *Una carta a Dios*

We hope that these brief adaptations, along with the poems referred to above, will whet the students' appetite and will provide the instructor with the opportunity to expand on the wealth and charm of Spanish literature.

8. Appendices include the answers to the section exercises, a discussion of important deceptive cognates, songs, a brief review of stress, syllabication and orthography, and tables of regular, irregular and stem-changing verbs.

9. A second color has been added to the text in order to highlight important grammatical concepts. We hope that this will clarify explanations and verb charts and will facilitate studying.

10. Throughout the text we have tried to inject a light, humorous touch, both in grammatical examples and exercises, as well as in our choice of proverbs, poems and songs.

Acknowledgments

We gratefully acknowledge the following reviewers for their valuable comments:
   Nelson Arana, University of South Dakota
   Rafael E. Correa, California State University, San Bernadino
   John Griggs, Glendale Community College
   John Koppenhaver, Wichita State University
   Marcie Paul, St. Norbert College
   Salvatore Poeta, Villanova University
   Jorge Silveira, Hampden–Sydney College
   Phil Thomason, Pepperdine University
   Lourdes Torres, University of Kentucky

We are indebted to the many users of EN BREVE, both at Queens College and at other universities who have offered suggestions for this revision. We also wish to thank Marsha L. Hall and Lupe Garcia Ortiz of Holt, Rinehart and Winston for their valuable assistance in the preparation of this edition.

Lesson 1

1 Gender of Nouns

2 Plural of Nouns

3 Idioms and Word Study

4 The Present Tense

1 Gender of Nouns

A. Spanish nouns are either masculine or feminine.

Most nouns ending in **-a** or denoting female beings are feminine.
Most nouns ending in **-o** or denoting male beings are masculine.

el libro *the book*	la mesa *the table*
el hijo *the son*	la hija *the daughter*
el hombre *the man*	la mujer *the woman*
el rey *the king*	la reina *the queen*

B. Nouns ending in **-ción, -sión, -dad, -tad, -tud, -umbre** are feminine.

la canción *the song*	la expresión *the expression*
la ciudad *the city*	la multitud *the multitude*
la libertad *the liberty*	la costumbre *the custom*

NOTE: **La persona,** the person, and **la víctima,** the victim, are feminine even when referring to a male.

Es una buena persona.	*He (or she) is a fine person.*
La víctima está ahora en el hospital.	*The victim (he or she) is now in the hospital.*

C. Nouns ending in **-ista** may be either masculine or feminine.

el artista *or* la artista	*the artist*
el pianista *or* la pianista	*the pianist*
el socialista *or* la socialista	*the socialist*

D. Days of the week are masculine, and are not capitalized.

el lunes	*(on) Monday*
el martes	*(on) Tuesday*

E. Names of rivers, oceans, seas, and mountains are generally masculine.

el Amazonas *the Amazon*	el Mediterráneo *the Mediterranean*
el Atlántico *the Atlantic*	los Andes *the Andes*

F. The letters of the alphabet are feminine.

la a, la be, la ce, la o, etc.

G. Many masculine nouns ending in **-o** have a feminine equivalent in **-a.**

el hermano *the brother*	la hermana *the sister*
el sobrino *the nephew*	la sobrina *the niece*
el suegro *the father-in-law*	la suegra *the mother-in-law*
BUT: el yerno *the son-in-law*	la nuera *the daughter-in-law*

H. There are many nouns whose gender cannot be determined by their ending.

el origen *the origin*	la sal *the salt*
el mes *the month*	la gente *the people*
el timbre *the bell, stamp*	la flor *the flower*
el tren *the train*	la tribu *the tribe*
el lápiz *the pencil*	la luz *the light*

I. A number of nouns ending in **-ma** are masculine.

el clima *the climate*	el poema *the poem*
el drama *the drama*	el problema *the problem*
el idioma *the language*	el tema *the theme, topic*

NOTE: The following nouns ending in -a are masculine.

el día *the day*	el cometa *the comet*
el mapa *the map*	el planeta *the planet*
el poeta *the poet*	

J. The following nouns ending in **-o** are feminine.

la mano *the hand*

la foto (la fotografía) *the photo*

la moto (la motocicleta) *the motorcycle*

la radio *the radio*

K. Before a feminine singular noun beginning with stressed **a-** or **ha**, **el** or **un** is used. The plural retains the feminine form of the article.

La mejor salsa, el hambre. *(Proverb)*

Gato escaldado del agua fría huye. *(Proverb)*

Han contaminado las aguas puras del lago.

Tengo un hambre atroz.

Hunger is the best sauce.

A scalded cat runs away from cold water.

They have polluted the pure waters of the lake.

I am famished. (I have a fierce hunger.)

L. Some nouns are used in the masculine or feminine but with different meanings.

el capital *the capital (money)*

el corte *the cut (of cloth or with a knife)*

el cura *the priest*

el frente *the front (battle)*

el guía *the guide (male)*

el orden *the order (arrangement)*

el Papa *the Pope*

el pez *the fish*

la capital *the capital (city)*

la corte *the court (of law)*

la cura *the cure*

la frente *the forehead*

la guía *the guidebook or the guide (female)*

la orden *the order (command)*

la papa *the potato (in Spanish America)*

la pez *the tar*

EXERCISE 1

Place the appropriate definite article before the following nouns.*

1. _____ juventud **2.** _____ tema **3.** _____ educación **4.** _____ cabeza
5. _____ artista *(fem.)* **6.** _____ inmortalidad **7.** _____ mano **8.** _____ día
9. _____ cumbre **10.** _____ Misisipí *(river)* **11.** _____ sobrina
12. _____ tren **13.** _____ artista *(masc.)* **14.** _____ flor **15.** _____ martes
16. _____ be **17.** _____ libertad **18.** _____ agente **19.** _____ mapa
20. _____ cura *(priest)*

---

*Answers to the exercises in the grammar sections will be found at the back of the book beginning on page 229. Students are advised to study the grammar thoroughly before attempting to write the answers. If they find the exercises difficult, they should restudy the grammar.

2 Plural of Nouns

A. In general, the plural of nouns is formed by adding **-s** to words ending in a vowel and **-es** to words ending in a consonant.

el pie *the foot*	los pies *the feet*
la puerta *the door*	las puertas *the doors*
el mineral *the mineral*	los minerales *the minerals*
la flor *the flower*	las flores *the flowers*

B. Nouns ending in **-z** change the **z** to **c** before adding **-es**.

el lápiz *the pencil*	los lápices *the pencils*
la voz *the voice*	las voces *the voices*
una vez *once*	dos veces *twice*

C. Nouns ending in an unstressed syllable ending in **-s** remain the same in the plural.

el martes *(on) Tuesday*	los martes *(on) Tuesdays*
la crisis *the crisis*	las crisis *the crises*
el paraguas *the umbrella*	los paraguas *the umbrellas*

D. Nouns ending in an accented vowel plus **-n** or **-s** lose the written accent in the plural. (See Appendix D.)

inglés, ingleses *English*	jardín, jardines *garden(s)*

Conversely, nouns ending in an unstressed vowel plus -n require a written accent in the plural to maintain the original stress.

examen	exámenes	*exam(s)*
origen	orígenes	*origin(s)*
joven	jóvenes	*young man or woman (young men or women)*

NOTE: Two nouns shift their stress in the plural.

carácter	caracteres	*character(s)*
régimen	regímenes	*regime(s), diet(s)*

E. Family names generally remain unchanged in the plural.

los García	*the Garcías*
los Fernández	*the Fernándezes*
los Blanco	*the Blancos*

F. With names designating relationship or rank, the masculine plural may include individuals of both sexes.

los hermanos	*the brothers* or *the brother(s) and sister(s)*
los hijos	*the sons* or *the children*

los padres	*the fathers* or *the father(s) and mother(s); parents*
los reyes	*the kings* or *the king(s) and queen(s)*

G. Some nouns are singular in English, but in Spanish may be singular or plural, depending on the meaning.

el consejo	*the piece of advice*	los consejos	*the advice*
el mueble	*the piece of furniture*	los muebles	*the furniture*
el negocio	*the business deal*	los negocios	*business*
la noticia	*the piece of news*	las noticias	*the news*

Perdí mucho dinero en este negocio porque seguí su consejo.	*I lost a lot of money on this deal because I followed his advice.*
Los consejos que dio Don Quijote a Sancho Panza eran excelentes.	*The advice that Don Quijote gave to Sancho Panza was excellent.*
Hoy recibí una buena noticia.	*Today I received a good piece of news.*
Prefiero escuchar las noticias en la radio.	*I prefer to listen to the news on the radio.*

NOTE: The collective noun *the people* governs a plural verb in English, while **la gente** in Spanish takes the singular form.

The romantic Argentinian song, *Isabelita,*†* includes the following lines.

La calle palpita,	*The street palpitates,*
la gente se agita,	*the people become excited,*
al verla pasar.	*on seeing her pass by.*

EXERCISE 2

Write the plural of the following.

1. la crisis **2.** la mujer **3.** el comedor **4.** la luz **5.** el jueves
6. el idioma **7.** el café **8.** la lumbre **9.** el corazón **10.** el portugués
11. la pared **12.** el paraguas **13.** el poeta **14.** el rey **15.** el examen
16. la ciudad **17.** la camarera **18.** la noticia

Idioms and Word Study

A. Idioms with **tener**.

tener (mucha) hambre	*to be (very) hungry*
tener (mucha) sed	*to be (very) thirsty*

---

*A single dagger (†) indicates that a more complete version of the song is included in Appendix C.

tener (mucho) calor	to be (very) warm
Él tiene calor.	He is warm.
tener frío	to be cold
Tenemos frío.	We are cold.
tener miedo	to be afraid
tener sueño	to be sleepy
tener (mucha) suerte	to be (very) lucky
tener prisa	to be in a hurry
(no) tener razón	to be (wrong) right
tener (cinco) años	to be (five) years old
¿Cuántos años tiene Ud.?	How old are you?
tener que (estudiar)	to have to (study), must (study)

B. Saber and conocer.

Saber means *to know a fact*; before an infinitive, it means *to know how to*. Conocer means *to know*, as *to be familiar with* or *to be acquainted with a person, place or thing.*

¿Conoce Ud. la capital del Perú?	Are you familiar with the capital of Peru?
¿Sabe Ud. que es Lima?	Do you know that it is Lima?
No conozco esta canción.	I do not know this song.
No conozco personalmente al gobernador pero sé cómo se llama y que sabe hablar español.	I don't know the governor personally but I know what his name is and that he knows how to speak Spanish.

C. The Verb gustar.

Gustar *(to please)* is usually translated in English as *to like*. The English subject (*I like, you like*, etc.) becomes the indirect object in Spanish (me, te, le, nos, os, les)* and the English object becomes the subject.

He likes these books should be changed mentally to *These books are pleasing to him*, Estos libros le gustan (or Le gustan estos libros, since the verb usually precedes the subject in this construction).

Nos gusta la película.	We like the film.
¿Por qué no te gusta?	Why don't you like it?

Normally, only the third person singular or the third person plural (gusta, gustan) is used. The other forms are used rather infrequently.

¿Te gusto?	Do you like me?
Sí, me gustas muchísimo.	Yes, I like you very much.

If the subject of gustar is an infinitive or a group of infinitives, the singular form (gusta) is always used.

---

*See Lesson 5, Section 2, for a complete treatment of object pronouns.

Nos gusta estudiar y hablar los idiomas extranjeros.	*We like to study and speak foreign languages.*
No les gusta trabajar demasiado.	*They don't like to work too hard.*

Following are examples of the **gustar** construction in two old-time favorite songs:

Me gustan todas, me gustan todas,	*I like them (fem.) all, I like them all,*
me gustan todas en general;	*I like them all in general;*
pero esa rubia, pero esa rubia,	*But that blonde, but that blonde,*
pero esa rubia me gusta más.	*But that blonde I like best.*

Me gusta la leche,	*I like milk,*
me gusta el café,	*I like coffee,*
pero más me gustan	*But I like best*
los ojos de usté (usted).	*Your eyes.*

A few other verbs follow the **gustar** construction. Among the most common are **faltar**, *to need, lack*; **importar**, *to matter*; **encantar**, *to charm, delight.*

No me importan las notas.	*I don't care about grades. (Grades don't matter to me.)*
Me encanta su manera de hablar.	*I am delighted by his way of speaking. (His way of speaking delights me.)*
No me falta nada.	*I don't need anything. (Nothing is lacking to me.)*

From a popular version of the refrain of *La cucaracha,*† the marching song of Pancho Villa's men in the Mexican revolution of 1910–1917.

La cucaracha, la cucaracha,	*The cockroach, the cockroach,*
ya no puede caminar,	*it can't go (walk) any more,*
porque no tiene, porque le falta	*because it does not have, because it lacks*
marijuana que fumar.	*marijuana to smoke.*

EXERCISE 3

A. ¿Sí o no?

1. Cuando tengo frío, tomo helado. **2.** Si tengo hambre, como. **3.** Si digo que es malo estudiar, tengo razón. **4.** Cuando tenemos sed, bebemos agua. **5.** En el verano tenemos calor. **6.** Tenemos que comer para vivir. **7.** Conozco bien la calle donde vivo. **8.** Es mejor bailar si tenemos sueño. **9.** Si veo un león en el bosque, tengo miedo. **10.** Sé que un hombre que tiene ochenta años es viejo. **11.** Corro cuando tengo prisa. **12.** Tengo suerte si gano diez mil dólares en la lotería.

B. Translate the words in parentheses with the proper form of **saber** or **conocer**.

1. El profesor siempre pregunta: *(Who knows?)* **2.** No estudia y por eso *(he doesn't know anything).* **3.** *(I am acquainted with)* **El sombrero de tres picos** pero *(I don't know)* quién escribió la novela. **4.** Les gusta la música pero *(they don't know how to dance).* **5.** *(I don't know)* a su prima pero quiero *(to make her acquaintance).*

C. Replace the subject in italics with the words indicated and change the verb if necessary.

1. Nos gusta *nuestra profesora.*
    a. el nuevo coche **b.** jugar al tenis **c.** estas corbatas **d.** los deportes
    e. el verano
2. Me gustan *los bailes latinos.*
    a. la comida mexicana **b.** la clase de matemáticas **c.** bailar contigo
    d. tus ideas **e.** el té con limón

D. Translate the English portion.

1. *(We do not like)* estudiar. **2.** *(She likes)* las novelas de Galdós. **3.** *(I like)* las flores. **4.** *(They like)* este abrigo. **5.** *(We don't care about)* el dinero. **6.** *(You need = lack)* tres vasos.

4

The Present Tense

A. Regular Verbs.

Spanish verbs are grouped in three conjugations according to their endings: -ar, -er, -ir. Models of the present tense of regular verbs follow.

tomar *to take*	
yo tomo	*I take (I am taking, I do take)*
tú tomas	*you (fam.) take*
él, ella, usted toma	*he, she, you (pol.), it takes*
nosotros (nosotras) tomamos	*we take*
vosotros (vosotras) tomáis	*you (fam. pl.) take*
ellos, ellas, ustedes toman	*they, you (pol. pl.) take*

comer *to eat*	escribir *to write*
como	escribo
comes	escribes
come	escribe
comemos	escribimos
coméis	escribís
comen	escriben

B. Use of Subject Pronouns.

The subject pronouns, except **usted** and **ustedes** (abbreviated **Ud., Uds.,** or **Vd., Vds.**), are usually omitted unless needed for clarity or emphasis:

Creo que sí.	*I think so.*
Ud. tiene razón.	*You are right.*
Tú dices que sí, y él dice que no, y nosotros no sabemos qué hacer.	*You say yes, and he says no, and we do not know what to do.*

English *you* has four possible equivalents in Spanish: the polite forms **usted** and **ustedes,** which take the third person forms of the verb, and the familiar **tú** and **vosotros,** used in addressing close friends, most relatives, children, animals, and in prayer. The **tú** form is very important and of high frequency. The **vosotros** form, however, is not used in Spanish America, where it is replaced by **ustedes. Vosotros** should not be completely neglected, however, since it is widely used in Spain.

The **vosotros** form is also used a great deal in poetry. The following is the opening stanza of a witty poem in defense of women, written about 300 years ago. The author was the brilliant Mexican nun Sor Juana Inés de la Cruz (1651–1695).

Hombres necios que acusáis	*You foolish men, who accuse*
a la mujer sin razón,	*women without reason,*
sin ver que sois la ocasión	*without seeing that you are the cause*
de lo mismo que culpáis ...	*of the very thing you blame . . .*

Compound subjects with **yo** take the first person plural form of the verb; with **tú** the second person plural form is used in Spain, and the third person plural in Spanish America.

María y yo tenemos hambre.	*María and I are hungry.*
Tú y ella habláis (hablan) muy bien.	*You and she speak very well.*

C. Stem-changing (radical-changing) verbs.

A number of verbs have a change in the vowel **e** or **o** of the stem.

1. The change of **e** to **ie** or **o** to **ue** takes place in all persons of the singular and in the third person plural of all three conjugations. Note that these changes occur in the stressed syllables. (See Appendix D for rules of syllabication and stress.)

pensar *to think*	volver *to return*	sentir *to feel*	dormir *to sleep*
pienso	vuelvo	siento	duermo
piensas	vuelves	sientes	duermes
piensa	vuelve	siente	duerme
pensamos	volvemos	sentimos	dormimos
pensáis	volvéis	sentís	dormís
piensan	vuelven	sienten	duermen

Other common stem-changing verbs are:

e > ie

atravesar *to cross*
calentar *to heat*
comenzar *to begin*
confesar *to confess*
defender *to defend*
despertar *to awaken*
divertir *to amuse*
empezar *to begin*
encender *to light*
entender *to understand*
herir *to wound*
mentir *to lie*
negar *to deny*
nevar to snow
perder *to lose*
preferir *to prefer*
querer* *to want, love*
referir *to refer, tell*
sentar *to seat*
sentir *to feel, regret*
sugerir *to suggest*
temblar *to tremble*
tropezar *to stumble*

o > ue

acordarse *to remember*
acostar *to put to bed*
almorzar *to have lunch*
aprobar *to approve*
colgar *to hang*
contar *to count*
costar *to cost*
encontrar *to meet, find*
llover *to rain*
morir *to die*
mostrar *to show*
mover *to move*
poder* *to be able*
probar *to try*
recordar *to remember*
rogar *to beg (ask)*
soler *to be accustomed to*
sonar *to ring, sound*
soñar *to dream*
volar *to fly*

* **Querer** and **poder** are irregular in a few other tenses.

Compounds of the above verbs, such as **devolver, envolver, demostrar, consentir, resonar,** etc., follow the same pattern.

NOTE: The verb **jugar,** *to play,* changes **u** to **ue:** juego, juegas, juega, jugamos, jugáis, juegan.

The following *copla* contains four examples of stem-changing verbs, two **o > ue** in line one, and two **e > ie** in line two.

Si duermo, sueño contigo,   *If I sleep, I dream of you,*
si despierto, pienso en ti.   *if I awake, I think of you.*
Dime tú, compañerita,   *Tell me, my darling,*
si te pasa lo que a mí.   *if the same happens to you*
                                  as to me.

2. Third conjugation (-ir) verbs *only* may have another type of stem change: e > i

pedir *to ask for, request*	
pido	pedimos
pides	pedís
pide	piden

Other common verbs in this category are:

corregir *to correct*   seguir *to follow, continue*
elegir *to elect, select*   servir *to serve*
reñir *to scold, quarrel*   vestir(se) *to dress*
repetir *to repeat*

Compounds of these verbs, such as **conseguir,** *to obtain;* **despedir,** *to send away, dismiss;* **impedir,** *to prevent,* etc., follow the same pattern.

NOTE: Vocabularies generally indicate the type of stem change in parentheses: **encontrar (ue), perder (ie), sentir (ie), pedir (i).**

D. Orthographic-changing verbs.*

In order to retain the original sound of the stem in its infinitive form, some verbs of the second and third conjugations change their spelling in the first person singular. The remaining forms are regular.
   If the stem of the infinitive ends in a consonant + **cer** or **cir, c > z.**
   If the infinitive ends in **-ger** or **-gir, g > j.**
   If the infinitive ends in **-guir, gu > g.**

*The orthographic table in Appendix D will be a very helpful reference for these verbs.

vencer	to conquer, win	venzo, vences, vence, vencemos, vencéis, vencen
torcer (ue)	to twist	tuerzo, tuerces, etc.
coger	to catch, take	cojo, coges, coge, cogemos, cogéis, cogen
recoger	to gather, pick up	recojo, recoges, etc.
corregir (i)	to correct	corrijo, corriges, etc.
dirigir	to direct	dirijo, diriges, etc.
seguir (i)	to follow	sigo, sigues, sigue, seguimos, seguís, siguen
conseguir (i)	to obtain	consigo, consigues, etc.

E. Reflexive verbs.

A reflexive verb is formed by placing the reflexive pronoun* in front of the conjugated verb.

lavarse *to wash (oneself)*			
me lavo	*I wash (myself)*	nos lavamos	*we wash (ourselves)*
te lavas	*you wash (yourself)*	os laváis	*you wash (yourselves)*
se lava	*he washes (himself)*	se lavan	*they wash (themselves)*
	she washes (herself)		*you wash (yourselves)*
	you wash (yourself)		

F. There are a number of verbs of high frequency which have some irregularity in the present tense.

1. Many are irregular only in the first person singular and of these the irregularity is often a **-go** ending.

hacer	to do	ha**go**, haces, hace, hacemos, hacéis, hacen
poner	to put	pon**go**, pones, pone, ponemos, ponéis, ponen
salir	to leave	sal**go**, sales, sale, salimos, salís, salen
valer	to be worth	val**go**, vales, vale, valemos, valéis, valen

2. These two verbs have an **i** before the **-go** ending.

traer	to bring	traigo, traes, trae, traemos, traéis, traen
caer	to fall	caigo, caes, cae, caemos, caéis, caen

3. **Oír** has the above change and also has some forms with a **y** and some with a written accent.**

oír	to hear	oigo, oyes, oye, oímos, oís, oyen

---

*See Lesson 5, Section 3, for a complete treatment of reflexive pronouns and verbs.
**An unstressed *i* between vowels always becomes a *y*.

4. Tener, venir, and **decir** have a **-go** in the first person and then behave like stem-changing verbs.

decir	*to say*	**digo,** dices, dice, decimos, decís, dicen
tener	*to have*	**tengo,** tienes, tiene, tenemos, tenéis, tienen
venir	*to come*	**vengo,** vienes, viene, venimos, venís, vienen

5. Except for the initial letter, **dar** and **ir** follow the same pattern.

dar	*to give*	**doy,** das, da, damos, dais, dan
ir	*to go*	**voy,** vas, va, vamos, vais, van

6. Caber, saber, and **ver** are also irregular only in the first person singular.

caber	*to fit*	**quepo,** cabes, cabe, cabemos, cabéis, caben
saber	*to know*	**sé,** sabes, sabe, sabemos, sabéis, saben
ver	*to see*	**veo,** ves, ve, vemos, veis, ven

7. The very important verbs **ser** and **estar** are irregular in their own fashion.

estar	*to be*	**estoy, estás, está, estamos, estáis, están**
ser	*to be*	**soy, eres, es, somos, sois, son**

8. The auxiliary verb **haber,** *to have,* is used to form the compound tenses and will be treated in Lesson 4, Section 6. It is irregular in the present tense.

haber	*to have*	**he, has, ha, hemos, habéis, han**

9. The verb **oler,** *to smell,* begins with an **h** in the forms where it has a stem change.

huelo	olemos
hueles	oléis
huele	**huelen**

10. Verbs ending in **-uir** (except **-guir**) insert a **y** before the ending in all forms of the singular and in the third person plural.

construir	*to construct*
construyo	construímos
construyes	construís
construye	construyen

Other verbs following this pattern:

destruir *to destroy*
distribuir *to distribute*
huir *to flee*
incluir *to include*

11. A number of verbs ending in **-ecer, -ocer, -ucir** have **-zco** as the ending of the first person singular. (This change is indicated by **-zc** in the vocabulary.)

merecer	*to deserve*	mere**zco**, mereces, merece, merecemos, merecéis, merecen
conocer	*to know*	cono**zco**, conoces, conoce, conocemos, conocéis, conocen
conducir	*to lead, drive*	condu**zco**, conduces, conduce, conducimos, conducís, conducen

Other verbs of this type:

aborrecer	*to hate*	padecer	*to suffer*
agradecer	*to thank*	parecer	*to seem*
aparecer	*to appear*	permanecer	*to remain*
carecer	*to lack*	pertenecer	*to belong*
establecer	*to establish*	producir	*to produce*
favorecer	*to favor*	reconocer	*to recognize*
obedecer	*to obey*	traducir	*to translate*
ofrecer	*to offer*		

12. Certain verbs ending in **-iar** stress the **i** in all forms of the singular and in the third person plural.

enviar *to send*	
envío	enviamos
envías	enviáis
envía	envían

Other common verbs that follow the above pattern are **confiar,** *to confide;* **fiarse,** *to trust;* and **guiar,** *to guide.*

NOTE: Many verbs ending in **-iar** are regular **-ar** verbs and do not stress the **i**: **cambiar,** *to change;* **copiar,** *to copy;* **estudiar,** *to study;* **limpiar,** *to clean;* **odiar,** *to hate,* etc.

13. All verbs ending in **-uar** (except **-guar**) stress the **u** in all forms of the singular and in the third person plural.

continuar *to continue*	
continúo	continuamos
continúas	continuáis
continúa	continúan

Other verbs of this type are **acentuar,** *to emphasize;* and **graduarse,** *to graduate.*

G. Special uses of the present tense.

1. As in English, the present may imply immediate or future time.

Salimos para España el jueves.	*We are leaving for Spain on Thursday.*
Bueno, tomo café.	*O.K., I'll take coffee.*
Si lo encuentro, lo mato.	*If I find him, I'll kill him.*

2. The present progressive in English (present tense of the verb *to be* plus *present participle*) has an equivalent in Spanish. Spanish uses the present tense of **estar** plus the present participle. (See Lesson 5, Section 6.) It is often used instead of the regular present to emphasize or intensify the action in progress.

Estos niños estudian mucho, pero en este momento están mirando la televisión.	*These children study a lot, but at this moment they are watching television.*

3. To express an idea or action in the past that continues into the present, Spanish uses the third person singular of the verb **hacer** *(to make)* + *period of time* + **que** + *main verb* in the present tense.

Hace tres años que vivo aquí.	*I have lived (or I have been living) here for three years. (* literally: *it makes three years that I live here.)*
¿Cuánto tiempo hace que estudias francés?	*How long have you been studying French?*

If the idea is negative, the present perfect may be used.

Hace tres días que no la he visto. (Hace tres días que no la veo.)	*I haven't seen her for three days.*

The preposition **desde** *(since)* is used in a similar construction, as in the following examples.

¿Desde cuándo estudias francés?	*Since when have you been studying French?*
Estudio francés desde septiembre.	*I have been studying French since September.*

4. The verb **llevar** + *period of time* + *present participle* may be used instead of the **hace ... que** construction.

Llevamos muchos años trabajando aquí. (Hace muchos años que trabajamos aquí.)	*We have been working here for many years.*

If a negative idea is being expressed, **sin** + *infinitive* is used.

Lleva tres días sin salir de casa. (Hace tres días que no sale de casa.)	*He has not left the house for three days.*

EXERCISE 4

A. Rewrite the following sentences, replacing the subjects as indicated and making any other necessary changes.

1. *Juan* vende el coche.
   a. nosotros   **b.** ellos   **c.** vosotros   **d.** tú   **e.** yo
2. *Nosotros* esperamos verla.
   a. Pedro   **b.** tú   **c.** yo   **d.** María y Elena   **e.** vosotros
3. *Mi hermano* vuelve a casa temprano.
   a. nosotros   **b.** yo   **c.** ellos   **d.** vosotros   **e.** tú
4. *Nosotros* no cerramos nunca la ventana.
   a. vosotros   **b.** tú   **c.** Uds.   **d.** yo   **e.** ella
5. *El camarero* sirve bien la comida.
   a. yo   **b.** Ud.   **c.** vosotros   **d.** mi hermano y yo   **e.** tú
6. *Yo* prefiero saberlo.
   a. tú   **b.** vosotros   **c.** Juan y Ana   **d.** la gente   **e.** nosotros

B. Write the appropriate form of the present tense of the following verbs.

1. ellos (traducir, estar, pensar, ir, tener, salir)   **2.** yo (traer, saber, coger, conocer, seguir, venir)   **3.** nosotros (merecer, decir, ser, caer, conseguir, vencer)   **4.** él (querer, poder, oír, decir, lavarse, seguir)   **5.** yo (salir, dar, ser, vencer, poner, hacer)   **6.** tú (oír, ser, estar, dormir, decir, venir)   **7.** Uds. (enviar, acostarse, continuar, construir, coger)   **8.** vosotros (tomar, saber, vivir, volver, pensar)

C. Translate.

1. Hace dos años que espero casarme contigo.   **2.** Hace tres horas que comemos y ahora me duele el estómago.   **3.** Desde el mes pasado viven en Buenos Aires.   **4.** Estoy enamorado de ti desde el primer día que te conocí.   **5.** Hace un año que no fuman.   **6.** Llevo tres horas leyendo esta novela.   **7.** Lleva dos semanas sin recibir una carta de su novia.

Basic Class Exercises*

1

I. Place the appropriate definite article before each noun, then circle the one that is not related to the others.

EXAMPLE: mes   mapa   día   año
            el mes   (el mapa)   el día   el año

*In this section, *Basic Class Exercises,* the numbers of the exercises correspond to the number of the grammar section in which the grammar point involved is explained, and provide a complete review of the material in the lesson. If the student has difficulty with an exercise, he/she is advised to restudy the appropriate section together with the corresponding section exercise and the answers in Appendix A.

1. tren	coche	avión	sal
2. lunes	miércoles	libertad	viernes
3. mano	Amazonas	pie	nariz
4. legumbre	carne	paraguas	pescado
5. ciudad	pueblo	estado	juventud
6. comida	restaurante	pianista (m.)	camarera

II. Change the italicized articles and nouns to the plural. If necessary, also change the verb.

EXAMPLE: Escribimos *la lección.*   *Escribimos las lecciones.*
                     La cruz es roja.   *Las cruces son rojas.*

1. No tenemos clase *el miércoles.* **2.** Vamos a leer *el drama.* **3.** Tenemos que vencer *la crisis.* **4.** *El juez* ya está en la corte. **5.** El capitán dio *la orden* para el ataque. **6.** Miran *el jardín.* **7.** *El artista* llegó tarde. **8.** *El inglés y la francesa* están en la playa.

III. A. Answer the following questions using an idiom with **tener**.

1. ¿Cuándo comes? **2.** ¿Cuándo te pones el abrigo? **3.** ¿Cuándo toma tu padre un taxi? **4.** ¿Cuándo vamos a la playa? **5.** ¿Qué tenemos que hacer para aprender bien el español? **6.** ¿Tienes suerte si ganas un millón de dólares en la lotería? **7.** ¿Cuántos años tienes? **8.** ¿Cuándo tomas agua? **9.** ¿Cómo te sientes cuando ves un perro grande? **10.** ¿Cuándo nos acostamos?

B. Use the proper form of **saber** or **conocer**.

1. Es importante _____ nadar. **2.** Mi compañero es muy popular y _____ a todo el mundo. **3.** ¿Quién _____ la respuesta? **4.** Yo _____ quién es pero no la _____ personalmente. **5.** Nosotros _____ donde viven. **6.** ¿_____ tú Madrid bien?

C. *"A new acquaintance."* Answer in Spanish.

1. ¿Te gusta ir a la universidad? ¿Por qué? **2.** ¿Qué clase te gusta más? ¿Por qué? **3.** ¿Te gusta más mirar la televisión o ir al cine? ¿Por qué? **4.** ¿Te gustan los deportes? ¿Cuál te gusta más? **5.** ¿Les gusta a tus padres cuando hablas mucho por teléfono? ¿Por qué? **6.** ¿Te importan mucho los estudios?

IV. A. Fill in the blanks with the proper form of the present tense of the verb indicated.

1. Yo no (conocer) _____ su idioma. **2.** Mi amigo nunca (devolver) _____ el dinero que me debe. **3.** Los jóvenes no (decir) _____ eso. **4.** ¿A qué hora (venir) _____ tú a mi casa? **5.** Yo no (recoger) _____ las flores de mi jardín. **6.** Los Rodríguez (preferir) _____ quedarse aquí. **7.** El ama de casa (despedir) _____ a la criada. **8.** Los chicos (huir) _____ cuando (jugar) _____ y (romper) _____ una ventana. **9.** Yo no (saber) _____ qué hacer. **10.** Nosotros (ser) _____ socialistas. **11.** ¿(Estar) _____ cansadas vosotras? **12.** Yo no (oír) _____ nada. **13.** ¿Te (seguir) _____ siempre tu perro? **14.** Mañana yo te (traer) _____ flores.

B. *"The end of a wonderful summer."* Relate the story to the class in the third person singular. The first sentence will be:

Mañana piensa ...

1. Mañana pienso ir a la playa. **2.** Cuando tengo calor me gusta tomar el sol. **3.** En la playa veo a muchos jóvenes—algunos débiles y otros fuertes. **4.** Yo soy muy fuerte. **5.** Durante el invierno hago ejercicios en el gimnasio porque en el verano me pongo el traje de baño y puedo mostrar mis músculos. **6.** Me divierto mucho en el verano. **7.** En el invierno llevo un traje de invierno y cubro los músculos de mi cuerpo. **8.** Hoy le digo a mi mamá que voy a vivir en una isla del Caribe donde puedo ir a la playa todo el año.

C. Translate.

1. We have been studying French for four years. **2.** They have been sleeping for ten hours. **3.** Since when have you been playing *(tocar)* the piano? **4.** They have been in Ecuador for two months.

Elective Exercises*

V. Answer the following questions in Spanish as if they were directed to you personally. Note that some require a *nosotros* verb in the answer.

1. ¿Qué tienen que hacer Uds. esta noche? **2.** ¿A quién piden Uds. dinero? **3.** ¿Dónde duerme Ud. mejor—en casa o en la clase? **4.** ¿Con qué coge Ud. el lápiz? **5.** ¿Qué hacen Uds. en la clase de español? **6.** ¿Qué idioma habláis en casa? **7.** ¿Conoces la ciudad de Buenos Aires? **8.** ¿Quién tiene razón siempre? ¿Por qué?

VI. *"A sympathetic teacher."* Translate.

1. I like Spanish very much. **2.** I cannot study a lot, however, because I work every day. **3.** Sometimes I am very sleepy and I sleep in class. **4.** The students smile when they see me sleep but the professor does not say anything. **5.** When the class ends he comes and wakes me up (awakens me). **6.** He says, "I understand why you are tired." **7.** I say, "Thank you, professor. You are very kind *(amable)*." **8.** I pick up *(coger)* my books and go out of the classroom.

VII. *"Does father know best?"* Read the following dialogue and answer the questions below.

PADRE: Esta noche te quiero en casa a la una.
ELENA: Pero papá, es muy temprano. José y yo vamos al baile primero, luego a tomar algo en un café, después ... no sé qué vamos a hacer después.
PADRE: Eso es. Temo el «después». Te quiero en casa antes del «después».

---

*This section, *Elective Exercises*, is supplementary to the *Basic Class Exercises* and provides optional exercises for further practice at the discretion of the instructor.

1. ¿A qué hora dice el padre que Elena tiene que estar en casa? **2.** ¿Por qué dice ella que es muy temprano? **3.** ¿Qué puede hacer ella después?
4. ¿Quién tiene razón, el padre o la hija? ¿Por qué?

VIII. Answer the questions after looking at the drawing.

1. ¿Qué bebe la madre? **2.** ¿Qué hace el niño? **3.** ¿Qué hay en la pared?
4. ¿Qué busca el perro? **5.** ¿Quién es la mujer? **6.** ¿Qué lleva la criada en la bandeja? **7.** ¿Por qué deja caer la bandeja? **8.** ¿Qué más puede Ud. decir del dibujo?

criada *maid;* **bandeja** *tray;* **dejar caer** *to drop;* **ratoncito** *mouse;* **cafetera** *coffee pot;* **taza** *cup;* **algo que comer** *something to eat;* **tenedor** *fork;* **cuchara** *spoon;* **cucharita** *teaspoon;* **vaso** *glass;* **jarro** *jug;* **cuchillo** *knife;* **plato** *plate;* **comida** *meal;* **gritar** *to shout;* **cuadro** *picture.*

Vocabulary

At the end of each lesson, a Spanish–English vocabulary covers the words used in the exercises of the lesson. Some simple words and certain words and expressions which have been specifically treated in the lesson are not included here. The vocabularies at the end of the book should be consulted if necessary.

abrigo coat
acostarse (ue) to go to bed
acrtiz *f.* actress
(el) **ama de casa** housewife
avión *m.* airplane
baile *m.* dance
bosque *m.* forest
coche *m.* car
camarero (-a) waiter, waitress
casarse to get married
comedor *m.* dining room
corbata necktie
cruz *f.* cross
cubrir to cover
cuerpo body
cumbre *f.* peak
débil weak
deporte *m.* sport
despedir (i, i) to discharge, fire
devolver (ue) to return (something)
dibujo drawing
dirección direction, address
divertirse (ie, i) to enjoy oneself
doler (ue) to ache, pain
enamorado (-a) in love
eso es that's it
estómago stomach
exigir to demand, require
flor *f.* flower

fuerte strong
fumar to smoke
gimnasio gym
helado ice cream
huir to flee
idioma *m.* language
juez *m.* or *f.* judge
juventud *f.* youth
ladrón *m.* thief
legumbre *f.* vegetable
lumbre *f.* light
llevar to carry; wear
muchedumbre *f.* crowd
nadar to swim
novio (-a) boy (girl)friend, fiancé(e)
paraguas *m.* umbrella
pescado fish
playa beach
ponerse (irreg.) to put on
quedarse to remain
respuesta answer
romper to break
sal *f.* salt
tema *m.* theme, topic
temer to fear
traje *m.* suit;
  —**de baño** bathing suit

Lesson 2

1 The Definite Article

2 The Neuter Article

3 The Indefinite Article

4 Idioms and Word Study

5 The Imperfect Tense

6 The Preterite Tense

1

The Definite Article

A. The definite article has four forms in Spanish.

el libro (masculine singular)	*the book*
los libros (masculine plural)	*the books*
la casa (feminine singular)	*the house*
las casas (feminine plural)	*the houses*

B. Uses of the Definite Article.

The definite article is used in Spanish but not in English in the following instances:

21

1. With nouns used in a general sense, and also with abstract nouns.

Me gustan los animales.   *I like animals.*
Los españoles comen tarde.   *Spaniards dine late.*
La leche es necesaria para la salud.   *Milk is necessary for health.*
El tiempo vuela. *(Proverb)*   *Time flies.*

La vida es sueño (Life is a Dream) is the title of the famous play by Pedro Calderón de la Barca (1600–1681). A dramatic soliloquy at the end of Act II finishes with these oft-quoted lines:

¿Qué es la vida? Un frenesí.   *What is life? A frenzy.*
¿Qué es la vida? Una ilusión,   *What is life? An illusion,*
una sombra, una ficción,   *a shadow, a fiction,*
y el mayor bien es pequeño;   *and the greatest good is small;*
que toda la vida es sueño,   *for all life is a dream,*
y los sueños sueños son.   *and dreams themselves are dreams.*

2. With days of the week and with seasons of the year. Note that the definite article replaces *on* with days of the week.

Vamos a tener un examen el jueves.   *We are going to have an exam on Thursday.*
Van a la iglesia los domingos.   *They go to church on Sundays.*
La primavera es mi estación favorita.   *Spring is my favorite season.*
No me gusta el invierno.   *I do not like winter.*

The article is omitted after **ser** with days of the week.

Hoy es lunes.   *Today is Monday.*

The article may be omitted after **en** with seasons.

Estamos en (el) otoño.   *We are in autumn.*

3. With modified expressions of time.

El año pasado fuimos a España.   *Last year we went to Spain.*
Visitaré a mi tía la semana que viene.   *I shall visit my aunt next week.*

4. With titles (except **don*** and **doña**; **Santo**, **Santa**, and **San**), when speaking *about* a person.

La señora López no está aquí.   *Mrs. López is not here.*
El general Gómez es su tío.   *General Gómez is his uncle.*
Santa Teresa y San Juan fueron escritores místicos del siglo XVI.   *Saint Teresa and Saint John were mystic writers of the sixteenth century.*

***Don** and **doña** are titles of respect used before a first name, and have no English equivalent.

In direct address the article is not used.

¿Cómo está Ud., señorita García?　　*How are you, Miss García?*

The following popular *copla* contains a good illustration of how **don** is used.

Cuando tenía dinero
me llamaban don Tomás;
y ahora que no lo tengo,
me llaman Tomás no más.

*When I had money
they used to call me don Tomás;
and now that I do not have it,
they call me Tomás, nothing
more.*

5. With names of languages.

El español es importante.
Les gusta más el francés que
el alemán.

*Spanish is important.
They like French more than
German.*

The article is omitted immediately after **hablar** and is often omitted after the verbs **aprender, enseñar, entender, escribir, estudiar, leer,** and **saber.**

Hablan italiano y portugués.

*They speak Italian and
Portuguese.*

Habla bien (el) inglés.
Estamos aprendiendo (el) español.

*He speaks English well.
We are learning Spanish.*

The article is omitted after **en**, and generally after **de**.

Está escrito en ruso.
Una clase de inglés
El profesor de latín

*It is written in Russian.
An English class
The Latin teacher*

6. The definite article, rather than the possessive adjective, is usually used with parts of the body and articles of clothing when used as the object of a verb and the possessor is the subject of the sentence.

Se lava las manos.
Se puso el abrigo.

*He / she is washing his/her hands.
He / she put on his/her coat.*

BUT:　Sus manos están muy sucias.　　*His / her / their hands are very dirty.*

7. In telling time. (See Lesson 12, Section 2 for a more complete treatment.)

Es la una.　*It is one o'clock.*
Son las dos.　*It is two o'clock.*

a la una　*at one o'clock*
a las dos　*at two o'clock*

8. Before units of weight and measure, while English uses the indefinite article.

treinta pesos el kilo
ochenta centavos la docena

*thirty pesos a kilo
eighty cents a dozen*

9. Before the names of certain countries, although recent usage has been to omit the article in many cases.

la Argentina	el Japón
el Brasil	el Paraguay
el Canadá	el Perú
el Ecuador	el Uruguay
El Salvador*	los Estados Unidos

Hay problemas de inflación en (la) Argentina y en (el) Brasil.	*There are problems of inflation in Argentina and Brazil.*

The article is always used with geographic names when modified.

la España medieval	*medieval Spain*
la América del Sur	*South America*

Several cities use the definite article.

La Habana es la capital de Cuba.	*Havana is the capital of Cuba.*
La Coruña está en Galicia.	*La Coruña is in Galicia.*

10. Before the words **escuela** and **iglesia**.

Voy a la escuela todos los días.	*I go to school every day.*
Estaban en la iglesia muy temprano.	*They were in church very early.*

C. The prepositions **a** and **de** combine with the masculine singular article **el** to form **al** and **del**. These are the only contractions in the Spanish language.

El hijo del alcalde fue al supermercado del pueblo.	*The mayor's son went to the town's supermarket.*

EXERCISE 1

Insert the definite article, if necessary.

1. Hoy es _____ domingo. **2.** _____ honor vale mucho. **3.** Tenemos que calentar _____ agua fría. **4.** ¿Cómo está Ud., _____ Sr. García? **5.** Vamos al cine _____ sábado. **6.** _____ español es fácil. **7.** _____ señorita Morales es inteligente. **8.** _____ hambre es una cosa horrible. **9.** Hablan _____ francés. **10.** Escribimos en _____ español. **11.** Me pongo _____ sombrero. **12.** Es _____ una. **13.** Estamos estudiando _____ España antigua. **14.** Compro el azúcar a diez pesos _____ kilo.

*The article in El Salvador is part of the name of the country.

2

The Neuter Article

The neuter article **lo** is used:

A. Before a masculine singular adjective or past participle which then has the force of an abstract noun.

Lo importante viene ahora.	*The important part (what is important) comes now.*
Hay que distinguir entre lo bueno y lo malo.	*One must distinguish between (the) good and (the) bad (what is good and what is bad).*
A lo hecho, pecho. *(Proverb)*	*To what has been done, brave heart. (No use crying over spilt milk.)*

B. Before an adjective with the meaning of *how* (**lo** + *adj.* + **que**).

No se dan cuenta de lo hermosas que son las ciudades de ese país.	*They do not realize how beautiful the cities of that country are.*
Me sorprende saber lo ricos que son.	*I am surprised to learn how rich they are.*

This type of sentence may also be expressed by using **qué** instead of **lo ... que**.

No se dan cuenta de qué hermosas son las ciudades de ese país.
Me sorprende saber qué ricos son.

C. Before adverbs with the meaning of *how* (**lo** + *adv.* + **que**).

Ud. no sabe lo bien que lo hacen.	*You don't know how well they do it.*
Se fijaban en lo despacio que andaba la anciana.	*They were noticing how slowly the old woman was walking.*

As with adjectives in the above section, **qué** may be substituted for **lo ... que**.

Ud. no sabe qué bien lo hacen.
Se fijaban en qué despacio andaba la anciana.

D. In many prepositional phrases.

a lo lejos	*in the distance*
lo menos, por lo menos	*at least*
lo más pronto posible	*as soon as possible*
lo de menos	*of least importance*
lo de siempre	*the same as always*
por lo visto	*evidently*
Por lo menos vino lo más pronto posible.	*At least he came as soon as possible.*

EXERCISE 2

Translate the English portion of the following sentences.

1. Recuerdo *how tall she was.* (two ways) **2.** Ahora viene *the best part.* **3.** Le encanta *the mysterious.* **4.** No te puedes imaginar *how well he plays* el piano. (two ways) **5.** Venga a verme *as soon as possible.* **6.** *What is beautiful* es eterno.

3 The Indefinite Article

A. The indefinite articles are **un** and **una**.

un niño   *a boy*   una niña   *a girl*

The plural forms, **unos** and **unas**, are usually omitted but may be used in the sense of *some, a few.*

Compré (unos) libros y cuadernos.   *I bought some books and notebooks.*

Unos, unas may also mean *about, approximately.*

Está a unos veinte kilómetros de aquí.   *It is about twenty kilometers from here.*

B. The indefinite article is generally omitted in Spanish.

1. After the verb **ser,** before an unmodified noun indicating profession, nationality, religion, or political affiliation.

No es médico, sino dentista.	*He is not a doctor, but a dentist.*
Es americano.	*He is (an) American.*
Es católica.	*She is (a) Catholic.*
Es republicano ahora, pero por muchos años fue socialista.	*He is a republican now, but for many years he was a socialist.*

BUT: Es un abogado muy bueno.   *He is a very good lawyer.*

2. Often after a negative word.

No tiene pluma.	*He does not have a pen.*
Salió sin abrigo.	*He went out without an overcoat.*
Los jóvenes nunca llevan sombrero.	*Young people never wear a hat.*

3. Sometimes, even when the sentence is not negative, if the word *a* is not considered essential.

Tiene lápiz, pero no quiere escribir la tarea.	*He has a pencil, but he does not want to write the homework.*
Prefiere escribir con pluma.	*He prefers to write with a pen.*

BUT: When *a* means *one,* and *some* means *several,* the indefinite article is used.

Tengo un coche, no dos.
Compré unos libros de español.

I have one car, not two.
I bought some Spanish books.

4. Before certain common adjectives.

cierto caballero
otra vez
tal cosa
Mañana será otro día. *(Proverb)*
De tal palo, tal astilla. *(Proverb)*

a certain gentleman
another time, again
such a thing
Tomorrow is (will be) another day.
From such a stick, such a splinter.
(Like father, like son, or A chip
off the old block.)

C. Un rather than **una** is generally used before a feminine singular noun beginning with *stressed* **a** or **ha**.

un ama de casa
un alma perdida

a housewife
a lost soul

BUT: una alcoba

a bedroom

EXERCISE 3

Insert the indefinite article, if necessary.

1. Mi hermano es _____ abogado. **2.** No tengo_____ fósforos. **3.** No quiero salir con _____ otro chico. **4.** Ese hombre es _____ escritor muy conocido.
5. Le gusta salir sin _____ corbata. **6.** Vendió _____ silla y _____ lámpara.
7. Busco _____ cierto libro sobre este tema.

4

Idioms and Word Study

A. Weather expressions.

¿Qué tiempo hace?
Hace (mucho) calor.
Hace fresco.
Hace (mucho) frío.
Hace buen (mal) tiempo.
Hace (hay) viento.
Hace (hay) sol.
Hay luna.
Está despejado.
Está nublado.
Llovizna.
Llueve. *(from* llover)
Nieva. *(from* nevar)

How is the weather?
It is (very) warm.
It is cool.
It is (very) cold.
The weather is good (bad).
It is windy.
It is sunny.
The moon is out.
It is clear.
It is cloudy.
It is drizzling.
It rains, it is raining.
It snows, it is snowing.

B. *To leave.*

salir	*to leave (go out), depart*
dejar	*to leave (behind), abandon*

El profesor distraído dejó su
pasaporte en casa cuando
salió para el aeropuerto.

*The absent-minded professor left
his passport at home when he
left for the airport.*

C. Useful expressions: Simple greetings and good-byes.

Le (te) presento a mi amigo Carlos.	*May I introduce my friend Carlos.*
Mucho gusto (en conocerlo, en conocerte.)	*Very pleased (to meet you).*
Encantado (-a).	*Delighted.*
El gusto es mío.	*The pleasure is mine.*
Hola, ¿qué tal?	*Hi, how are things?*
Bien, gracias, ¿y Ud.? (¿y tú?)	*Fine, thanks, and you?*
Hasta luego; hasta pronto; hasta la vista.	*So long.*
Adiós; (que le vaya bien).	*Good-bye; (may things go well for you.)*

EXERCISE 4

Fill in the blanks with one of the words or expressions in this section.

1. En el invierno hace viento, nieva y _____ . **2.** Tengo calor cuando _____ .
3. Por la noche cuando _____ se ve mejor. **4.** Los barcos de vela casi vuelan
cuando _____ . **5.** Por la noche no _____ . **6.** Cuando _____ las montañas
están blancas. **7.** Si _____ , necesito un paraguas. **8.** ¿A qué hora _____ el
tren de las nueve? **9.** Yo _____ para España mañana. **10.** ¿Por qué _____
solo a tu hermano?

The Imperfect Tense

A. Formation of the imperfect tense.

1. The imperfect tense is formed as follows: Verbs of the first conjugation drop
the infinitive ending (**-ar**) and add: **-aba, -abas, -aba, -ábamos, -abais, -aban.**

comprar *to buy*	
compraba	*I bought (used to buy, was buying, would buy*)*
comprabas	*you bought*
compraba	*he (she, you) bought*
comprábamos	*we bought*
comprabais	*you bought*
compraban	*they (you) bought*

* *Would* in the sense of *used to* requires the imperfect. In English *would* is also used to form the
conditional. See Lesson 3, Section 6.

2. Verbs of the second and third conjugations drop the infinitive ending (-er and -ir) and add: -ía, -ías, -ía, -íamos, -íais, -ían.

comer — to eat — comía, comías, comía, comíamos, comíais, comían
vivir — to live — vivía, vivías, vivía, vivíamos, vivíais, vivían

3. Note that all verbs, including stem-changing and irregular verbs, are regular in the imperfect tense, except for **ir, ser** and **ver.**

ir — to go — iba, ibas, iba, íbamos, ibais, iban
ser — to be — era, eras, era, éramos, erais, eran
ver — to see — veía, veías, veía, veíamos, veíais, veían

B. Uses of the imperfect tense.

1. The imperfect tense describes what *was happening* or *used to happen* in the past. It is used for background or descriptions of persons or things as well as for habitual or customary actions. It expresses an action or state *which existed at the time spoken about* without reference to the beginning or end of the action or state.

El verano pasado me levantaba tarde porque no trabajaba.

Last summer I got (used to get) up late because I was not working.

Íbamos a la playa todos los días porque hacía calor.

We went (used to go) to the beach every day because it was warm.

Cuando éramos jóvenes vivíamos en México.

When we were young we lived in Mexico

Nuestra casa era muy grande.

Our house was very big.

The *copla* about **don Tomás,** which was used earlier in this lesson, contains two examples of the imperfect tense in its first two lines.

Cuando tenía dinero
me llamaban don Tomás ...

When I had money
they used to call me don Tomás . . .

The popular Mexican song *Allá en el rancho grande*[†] has several imperfect tense forms in its opening stanza.

Allá en el rancho grande,
allá donde vivía,
había una rancherita
que alegre me decía,
que alegre me decía ...

There on the big ranch,
there where I used to live,
there was a cute ranch girl,
who happily used to say to me,
who happily used to say to me . . .

2. The imperfect tense is used for an action or condition that was in progress when another action took place (preterite).

Iban al centro cuando vieron a Juan.	*They were going downtown when they saw Juan.*
Mientras hablaban los soldados estalló la bomba.	*While the soldiers were talking the bomb exploded.*

3. The imperfect tense is also used for telling time in the past.

¿Qué hora era?	*What time was it?*
Era la una; eran las dos.	*It was one o'clock; it was two o'clock.*

4. The imperfect is used for age, physical description, or possession.

Juanito tenía diez años.	*Juanito was ten years old.*
La casa tenía muchas ventanas.	*The house had many windows.*
Juan era muy alto.	*Juan was very tall.*
El jardín estaba rodeado de árboles.	*The garden was surrounded by trees.*

5. The past progressive in English (*was* or *were* plus *present participle*) has an exact equivalent in Spanish, the imperfect of **estar** plus the present participle (See Lesson 5, Section 6). It is often used instead of the regular imperfect to emphasize or intensify the action in progress. The progressive is, however, less frequent in Spanish than in English.

Estaba lloviendo (llovía) cuando salí.	*It was raining when I left.*

6. You will remember from Lesson 1, Section 4, F.3, that to express an action that began in the past and continues into the present, Spanish uses the following construction: **Hace** + *period of time* + **que** + *verb in present*.

Hace dos horas que estudio esta lección.	*I have been studying this lesson for two hours.*

To express an action or idea that began in the past and continued up to another point of time in the past when something else happened, Spanish uses the following formula in the imperfect tense: **Hacía** + *period of time* + **que** + *verb in imperfect*.

Hacía dos horas que estudiaba cuando entraron mis amigos.	*I had been studying for two hours when my friends came in.*
Hacía tres años que vivíamos aquí cuando decidimos comprar muebles.	*We had been living here for three years when we decided to buy furniture.*

7. As pointed out in Lesson 1, Section 4, F.4, **llevar** + *present participle* may also be used in the above construction.

Llevaba mucho tiempo quejándose
de su jefe. (Hacía mucho tiempo
que se quejaba de su jefe.)

*He had been complaining about his
boss for a long time.*

Llevábamos cinco años sin
hablarnos. (Hacía cinco años
que no nos hablábamos.)

*We had not spoken to one another
for five years.*

EXERCISE 5

A. Change the following verbs to the imperfect tense.

1. nosotros: tomamos, comemos, vivimos, hacemos, queremos **2.** yo: saco,
cojo, comienzo, hago, soy **3.** Ud.: encuentra, vuelve, siente, pide, pone
4. tú: dices, pagas, lees, empiezas, te vistes **5.** vosotros: sabéis, robáis,
preferís, habláis, podéis **6.** ellas: riñen, se divierten, empiezan, tienen, van

B. Translate.

1. Hacía muchos años que yo no veía a mi amiga Consuelo. **2.** Hacía
tres horas que comíamos cuando me puse enfermo. **3.** Hacía un año que
vivíamos en Buenos Aires cuando tuvimos que regresar a los Estados Unidos.
4. ¿Cuánto tiempo hacía que esperabas el tren? **5.** Llevábamos dos meses
viajando por el país cuando conocimos al Presidente.

The Preterite Tense

A. Formation of the preterite tense.

1. Regular verbs of the first conjugation form the preterite tense by
dropping the infinitive ending (**-ar**) and adding: **-é, -aste, -ó, -amos, -asteis,
-aron.**

hablar *to speak*	
hablé *I spoke, I did speak*	hablamos *we spoke*
hablaste *you spoke*	hablasteis *you spoke*
habló *he, she, you spoke*	hablaron *they, you spoke*

Second and third conjugation verbs drop the infinitive ending (**-er, -ir**) and
add **-í, -iste, -ió, -imos, -isteis, -ieron.***

vender   *to sell*   vendí, vendiste, vendió, vendimos, vendisteis,
                           vendieron
abrir   *to open*   abrí, abriste, abrió, abrimos, abristeis, abrieron

*The accent is no longer used in monosyllabic verb forms: **vi, vio.**

2. Stem (Radical)-Changing Verbs.

First (-**ar**) and second (-**er**) conjugation verbs do not have a stem change in the preterite tense. Only *third* (-**ir**) conjugation verbs have a stem change from **e** to **i**, but only in the *third* person singular and the *third* person plural.

sentir	*to feel*	sentí, sentiste, sintió, sentimos, sentisteis, sintieron
servir	*to serve*	serví, serviste, sirvió, servimos, servisteis, sirvieron

Two verbs, **dormir** and **morir**, change the **o** to **u** in the third persons singular and plural.

dormir	*to sleep*	dormí, dormiste, durmió, dormimos, dormisteis, durmieron
morir	*to die*	morí, moriste, murió, morimos, moristeis, murieron

In vocabularies, stem changes of third conjugation verbs are indicated as follows: **sentir (ie, i); pedir (i, i); morir (ue, u)**.

3. Orthographic-Changing Verbs.*

a. In order to preserve the original sound of the final consonant of the stem, the following spelling changes occur in the *first* person singular of *first* conjugation verbs only.

c *to* qu sacar		g *to* gu pagar		z *to* c comenzar	
saqué	sacamos	pagué	pagamos	comencé	comenzamos
sacaste	sacasteis	pagaste	pagasteis	comenzaste	comenzasteis
sacó	sacaron	pagó	pagaron	comenzó	comenzaron

b. Second conjugation verbs whose stem ends with a vowel change the **i** of the third person singular ending (**-ió**) and the third person plural ending (**-ieron**) to a **y**. They also take a written accent on the **i** of all the other forms (first and second persons singular and plural).

leer	*to read*	leí, leíste, leyó, leímos, leísteis, leyeron

Other verbs of this type are **caer, creer, poseer.**

The third conjugation verb **oír** also follows the above pattern.

oír	*to hear*	oí, oíste, oyó, oímos, oísteis, oyeron

c. Third conjugation verbs ending in -**uir** (except for verbs ending in -**guir**) change the **i** of the third persons singular and plural to **y**, as with second conjugation verbs.

construir	*to build*	construí, construiste, construyó, construimos, construisteis, construyeron

*Consult the orthographic table in Appendix D.

Other verbs of this type are: **atribuir, concluir, constituir, contribuir, destruir, disminuir, distribuir, excluir, huir, incluir, influir, instruir.**

d. Verbs ending in **-guar** require a dieresis over the **u** in the first person singular.

averiguar   *to find out*   averigüé, averiguaste, etc.

4. There are a number of common verbs that have an irregular stem in the preterite and take a special set of endings: **-e, -iste, -o, -imos, -isteis, -ieron.**

Notice that there are no written accents on any of the above endings. Study the following verbs.

andar	*to go*	anduve, anduviste, anduvo, anduvimos, anduvisteis, anduvieron
caber	*to fit*	cupe, cupiste, cupo, cupimos, cupisteis, cupieron
estar	*to be*	estuve, estuviste, estuvo, estuvimos, estuvisteis, estuvieron
haber*	*to have*	hube, hubiste, hubo, hubimos, hubisteis, hubieron
poder	*to be able*	pude, pudiste, pudo, pudimos, pudisteis, pudieron
poner	*to put*	puse, pusiste, puso, pusimos, pusisteis, pusieron
saber	*to know*	supe, supiste, supo, supimos, supisteis, supieron
tener	*to have*	tuve, tuviste, tuvo, tuvimos, tuvisteis, tuvieron
hacer**	*to do, make*	hice, hiciste, hizo, hicimos, hicisteis, hicieron
querer	*to want, love*	quise, quisiste, quiso, quisimos, quisisteis, quisieron
venir	*to come*	vine, viniste, vino, vinimos, vinisteis, vinieron

Verbs whose irregular preterite stem ends in **j** drop the **i** of the third person plural ending.

decir	*to say, tell*	dije, dijiste, dijo, dijimos, dijisteis, dijeron
traer	*to bring*	traje, trajiste, trajo, trajimos, trajisteis, trajeron

Verbs whose infinitive ends in **-ucir** take the following endings: **-uje, -ujiste, -ujo, -ujimos, -ujisteis, -ujeron.**

traducir	*to translate*	traduje, tradujiste, tradujo, tradujimos, tradujisteis, tradujeron

*Remember that **haber** is the auxiliary verb used in forming compound tenses (See Lesson 4, Section 6) and should not be confused with **tener. Hemos comido**—*We have eaten.*
** Note the change of **c** to **z** in the third person singular to preserve the original sound of the infinitive.

Other verbs that follow the above patterns: **atraer,** *to attract;* **conducir,** *to conduct, drive;* **detener,** *to stop;* **disponer,** *to dispose;* **maldecir,** *to curse;* **producir,** *to produce;* **reducir,** *to reduce.*

5. The verbs **ir** and **ser** have the same forms in the preterite.

fui	*I went or I was*	fuimos	*we went or we were*
fuiste	*you went or you were*	fuisteis	*you went or you were*
fue	*he, she, it, you went or he, she, it was, you were*	fueron	*they, you went or they, you were*

6. The first conjugation verb **dar** takes the endings of the second and third conjugation verbs in the preterite.

dar *to give* di, diste, dio, dimos, disteis, dieron

7. A small number of second and third conjugation verbs whose stem ends in **ll** or **ñ** drop the **i** of the third person endings **-ió** and **-ieron.**

zambullir	*to dive*	zambulló, zambulleron
gruñir	*to grumble*	gruñó, gruñeron

Other verbs of this type: **bullir** *to boil;* **reñir** *to scold, quarrel;* **tañer** *to ring, toll;* **teñir,** *to dye.*

EXERCISE 6A

Write the preterite of the following verbs.

1. nosotros: tomamos, comemos, vivimos, hacemos, queremos **2.** Ud.: encuentra, vuelve, siente, pide, pone **3.** yo: saco, cojo, comienzo, hago, puedo **4.** tú: dices, pagas, lees, empiezas, te vistes **5.** vosotros: sabéis, robáis, preferís, habláis, podéis **6.** ellas: riñen, se divierten, empiezan, tienen, van

B. Uses of the preterite tense.

1. The preterite tense expresses the beginning, end, or completeness of an action or state within a definite time in the past.

Abrió la puerta, entró, encendió la luz, se sentó y comenzó a leer. Leyó por dos horas.	*He opened the door, entered, turned on the light, sat down and began to read. He read for two hours.*
Felipe II fue rey de España por cuarenta años.	*Philip II was king of Spain for forty years.*

The following popular folk poem, recounting a rapid courtship, has a preterite in each line.

El domingo la vi en misa,	*On Sunday I saw her at mass,*
el lunes le sonreí,	*on Monday I smiled at her,*
el martes me presentaron,	*on Tuesday they introduced me,*
el miércoles fui a su casa,	*on Wednesday I went to her house,*
el jueves me declaré,	*on Thursday I proposed,*
el viernes le di el anillo	*on Friday I gave her the ring,*
y el sábado me casé.	*and on Saturday I was married.*

2. The preterite is also used when a repeated action is considered as a single unit.

El verano pasado fuimos a la playa todos los días.	*Last summer we went to the beach every day.*
Visité a mi abuela cuatro veces el mes pasado.	*I visited my grandmother four times last month.*

C. Contrastive usage of preterite and imperfect tenses.*

1. The preterite tense is used to express what took place while another action or condition was in progress (imperfect).

Mientras comíamos, llegó Juan.	*While we were eating, Juan arrived.*
Felipe II era rey de España cuando la Armada Invencible fue vencida.	*Philip II was king of Spain when the Invincible Armada was defeated.*

Study the following sentences which further illustrate the uses of the imperfect and preterite.

Le hablaba todos los días.	*I used to speak to him every day.*
Le hablé ayer.	*I spoke to him yesterday.*
—¿Qué hacía Ud. cuando estalló el fuego? —Miraba la televisión.	*"What were you doing when the fire broke out?" "I was watching television."*
—¿Qué hizo Ud. cuando estalló el fuego? —Me tiré por la ventana.	*"What did you do when the fire broke out?" "I jumped out of the window."*

The following *décima* (ten-line stanza) from Act I of *La vida es sueño* by Calderón de la Barca contains many good examples of imperfect and preterite verbs.

Cuentan de un sabio que un día	*They tell of a wise man who one day*
tan pobre y mísero estaba,	*was so poor and wretched,*
que sólo se sustentaba	*that he sustained himself only*

*As pointed out in Section 5, B, of this lesson, *was* or *were* + *present participle* or *used to* + *infinitive* always call for use of the imperfect tense.

de unas yerbas que cogía.	on some herbs which he gathered.
«Habrá otro»— entre sí decía—	"Can there be another," he said to himself,
«más pobre y triste que yo»	"poorer and sadder than I?"
Y cuando el rostro volvió	And when he turned his face,
halló la respuesta, viendo	he found the answer, seeing
que iba otro sabio cogiendo	that another wise man went along picking up
las hojas que él arrojó.	the leaves that he threw away.

Many examples of the imperfect and preterite are also found in the following Chilean folk song.

A cantar a una niña yo le enseñaba,	I was teaching a girl to sing,
y un beso en cada nota ella me daba;	and she gave me a kiss at each note;
y aprendió tanto, y aprendió tanto,	and she learned so much, and she learned so much,
que de todo sabía, menos del canto.	that she knew about everything, except singing.

2. Some verbs take on a special meaning in the preterite tense.

querer	to want	quise	I tried (but failed); **no quise** I refused
poder	to be able	pude	I managed to, I succeeded in; **no pude** I could not, did not succeed in
saber	to know	supe	I learned (found out)
conocer	to know	conocí	I met (made the acquaintance of)

Sabía la verdad, y por eso no quería ir con ellos.	He knew the truth and therefore did not want to go with them.
Cuando supo la verdad, no quiso ir con ellos.	When he found out the truth, he refused to go with them.
Yo los conocía antes de ir a Madrid.	I knew them before going to Madrid.
Los conocí en Madrid.	I met them in Madrid.
Queríamos ayudarle pero no podíamos hacer nada.	We wanted to help him, but were unable to do anything.
Quiso abrir la puerta pero no pudo.	He tried to open the door, but could not.

EXERCISE 6B

Fill in the blanks with the appropriate imperfect or preterite tense form of the infinitive in parentheses.

1. (Ser) _____ las siete. **2.** La casa (tener) _____ muchas puertas.
3. Anoche nosotros (conocer) _____ por primera vez a su sobrina. **4.** ¿No

(saber) _____ tú que él (tener) _____ tres hermanos? **5.** María (ser) _____ muy alta cuando (tener) _____ doce años. **6.** Hola, Pedro, ¿a qué hora (ir) _____ al cine anoche? Yo no te (ver) _____ . **7.** Mi padre (comprar) _____ un coche que (ser) _____ grandísimo. **8.** (Hacer) _____ cuatro años que ellos (ser) _____ novios cuando se casaron. **9.** ¿Por qué (dejar) _____ Luisa a su novio sin decirle nada? **10.** Yo (almorzar) _____ temprano porque (tener) _____ hambre.

Basic Class Exercises

1

I. Translate the English into Spanish.

1. ¿Adónde fue Ud., *Mrs. Romero?* **2.** Como amenazaba llover, me llevé *my umbrella.* **3.** En España toman *wine* con la comida. **4.** *Wine* está muy caro estos días. **5.** Andrés vino a casa *on Saturday.* **6.** *Last week* hizo mucho frío.
7. Ayer fue *Monday.* **8.** *Mr. Pérez* tenía razón. **9.** *Spanish and French* son lenguas romances. **10.** Los huevos estaban a noventa pesetas *a dozen.*

2

II. Fill in the blanks with one of the following expressions and translate the sentences into English: *a lo lejos, lo cansada, por lo menos, lo pintoresco, lo difícil.*

1. _____ es escribirlo. **2.** No te puedes imaginar _____ que estaba Elena.
3. _____ se distinguían las montañas. **4.** _____ de España es la arquitectura de las casas del sur. **5.** Tiene _____ cincuenta años.

3

III. *"Mis hermanos."* Fill in the blanks with the indefinite article, if necessary.

1. Vivo en _____ casa muy grande. **2.** Tengo _____ hermano y tres hermanas. **3.** _____ de mis hermanas es doctora. **4.** Me gusta salir sin _____ sombrero. **5.** Cuando hace frío, mi hermana dice que _____ sombrero mantiene el calor. **6.** _____ otra hermana es profesora. **7.** Dice que soy _____ alma perdida porque estudio muy poco. **8.** Es muy desagradable tener _____hermanos mayores.

4

IV. A. *"¿Qué tiempo hace?"* Complete the sentences with an expression from Section 4. More than one answer is possible.

EXAMPLE: Tenemos frío cuando ...
             Tenemos frío cuando hace frío.

1. Tengo calor cuando ... **2.** Tomo un paraguas cuando ... **3.** A veces pierdo el sombrero cuando ... **4.** A veces llueve, pero no mucho, cuando ... **5.** El cielo está muy claro cuando ... **6.** Me pongo un suéter cuando ... **7.** A veces me quedo en casa cuando ... **8.** Hay muchas nubes cuando ... **9.** Me gusta dar un paseo cuando ... **10.** Los niños tiran bolas de nieve cuando ...

B. *"Popularity can bring Ana problems."* Fill in the blanks with the appropriate form of **salir** or **dejar**.

1. Roberto y yo _____ juntos muchas veces. **2.** Ahora Roberto me dice que me va a _____ si yo _____ con otros chicos. **3.** Es un problema porque prefiero _____ con Roberto pero al mismo tiempo no quiero _____ a los otros chicos. **4.** ¿Cómo voy a _____ de este dilema?

5

V. A. *"How were things?"* Complete the sentences in the imperfect tense to show how things used to be, without reference to the beginning or end of the action.

EXAMPLE: Ahora salgo de casa muy temprano. Antes _____ muy tarde.
             Ahora salgo de casa muy temprano. Antes salía muy tarde.

1. Ahora tengo treinta años. Cuando me casé _____ veinte años. **2.** Ahora como mucho. Antes _____ poco porque estaba enfermo. **3.** María me visita a menudo. Antes ella me _____ raras veces. **4.** Ahora tenemos una casa grande. Antes _____ una casa pequeña. **5.** Ahora vuelves a casa temprano. Antes _____ bastante tarde. **6.** Ahora me despierto a las ocho. Durante las vacaciones _____ a las diez. **7.** Ahora los estudiantes entienden el problema. Ayer no lo _____. **8.** Ahora tú eres muy grande. Cuando niño, _____ bastante pequeño. **9.** Este año Carmen y yo vamos a la universidad. El año pasado _____ al colegio. **10.** Este mes hace calor. El mes pasado _____ frío.

B. Translate.

1. They have been studying for two hours. **2.** They had been studying for two hours. **3.** It had been raining for three weeks. **4.** He had been waiting for her letter for a month.

6

VI. A. Complete the sentences with a form of the preterite tense to indicate a completed action. Note how this differs from the ongoing action of the imperfect, which indicates no beginning or ending.

EXAMPLE: El año pasado yo iba a la playa cuando hacía calor.

             Este año yo _____ a la playa sólo una vez.
             Este año yo fui a la playa sólo una vez.

1. Ayer aunque hacía frío, salí con Julia. Ayer _____ mucho frío, pero hoy hace calor. **2.** Anoche María no se sentía bien y se acostó. Anoche María no _____ bien pero hoy está mejor. **3.** ¿Qué decían tus padres cuando llegabas tarde? ¿Qué _____ tus padres cuando _____ tarde anoche? **4.** Siempre nos divertíamos en casa de nuestros abuelos. Sin embargo anoche no _____ mucho. **5.** En esa clase los estudiantes leían muchas novelas, pero el año pasado _____ pocas. **6.** Tú traducías bien las frases en la clase de español. ¿Por qué tú no _____ este párrafo en el libro? **7.** Pablo siempre pedía sopa en este restaurante pero hoy _____ una ensalada. **8.** Antes lavabais la ropa en la máquina de lavar. ¿Por qué no la _____ en la máquina hoy?

B. Complete the sentences using the correct form of the imperfect or preterite tense of the infinitive in parentheses.

1. (Ser) las nueve cuando yo (llegar) _____ . **2.** ¿Cuántos años _____ (tener) _____ tú cuando (venir) _____ a este país? **3.** Yo (ir) _____ en mi coche cuando (chocar) _____ con un árbol porque (pensar) _____ en mi novia. **4.** Al final del semestre el profesor me (dar) _____ una *F,* y yo le (mandar) _____ una carta de protesta. **5.** Él me (escribir) _____ una carta muy amable, pero no (cambiar) _____ la nota. **6.** (Hacer) _____ cinco años que nosotros nos (conocer) _____ cuando (casarse) _____. **7.** (Hacer) _____ cinco meses que nosotros (estar) _____ casados cuando (divorciarse) _____. **8.** Su marido (ser)_____ muy alto y guapo. **9.** ¿Cuántos cuartos de baño (tener) _____ tu apartamento? **10.** ¿Qué tiempo (hacer) _____ cuando tú (llegar) _____ ayer?

C. *"A day at the beach."* Fill in the blanks with the appropriate imperfect or preterite tense of the verb in parentheses.

1. Ayer yo _____ (querer) ir a la playa. **2.** _____ (llamar) a mis amigos y nosotros _____ (decidir) salir a las diez. **3.** _____ (hacer) sol pero _____ (haber) algunas nubes en el cielo. **4.** _____ (preparar) nuestras cosas y _____ (salir). **5.** Cuando nosotros _____ (llegar) a la playa, el cielo _____ (estar) nublado y después de algunos minutos _____ (empezar) a llover. **6.** Nosotros no _____ (poder) nadar y _____ (tener) que volver a casa.

D. The following story is based on the famous windmill episode (Part I, Chapter 8) of *Don Quijote.* Retell the story, changing the present tenses to the preterite or imperfect.

> Don Quijote, el famoso caballero andante, va montado a caballo, acompañado por Sancho Panza, su leal escudero. A lo lejos, don Quijote ve unos veinte molinos de viento y cree que son gigantes. Le dice a Sancho que va a matarlos porque son malos. Sancho le dice que no son gigantes sino molinos de viento.
>
> Don Quijote no le hace caso. Sin tener miedo apunta su lanza a uno de los molinos y ataca las aspas, creyendo que son brazos. De repente el viento hace volver las aspas y cuando llega don Quijote, un aspa le da un golpe que le hace rodar al suelo con su pobre caballo. Los dos se hacen mucho daño.
>
> Sancho corre a ayudarlo y le dice: —Te digo que no son gigantes sino molinos de viento.
>
> No lo cree don Quijote. Dice que su enemigo, el mago Frestón siempre convierte a sus enemigos en otras cosas para quitarle la gloria. Cuando se siente mejor se levanta y los dos siguen su camino en busca de otras aventuras.

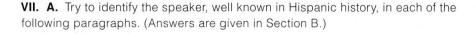

Elective Exercises

VII. A. Try to identify the speaker, well known in Hispanic history, in each of the following paragraphs. (Answers are given in Section B.)

1. Nací en Castilla en 1451. En 1469 me casé con Fernando de Aragón. Fernando y yo unimos nuestros reinos en 1479. En 1492 conquistamos la ciudad de Granada. En el mismo año mandé a Cristóbal Colón a buscar una nueva ruta a las Indias. ¿Quién fui yo?

2. Nací en Alcalá de Henares en Castilla en 1547. Escribí poesías, dramas y novelas. En 1605 publiqué la primera parte de una novela famosísima, *Don Quijote de la Mancha*. La segunda parte apareció diez años más tarde. Morí en 1616, el mismo año que Shakespeare. ¿Quién fui yo?

3. Nací en Caracas en 1783. Tomé parte en la rebelión de las colonias contra la dominación española. Uno de los países creados después de la derrota de los españoles fue nombrado en mi honor. ¿Quién fui yo?

4. Nací en Bélgica en 1840. Me casé con Maximiliano, archiduque de Austria, en 1857. De 1864 a 1867 mi esposo fue emperador de México, apoyado por Napoleón III. Maximiliano fue fusilado por los mexicanos en 1867. Yo viví el resto de mi vida en Europa, donde morí en 1927. ¿Quién fui yo?

B. Say or write something about Isabel la Católica, Miguel de Cervantes, Simón Bolívar, and Empress Carlota.

VIII. A. *"Love Unrequited, Alas!"* Translate the following sentences.

1. Mr. López, did you take Miss García to the movies last night? **2.** No, she said she was busy, but later I saw the liar with another man. **3.** It was snowing when I kissed her the first time, but she left me last month. **4.** Now when it snows I throw snowballs at her picture.

B. *"Wine or Water?"* This sign actually existed. Translate.

1. We saw a sign that said, "Water is good for frogs." **2.** Evidently for the French, Italians and Spanish, wine is better than *(mejor que)* water. **3.** They prefer to drink wine with (the) meals.

IX. A. Tell how you spent the previous day. *(Ayer me levanté a las siete, tomé el desayuno, salí de casa para ...)* The other students will ask you questions on what you said. *(¿Por qué te levantaste tan temprano?, etc.)*

B. The following frame story tells of a typical accident in the life of a small boy which ends happily here. Relate the story by answering the questions.

1. ¿Qué tiempo hacía?
2. ¿Qué hacía el niño?

b.

3. ¿Qué le pasó?

c.

4. ¿Qué empezó a hacer?

d.

5. ¿Quién lo vio?
6. ¿Cómo era el hombre?

e.

7. ¿Qué hizo el hombre?

f.

8. ¿Por qué sonreía el niño?

Useful vocabulary for answers: **correr** *to run;* **tropezar (con)** *to trip (on);* **piedra** *stone;* **llorar** *to cry;* **alto** *tall;* **delgado** *thin;* **secar** *to dry;* **lágrima** *tear;* **dólar** *dollar.*

X. Review of Lesson 1.

A. Supply the appropriate definite article and change to the plural.

EXAMPLE: _____ poeta *el poeta los poetas*

1. _____ luz **2.** _____ poema **3.** _____ mano **4.** _____ función
5. _____ capitán **6.** _____ cura *(priest)* **7.** _____ bailarín
8. _____examen **9.** _____ legumbre **10.** _____ miércoles
11. _____ francés **12.** _____ amistad

B. *"This is not a typical class!"* Change the following sentences to the present tense.

1. Los alumnos tuvieron miedo cuando entró el profesor. **2.** Siempre gritaba y castigaba a los muchachos. **3.** Algunos muchachos pusieron una tachuela en su silla y cuando se sentó empezó a gritar; pero no pudo castigar a nadie porque no sabía quién era el criminal. **4.** Para él, el día estaba lleno de crisis. **5.** Empecé a odiar la escuela, pero al mismo tiempo me divertía mucho y no quería graduarme.

Vocabulary

abogado lawyer
amable kind, friendly
amenazar to threaten
amistad *f.* friendship
andante: caballero— knight errant
anoche last night
antiguo old, ancient
anuncio announcement
apoyar to support
apuntar to aim
(el) **aspa** *f.* wing (blade of a windmill)
arrugado wrinkled
azúcar *m.* sugar
bailarín *m.* dancer
baño bath
barco boat;—**de vela** sailboat
Bélgica Belgium
bola ball
busca search; **en—de** in search of
caballo horse; **a—** on horseback
calentar (ie) to warm up
cambiar to change
camino road
castigar to punish

colegio elementary or secondary school
conquistar to conquer
convertir (ie, i) to convert
creado created
chocar to collide
derrota defeat
desagradable unpleasant
docena dozen
encantar to charm, enchant
enemigo enemy
escudero squire
fósforo match
fusilar to execute
gigante *m.* giant
golpe *m.* blow
guapo handsome
huevo egg
justicia justice, law
kilo kilogram (2.2 pounds)
lanza lance
leal loyal
mantener *(irreg.)* to maintain
marido husband

menudo: a— often
molino mill;—de viento windmill
montado mounted
nieve *f.* snow
nombrar to appoint
nota grade
nube *f.* cloud
odiar to hate
paseo walk; dar un— to take
  a walk
peseta *peseta* (unit of currency
  in Spain)
pintoresco picturesque
reino kingdom

reloj *m.* watch, clock
reñir (i, i) to quarrel; to scold
rodar (ue) to roll
seguir (i, i) to continue; to follow
sobrino nephew
sonreír to smile
suelo ground
tachuela thumbtack
unir to unite
valer *(irreg.)* to be worth
volar (ue) to fly
volver (ue) to turn; to return
volverse (ue) to turn around;
  to become

Lesson 3

1 Adjectives

2 Adverbs

3 *Estar* and *Ser*

4 Idioms and Word Study

5 The Future Tense

6 The Conditional Tense

1 Adjectives

A. Adjectives must agree in gender and in number with the noun they modify. Most masculine adjectives end in **-o**; the feminine in **-a**.

el libro rojo *the red book*
los libros rojos *the red books*

la flor roja *the red flower*
las flores rojas *the red flowers*

A Spanish folk song:

Eres alta y delgada	*You are tall and slender*
Como tu madre,	*Like your mother,*
Morena salada, como tu madre.	*Bewitching brunette, like your mother.*

Adjectives that do not end in -o or -a are the same in the feminine as in the masculine.

el sombrero verde *the green hat*	los sombreros verdes *the green hats*
la pared verde *the green wall*	las paredes verdes *the green walls*
el niño cortés *the polite boy*	los niños corteses *the polite boys*
la niña cortés *the polite girl*	las niñas corteses *the polite girls*

EXCEPTIONS:

1. Adjectives ending in **-án** and **-ón** are made feminine by adding **-a** and dropping the accent.

holgazán, holgazana	*lazy*
burlón, burlona	*mocking*

2. Adjectives ending in **-dor** are made feminine by adding **-a**.

hablador, habladora	*talkative*

3. Adjectives of nationality ending in a consonant are made feminine by adding **-a,** and dropping the accent if there is one.

español, española	*Spanish*
alemán, alemana	*German*
portugués, portuguesa	*Portuguese*

B. Plural of Adjectives.

Like nouns, adjectives that end in a vowel add **-s**. Those that end in a consonant add **-es** to form the plural.

m. sing.	m. pl.	fem. sing.	fem. pl.	
rojo	rojos	roja	rojas	*red*
azul	azules	azul	azules	*blue*
francés	franceses	francesa	francesas	*French*
cortés	corteses	cortés	corteses	*polite*

Like nouns, adjectives that end in **-z** change to **-c** before adding **-es**.

una mujer feliz	*a happy woman*
unas mujeres felices	*some happy women*

Adjectives that modify two or more nouns of different gender are normally masculine plural.

Juan y Luisa son altos.	*Juan and Luisa are tall.*

C. Position of Adjectives.

1. Descriptive adjectives generally follow the nouns they modify in order to distinguish the nouns from others of their class or to emphasize them.

una mesa redonda	*a round table*
un mensaje importante	*an important message*

la pared verde	*the green wall*
Su hermano es un autor famoso.	*Her brother is a famous author.*
Vive en una casa blanca.	*He lives in a white house.*

If, however, the adjective does not add a distinguishing characteristic or emphasis, but rather is readily associated with the noun, the descriptive adjective will frequently precede the noun.

Cervantes, el famoso autor	*Cervantes, the famous author*
su amable esposa	*your charming wife*
el incomparable Lope de Vega	*the incomparable Lope de Vega*
la blanca nieve	*the white snow*

The Marqués de Santillana (1398–1458) wrote a number of delightful *serranillas* (mountain songs). The third stanza of the popular *Serranilla de la Finojosa* begins:

En un verde prado	*In a green meadow*
de rosas y flores	*of roses and flowers*
guardando ganado	*tending cattle*
con otros pastores ...	*with other shepherds . . .*

Examples of the position of adjectives appear in the opening stanza of *Versos sencillos* (well known as the popular folk song *Guantanamera*) by the great Cuban patriot and writer, José Martí (1853–1895), and in his short two-stanza poem which follows it.

Yo soy un hombre sincero	*I am a sincere man*
de donde crece la palma,	*from where the palm tree grows,*
y antes de morirme quiero	*and before I die I want*
echar mis versos del alma.	*to pour forth the verses from my soul.*

Cultivo una rosa blanca	*I cultivate a white rose*
en julio como en enero,	*in July as in January,*
para el amigo sincero	*for the sincere friend*
que me da su mano franca.	*who gives me his open hand.*
Y para el cruel que me arranca	*And for the cruel one who tears from me*
el corazón con que vivo,	*the heart with which I live,*
cardo ni ortiga cultivo,	*neither thorn nor thistle do I cultivate,*
cultivo la rosa blanca.	*I cultivate the white rose.*

2. Articles, cardinal and ordinal numbers, as well as limiting adjectives, such as demonstratives, possessives and indefinites, usually precede the noun.

los idiomas	the languages
esta clase	this class
sus amigos	his friends
ocho días	eight days
la primera vez	the first time
algunos compañeros	some companions

D. Certain adjectives normally precede the noun modified and lose their final **-o** before a masculine singular noun. They are easy to remember if they are grouped as follows:

bueno—malo	good—bad
primero—tercero	first—third
alguno—ninguno	some—none

NOTE: **Algún** and **ningún** require a written accent.

un buen muchacho	a good boy
Hace mal tiempo.	The weather is bad.
el primer mes	the first month
el tercer hombre	the third man
algún desastre	some disaster
ningún derecho	no right

BUT: **una buena muchacha,** *a good girl;* **la primera (tercera) semana,** *the first (third) week;* **alguna vez,** *sometime;* **ninguna posibilidad,** *no possibility.*

Bueno and **malo,** however, may follow, especially when emphatic.

| Es un chico muy bueno. | He is a very good boy. |
| Fue una comida muy mala. | It was a very bad meal. |

Grande becomes **gran** before a masculine or feminine singular noun. It normally has the meaning of *great* but means *big* when it follows the noun.

Es una gran señora.	She is a great lady.
No es gran cosa.	It's not a big deal.
Lincoln fue un gran hombre y también fue un hombre grande.	Lincoln was a great man and he was also a big man.

Santo becomes **San** except before a name beginning with **Do-** or **To-**.

| San Juan *St. John* | Santo Domingo *St. Dominick* |
| San Pedro *St. Peter* | Santo Tomás *St. Thomas* |

E. A number of adjectives may be used before or after the noun with a difference in meaning. They usually follow the noun when used in their literal sense.

mi antiguo profesor	*my former teacher*
un monumento antiguo	*an ancient monument*
cierta vez	*a certain time*
una cosa cierta	*a sure thing*
el mismo libro	*the same book*
el profesor mismo	*the teacher himself*
un coche nuevo	*a new car (brand new)*
un nuevo coche	*a new car (a different one, not necessarily new)*
un viejo amigo	*an old friend (of long standing)*
un amigo viejo	*an old (aged) friend*
Los niños pobres no tienen nada que comer.	*The poor (indigent) children don't have anything to eat.*
Los pobres niños tienen un examen hoy.	*The poor (unfortunate) kids have an exam today.*

F. Adjectives may be used as nouns. In this case, they are preceded by a definite article or a demonstrative adjective.

El joven ayudó a la vieja.	*The young man helped the old lady.*
Los ricos a veces no comprenden los problemas de los pobres.	*The rich sometimes do not understand the problems of the poor.*
¿Cuál de estos vestidos prefieres, el rojo o el verde?	*Which of these dresses do you prefer, the red one or the green one?*
El francés se despidió de esa española.	*The Frenchman said good-bye to that Spanish lady.*
Arrímate a los buenos y serás uno de ellos. *(Proverb)*	*Get close to the good ones and you will be (become) one of them.*

G. Where English has a noun with adjective force modifying another noun, Spanish uses a prepositional phrase introduced by **de.**

un reloj de oro	*a gold watch*
una corbata de seda	*a silk tie*

EXERCISE 1

Write the correct form of the adjective in its proper place.

1. la chica (inglés) **2.** una niña (encantador) **3.** los temas (fácil) **4.** los lápices (azul) **5.** el dramaturgo Calderón (famoso) **6.** una muchacha (cortés) **7.** los parientes (alemán) **8.** los pinos (verde) **9.** mi profesor (viejo = *former*) **10.** mi tía (viejo) **11.** el capítulo (primero) **12.** el millonario (pobre) **13.** las casas (popular) **14.** la mujer (burlón) **15.** los animales (feroz) **16.** una actriz (grande) **17.** un orador (bueno) **18.** la lección (tercero) **19.** Domingo (Santo) **20.** las lecciones (difícil)

2 Adverbs

A. Just as English usually forms an adverb by adding **-ly** to the adjective *(clear, clearly)*, Spanish adds **-mente** to the feminine singular form of the adjective.

claro	claramente	*clearly*
absoluto	absolutamente	*absolutely*
horrible	horriblemente	*horribly*

When a written accent on the original adjective is retained in the adverb, the main spoken stress is on the first **e** of **-mente** and there is a secondary stress on the vowel bearing the written accent:

rápido	rápidamente	*rapidly*
fácil	fácilmente	*easily*
cortés	cortésmente	*politely*

There are many simple adverbs which do not end in **-mente**: **aquí**, *here*; **luego**, *then*; **bien**, *well*; **mal**, *badly*; **despacio**, *slowly*; etc.

B. In a series of two or more adverbs, **-mente** is added only to the last one.

Ud. lee clara y lentamente.	*You read clearly and slowly.*
Ella viste sencilla y elegantemente.	*She dresses simply and elegantly.*

C. Frequently an adverbial phrase replaces the adverb.

frecuentemente *or* con frecuencia	*frequently*
cuidadosamente *or* con cuidado	*carefully*

In some cases an adverbial phrase is the preferred way of expressing the idea.

con calma	*calmly*
sin piedad	*pitilessly*
de una manera alarmante	*in an alarming way*
or de un modo alarmante	

D. Adjectives are sometimes used in place of adverbs.

Corrió rápido por el camino.	*He ran rapidly along the road.*
Los niños juegan contentos.	*The children are playing happily.*
Se casaron y vivieron felices para siempre.	*They got married and lived happily ever after.*
Esto te costará caro.	*This will cost you dearly.*

Note that the adjective agrees with the subject in such cases.

E. An adverb precedes the adjective it modifies but normally is placed after the verb it modifies.

Es muy importante.	*It is very important.*
Son bastante ricos.	*They are quite rich.*
Ya no preparan bien sus lecciones.	*They no longer prepare their lessons well.*

EXERCISE 2

A. Give the adverbial form of the following adjectives.

1. feliz **2.** difícil **3.** alegre **4.** ruidoso **5.** inteligente **6.** lento

B. Replace the adverbs in the following sentences with adjectives.

1. Nosotros corrimos rápidamente. **2.** ¿Adónde fuiste tan apresuradamente, Elena? **3.** Ellos siempre trabajaban lentamente. **4.** Ellas sonreían felizmente.
5. Sus hijos vivían tranquilamente.

Estar and *Ser*

Both **estar** and **ser** mean *to be* in English. The basic function of **estar** is to express *location, state,* or *condition.* It should be noted that **estar** is derived from Latin *stare (to stand)* and that the past participle of *stare* is *status.*

A. Uses of **estar.**

1. To express location or condition of a person or thing.

Madrid está en España.	*Madrid is in Spain.*
¿Cómo están Uds.?	*How are you?*
Estamos cansados pero contentos.	*We are tired but content.*
No está aquí porque está enfermo.	*He is not here because he is ill.*
El café está frío y el pan está duro.	*The coffee is cold and the bread is hard.*
Las ventanas están abiertas.	*The windows are open.*

Estar is often used in the sense of *to be at home, to be in.*

¿Está el Sr. García?	*Is Mr. Garcia in?*
Lo siento, pero no está ahora.	*I am sorry, but he is not in now.*

2. With the present participle, to form the progressive tenses.

¿Qué estás haciendo?	*What are you doing?*
Estoy prestando atención al maestro.	*I am paying attention to the teacher.*
Estaban mirando la televisión.	*They were watching television.*

B. Uses of **ser.**

1. With predicate nouns and pronouns.

¿Quiénes son Uds.?	Who are you?
Somos turistas.	We are tourists.
¿Quién es ella?	Who is she?
Es mi hermana.	She is my sister.
Soy yo; es él.	It is I; it is he.

This construction appears in a popular *rima* of the Spanish romantic poet, Gustavo Adolfo Bécquer (1836–1870).

—¿Qué es poesía? dices mientras clavas	*"What is poetry?" you say as you fix*
en mi pupila tu pupila azul.	*upon my eyes your eyes of blue.*
—¿Qué es poesía?—¿Y tú me lo preguntas?	*"What is poetry?" And you ask me that?*
Poesía ...eres tú.	*Poetry . . . 'tis you!*

2. In most impersonal expressions.

Es posible, *it is possible;* **es importante,** *it is important;* **es necesario,** *it is necessary;* **es (una) lástima,** *it is a pity;* etc.

| Es necesario estudiar para aprender. | *It is necessary to study in order to learn.* |

NOTE: **Estar** is used in some common impersonal expressions.

| Claro está. | *Certainly, of course.* |
| Está bien. | *All right, O.K.* |

3. **Ser de** is used to denote origin, material, or ownership.

Son de España, pero ahora están en México.	*They are from Spain but they are in Mexico now.*
La ventana es de vidrio.	*The window is (made) of glass.*
¿De quién es? Es del profesor.	*Whose is it? It is the teacher's.*

4. To tell time of day and in dates.

¿Qué hora es?	*What time is it?*
Es la una; son las dos.	*It is one; it is two (o'clock).*
¿Qué hora era?	*What time was it?*
Era la una; eran las dos.	*It was one; it was two (o'clock).*
¿Cuál es la fecha?	*What is the date?*
Es el primero de enero.	*It is January 1st.*
Es el dos de mayo.	*It is May 2nd.*

5. When *to be* equals *to take place.*

| ¿Dónde es la fiesta? | *Where is the party (taking place)?* |
| La escena es en Madrid. | *The scene is in Madrid.* |

6. To form the true passive. (For a full explanation of the passive construction see Lesson 5, Section 5.)

La puerta fue abierta por el alumno. *The door was opened by the student. (an action)*

But **estar** is used for a resultant state or condition.

Ahora la puerta está abierta. *Now the door is open.*

7. With adjectives expressing an inherent quality or characteristic normally associated with a person or thing.

El hierro es duro. *Iron is hard.*
Nuestra casa es grande. *Our house is large.*
Elena es encantadora. *Elena is charming.*
Es alto y fuerte, pero no es simpático. *He is tall and strong, but he is not likable.*

Note the opening lines of a romantic *rima* by Bécquer.

Yo soy ardiente, yo soy morena, *I am ardent, I am dark-skinned,*
yo soy el símbolo de la pasión ... *I am the symbol of passion . . .*

8. **Ser** is normally used with the adjectives **joven** and **viejo** (*young* and *old*), **rico** and **pobre** (*rich* and *poor*) and **feliz** and **infeliz** (*happy* and *unhappy*), even though they may be regarded as changeable qualities.

Son pobres pero felices. *They are poor but happy.*
Cuando yo era joven, todos *When I was young, we were all rich.*
  éramos ricos.

But to emphasize a particular characteristic at a given moment, **estar** may be used.

¡Qué joven estás esta noche, viejo! *How young you look (or, are acting) tonight, old man!*
Hoy estoy muy feliz. *I feel very happy today.*

C. Contrast of **estar** and **ser** with adjectives.

Many adjectives may be used with either verb, but with a difference in meaning.

El chico es muy malo. *The boy is very bad. (behavior)*
El chico está malo. *The boy is ill.*

La sopa está muy buena. ⎫
La sopa está muy rica. ⎭ *The soup is (tastes) very good.*

La sopa es muy rica. *The soup is very good (nutritious).*

El profesor es muy aburrido.	*The teacher is very boring.*
Los estudiantes están aburridos.	*The students are bored.*
Mi novia es muy lista, pero nunca está lista a tiempo.	*My fiancée (girlfriend) is very bright, but she is never ready on time.*
Es muy viva.	*She is very lively.*
No sé si está viva o muerta.	*I don't know if she is alive or dead.*
Es muy pálido.	*He is very pale. (complexion)*
Está muy pálido ahora.	*He is very pale now. (illness or emotion)*
Es inteligente y bonita.	*She is intelligent and pretty.*
¡Qué bonita estás hoy!	*How pretty you look today!*
Este sillón es muy cómodo.	*This armchair is very comfortable.*
No estoy cómodo aquí.	*I am not comfortable here.*
Es seguro.	*It's safe. It's a sure thing.*
No estoy seguro.	*I'm not sure.*

EXERCISE 3

Fill in the blanks with the proper form of **estar** or **se**r in the present tense.

1. ¿Dónde _____ el caballo que prometiste vender? —Ya no lo quiero vender; _____ mejor. **2.** ¿Cuándo _____ el baile? **3.** Me dicen que tu reloj _____ de oro. **4.** La ventana ____ abierta por Pedro todas las mañanas. **5.** Camilo José Cela _____ un autor muy famoso. **6.** La nieve ____ blanca. **7.** La ventana _____ abierta *(open)*. **8.** La nieve ____ negra. **9.** Siempre dice que Dolores _____ hermosa y encantadora. **10.** El profesor _____ tan aburrido que todos los alumnos ____ aburridos. **11.** ¿De dónde _____ tu novio? **12.** Él _____ de México, pero ya no ____mi novio. **13.** Él _____ casado con otra chica. **14.** No quiero tomar el agua porque ____ muy caliente. **15.** Pepe, ¿qué _____ haciendo tú ahora? **16.** Querida, ¡qué hermosa ____ esta noche! **17.** Dicen que las españolas ____ muy vivas. **18.** _____ la una y veinte. **19.** ¿ _____ vosotros contentos ahora que tenéis bastante dinero? **20.** Tú no ____ un loco _____ un monstruo.

Idioms and Word Study

A. Idioms with **hacer.**

hacer una pregunta	*to ask a question*
hacer un papel	*to play a role*
hacer un viaje	*to take a trip*

hacer la(s) maleta(s)	*to pack one's bag(s)*
hacer(se) daño; lastimarse	*to hurt (oneself)*
hace (un año)	*(one year) ago*

B. General Expressions.

querer decir	*to mean*
volver a (correr)	*(to run) again*
al día siguiente	*the next day*
a menudo	*often*
en seguida	*at once, immediately*
ya no (no ... ya)	*no longer, not anymore*

Tengo que hacer la maleta.	*I have to pack my bag.*
Me hizo daño.	*He hurt me.*
Me hice daño en la mano.	*I hurt my hand.*
Eso no quiere decir nada.	*That doesn't mean anything.*
No volveré a hacerlo.	*I shall not do it again.*
Ya no viene a mi casa. } No viene ya a mi casa. }	*He doesn't come to my house anymore.*
Hace dos años que se fueron. } Se fueron hace dos años. }	*They went away two years ago.*

C. To pay attention.

hacer caso a (de)	*to pay attention to (heed)*
prestar atención	*to pay attention (listen attentively)*

Me dio muchos consejos, pero no le hice caso.	*He gave me a lot of advice, but I didn't pay attention to him.*
Tenemos que prestar atención al profesor cuando habla.	*We have to pay attention to the teacher when he speaks.*

EXERCISE 4

Complete the following sentences with *a, b,* or *c.*

1. Todos los profesores _____.
   a. aburren **b.** se hacen daño **c.** hacen preguntas
2. Cuando me preparo para viajar, _____.
   a. hago un papel **b.** hago la maleta **c.** grito
3. La charla era interesante y todos _____.
   a. dormían **b.** prestaban atención. **c.** salieron
4. Dijo Juan que me visitaría _____.
   a. muerto **b.** al día siguiente **c.** hace tres años
5. Nuestros padres saben que _____ importante en nuestro desarrollo.
   a. hacen un viaje **b.** hacen daño **c.** hacen un papel

6. Dijo que ya no volvería _____.
   a. a verlo **b.** a morir **c.** a matarme
7. Inmediatamente _____, «*en seguida*».
   a. viene después de **b.** quiere decir **c.** se escribe
8. Íbamos al cine _____.
   a. nadando **b.** durmiendo **c.** a menudo

The Future Tense

A. To form the future tense *(shall* or *will)* add the endings **-é, -ás, -á, -emos, -éis, -án** to the entire infinitive of all three conjugations. Except for the first person plural, all forms bear a written accent.*

tomar	*to take (I, you, he, she, it, we, they will take)*	tomaré, tomarás, tomará, tomaremos, tomaréis, tomarán
volver	*to return*	volveré, volverás, volverá, volveremos, volveréis, volverán
abrir	*to open*	abriré, abrirás, abrirá, abriremos, abriréis, abrirán

B. There are a number of important verbs that use an irregular stem, rather than the entire infinitive, to form the future. They may be grouped as follows:

1. The **e** of the infinitive ending is dropped.

caber	*to fit*	cabré, cabrás, etc.
haber	*to have (aux.)*	habré, habrás, etc.
poder	*to be able*	podré, podrás, etc.
querer	*to want, to love*	querré, querrás, etc.
saber	*to know*	sabré, sabrás, etc.

2. The **e** or the **i** of the infinitive is dropped and a **d** inserted.

poner	*to put*	pondré, pondrás, etc.
tener	*to have*	tendré, tendrás, etc.
venir	*to come*	vendré, vendrás, etc.
salir	*to leave*	saldré, saldrás, etc.
valer	*to be worth*	valdré, valdrás, etc.

3. **Decir** loses the **-ec-** of the infinitive and **hacer** loses the **-ce-** before the endings are added.

decir	*to say, to tell*	diré, dirás, etc.
hacer	*to do, to make*	haré, harás, etc.

*These endings are derived from the present indicative tense of the auxiliary verb **haber** (**he, has, ha, hemos, habéis, han**).

C. The future tense in Spanish corresponds in general to English usage.

Dice que vendrá temprano.	*He says that he will come early.*
Si llueve, nos quedaremos en casa.	*If it rains, we shall stay home.*
Mañana será otro día. *(Proverb)*	*Tomorrow is (will be) another day.*

There are a number of popular poems and songs that contain examples of the future tense. The song *¡Qué será, será!*, well known in an English version, is given here in Spanish.

Qué será, será,	*What will be, will be,*
Lo que va a ser, será,	*Whatever will be, will be,*
El tiempo te lo dirá,	*Time will tell,*
Qué será, será.	*What will be, will be.*
Cuando yo era chiquitito	*When I was a little child*
A mi mamita le pregunté,	*I asked my mother,*
—¿Seré yo guapo? ¿Seré yo rico?	*"Will I be handsome? Will I be rich?"*
Me contestó así:	*She answered me thus:*
—Qué será, será,	*What will be, will be,*
Lo que va a ser, será,	*Whatever will be, will be,*
El tiempo te lo dirá,	*Time will tell,*
Qué será, será.	*What will be, will be.*

D. The future tense is sometimes used to express conjecture or probability in the present time. The context shows whether probability or future time is indicated.

¿Qué hora será?	*I wonder what time it is?*
Serán las ocho.	*It must be eight o'clock.*
¿Dónde está Elsa? Estará en casa.	*Where is Elsa? She is probably at home.*
Estará allí a las diez.	*He will be there at ten.*
Tendrá veinte años.	*He must be twenty years old (or will be twenty years old.)*

E. Just as in English *to go + infinitive* expresses futurity, in Spanish **ir a** *+ infinitive* is similarly used.

¿Qué va a pasar?	*What is going to happen?*
Van a salir en seguida.	*They are going to leave at once.*

F. If English *will* expresses the idea of *to be willing to,* rather than future time, the verb **querer** is used.

¿Quiere Ud. ir a la pizarra?	*Will you (please) go to the board?*
¿Quiere Ud. prestarme cien pesos?	*Will you (are you willing to) lend me a hundred pesos?*
No quiero hacerlo.	*I won't (don't want to) do it.*

G. The present tense is frequently used to express future time.

Salen el jueves.

They are leaving (will leave) Thursday.

Te veo mañana.

I'll see you tomorrow.

EXERCISE 5

Write the proper form of the future tense of the following verbs.

1. Ud. (volver, dudar, saber, escribir, venir) **2.** Juan y yo (empezar, sentir, decir, entender, tener) **3.** tú (salir, comprender, llegar, poner, vivir) **4.** vosotros (devolver, poder, insistir, pedir, ser) **5.** ellos (dormir, caber, decir, valer, coger) **6.** yo (estar, venir, hacer, perder, salir)

The Conditional Tense

A. The conditional tense *(would + infinitive)* is formed by adding the endings of the imperfect tense of **haber (-ía, -ías, -ía, -íamos, -íais, -ían)** to the entire infinitive. The endings are the same for all three conjugations.

comprar	to buy (I, you, he, she, it, we, you, they would buy)	compraría, comprarías, compraría, compraríamos, compraríais, comprarían
vender	to sell	vendería, venderías, vendería, venderíamos, venderíais, venderían
escribir	to write	escribiría, escribirías, escribiría, escribiríamos, escribiríais, escribirían

B. The verbs that have an irregular stem in the future tense also use the same stem to form the conditional.

	Future	Conditional		Future	Conditional
caber	cabré	cabría	salir	saldré	saldría
haber	habré	habría	tener	tendré	tendría
poder	podré	podría	valer	valdré	valdría
poner	pondré	pondría	venir	vendré	vendría
querer	querré	querría	decir	diré	diría
saber	sabré	sabría	hacer	haré	haría

C. The conditional corresponds in general to English usage, that is, to express what **would** happen under certain conditions.

Yo no haría eso.

I would not do that.

Lo compraría, pero no tengo bastante dinero.

I would buy it but I don't have enough money.

As in English, the conditional expresses a future time relative to a past. Usually the future will follow a present tense, whereas the conditional will follow a past tense.

Dice que vendrá mañana.	*He says that he will come tomorrow.*
Dijo que vendría mañana.	*He said that he would come tomorrow.*

D. Just as the future may be used to express probability in the present time, the conditional is sometimes used to express probability or conjecture in the past.

¿Qué hora sería cuando llegaste? Serían las dos.	*What time could it have been when you arrived? It must have been two o'clock.*
Tendría cincuenta años cuando murió.	*He must have been fifty years old when he died.*
¿Dónde estaba Pedro? Estaría en casa.	*Where was Pedro? He must have been at home.*

E. Remember that in English *would* + *infinitive* sometimes expresses a habitual past action and therefore calls for the imperfect tense.

Jugábamos a las cartas cuando él venía a visitarnos.	*We would (used to) play cards when he would (used to) come to visit us.*

F. Note that *should* in English may indicate the conditional *(would)* or **deber** *(ought to)*.

Me gustaría ir.	*I should (would) like to go.*
Debo hacerlo.	*I should (ought to) do it.*

G. Just as *will* in English may denote desire in the present, *would* may do so in the past. The verb **querer** is used in such cases. The context will make the meaning clear.

Lo haría por Ud.	*I would do it for you.*
Dijo que no quería venderlo.	*He said that he would not (did not want to) sell it.*
No quiso hacerlo.	*He would not (did not want to, refused to) do it.*

H. One of the main uses of the conditional is in contrary-to-fact sentences, discussed in Lesson 7, Section 5.

Si Luis estuviera aquí, estudiaríamos.	*If Luis were here, we would study.*

EXERCISE 6

Change the conditional verbs in the sentences below, substituting the words indicated for the subjects.

1. *María* comprendería las instrucciones.
    a. yo **b.** nosotros **c.** Uds. **d.** tú **e.** vosotros
2. *Nosotros* preferiríamos el agua fría.
    a. Ud. **b.** tú **c.** vosotros **d.** yo **e.** Teresa
3. *Tú* no lo harías fácilmente.
    a. nosotros **b.** yo **c.** Pedro **d.** ellos **e.** vosotras
4. *Carlos* tendría veinte años cuando ocurrió el accidente.
    a. tú **b.** yo **c.** Uds. **d.** ellos **e.** Juan y yo

Basic Class Exercises

I. A. Make the adjective agree with the noun and place it in the appropriate position before or after the noun.

1. las lecciones (primero) **2.** las chicas (portugués) **3.** la casa (grande) **4.** el niño (tercero) **5.** hombre (ninguno) **6.** las cumbres (alto) **7.** una muchacha (hablador) **8.** los atletas (alemán) **9.** su hermana (burlón) **10.** las paredes (azul) **11.** su esposa (dulce) **12.** Antonio (Santo) **13.** los métodos (eficaz) **14.** una mujer (grande = *great*)

B. The two main characters of *Don Quijote de la Mancha* are Don Quijote and his squire, Sancho Panza. The image most often portrayed in Spain is that of Don Quijote, tall and lean, with a lance in his hand, riding a bony nag, and Sancho

Panza, short and fat, riding on a donkey. Complete the description with the appropriate form of the adjectives in parentheses in their proper place.

1. (famoso, español) Don Quijote y Sancho Panza son los dos personajes más _____ de toda la _____ literatura _____ . **2.** (alto y flaco, bajo y gordo) Don Quijote era un _____ hombre _____ y Sancho, su buen escudero, era _____ . **3.** (grande y rico) Sancho quería ser el gobernador de una _____ isla _____ . **4.** (bueno, hermoso) Don Quijote pensaba sólo en ayudar a los desgraciados y dedicar sus _____ obras _____ a su _____ Dulcinea _____ . **5.** (feo, lindo) Ella era realmente _____ pero a los ojos de don Quijote era la mujer más _____ del mundo. **6.** (ninguno, europeo, valiente) _____ hombre _____ de todas las _____ literaturas _____ era más _____ que don Quijote.

2

II. Answer the following questions using one or more adverbs.

1. ¿Cómo camina Ud.? **2.** ¿Cómo canta Ud.? **3.** ¿Cómo viven los novios en las películas? **4.** ¿Cómo viven después de casarse? **5.** ¿Cómo vuelan los aviones?

3

III. *"Pablo's Birthday Present."* Fill in the blanks with the appropriate form of **estar** or **ser** to learn more about it. Pablo is speaking.

1. Hoy _____ feliz. **2.** _____ mi cumpleaños y creo que mi novia va a darme un buen regalo. **3.** Ella _____ de México y yo _____ de Puerto Rico. **4.** Aunque nosotros _____ en los Estados Unidos, para nosotros _____ natural hablar español. **5.** Ahora _____ las ocho y la _____ esperando en nuestro restaurante favorito. **6.** Pronto llega y parece _____ muy cansada. **7.** Parece que no sabe que hoy _____ mi cumpleaños; me da un besito y nada más. **8.** Ahora yo _____ triste y le pregunto, "¿Sabes qué día _____ hoy?" **9.** Ella contesta, "Sí, _____ jueves." **10.** Cuando ve que yo _____ desilusionado, sonríe y saca un reloj de su bolsillo. **11.** _____ de oro. **12.** Ahora _____ muy feliz porque sé que me quiere mucho.

4

IV. Answer the following questions.

1. ¿Cuándo no le haces caso a tu madre o padre? **2.** ¿Cuándo no prestan Uds. atención a lo que dice su profesor? **3.** ¿Qué quiere decir *a menudo* en inglés? **4.** ¿Quién juega un papel importante en tu vida? ¿Por qué? **5.** ¿Qué hay que hacer para un viaje largo? **6.** ¿Cuánto tiempo hace que hiciste tu último viaje? **7.** ¿Te gustó el viaje. ¿Por qué?

5

V. *"Tomorrow will be different!"* Change the statements to tell how things will be different.

EXAMPLE: Hoy hice el papel de Romeo. Mañana _____ el papel de Macbeth.
Hoy hice el papel de Romeo. Mañana haré el papel de Macbeth.

1. Hoy estudiamos poco. Mañana _____ más. **2.** Hoy no pudimos ir al teatro. Mañana _____ ir. **3.** Hoy no presté mucha atención al profesor. Mañana le _____ más atención. **4.** Estás muy cansada hoy, Ana. Mañana _____ menos cansada. **5.** Mi profesora llegó tarde hoy. Mañana _____ temprano. **6.** Hoy te quiero mucho. Mañana te _____ más. **7.** Elena y Ana no vinieron conmigo hoy.

Mañana _____ conmigo. **8.** Hoy no hay tiempo para eso. Mañana _____ más tiempo. **9.** Hoy Roberto no sabe bien la lección. Mañana la _____ mejor. **10.** Hoy ellos no tienen bastante dinero. Mañana ellos lo _____ .

6

VI. Rewrite the following sentences, changing the main verb to the preterite or imperfect tense and making any other necessary changes.

EXAMPLE: Dice que vendrá a las seis.
           Dijo que vendría a las seis.

1. Sabemos que no llegarán a tiempo. **2.** Cree que no podrá hacerlo.
3. El profesor dice que sólo hará preguntas fáciles. **4.** No sé qué hora será.
5. Afirmamos que lo haremos en seguida. **6.** Aseguran que saldrán pronto para Puerto Rico. **7.** Él pregunta qué querrá decir eso. **8.** Está claro que no pasará nada.

Elective Exercises

VII. Answer in Spanish.

1. ¿Qué hora será? **2.** ¿Qué hora sería ayer cuando terminó la clase?
3. ¿Hablarían Uds. español o portugués en el Brasil? **4.** ¿Eres inglés (o inglesa)? **5.** ¿Estudiarás mucho el año que viene? **6.** ¿A qué hora llegará Ud. a casa esta tarde? **7.** ¿Qué quiere decir *en seguida*? **8.** ¿Eres una buena (un buen) estudiante? ¿Por qué?

VIII. *"True Love?"* Translate.

1. Would you *(tú)* die for me? **2.** Yes, sincerely. Why do you ask such a question? **3.** I am going to take out an insurance policy on your life. **4.** We'll see then if you will really die for me. **5.** She must be crazy! **6.** I will pack my bags at once and leave for China. **7.** No man is so stupid that he would see her again (use *volver a*). **8.** I said I would die for her but I meant that only figuratively.

IX. The following sentences were taken from translations made by students. Many of the mistakes obviously stem from the students' selecting the wrong word in an English–Spanish dictionary. Correct the errors by substituting the words in **b** below for the italicized incorrect words:

1. Elena compró un traje de baño muy pequeño para enseñar su lindo *cadáver*.
2. José y Ana dirán al cura que quieren *cansarse*. **3.** Eduardo perdió su trabajo y ya no puede *soportar* a su mujer e hijos. **4.** Viendo el peligro Carlos gritó:—*¡Reloj fuera!* **5.** Dolores nunca me *vuelve* el dinero que le presto.
6. Chicos, es *el segundo tiempo* que les pido que presten atención. **7.** Rosa se hizo daño en *los clavos* de los dedos. **8.** Inés quiere mucho a su *dulce corazón*.

a. Some of the vocabulary words are: **enseñar,** *to show, teach;* **cadáver,** *body (corpse);* **soportar,** *to tolerate, support (a weight);* **clavo** *nail (metal).*
b. **uñas,** *fingernails;* **novio; la segunda vez; devuelve; cuidado,** *careful, watch out;* **cuerpo; mantener,** *to support financially;* **casarse.**

X. Review of Lesson 2.

A. *"How do we see ourselves?"* Change the verbs (except **estar**) in the following passage to the appropriate preterite or imperfect tense: (**Se** here means *each other.*)

> Dos hombres se encuentran en la calle y se miran. Uno camina con un bastón en la mano. El otro tiene la cara muy arrugada y el pelo blanco. Se conocen, pero hace veinte años que no se ven. De repente se reconocen y empiezan a hablar, muy contentos de haberse encontrado. Después de media hora se despiden el uno del otro.
>
> «Qué viejo está Miguel», dice José para sí.
>
> «Pobre viejito», piensa Miguel.

B. The following paragraph is a brief summary of the great Argentinian epic poem, *Martín Fierro,* by José Hernández (1834–1886). Retell the story in the past, changing the present tense of the verbs to the imperfect or preterite. (The verbs already in the past should be changed to *se habían ido* and *había abandonado.*)

> Me llamo Martín Fierro y soy un gaucho payador*. Me gusta tocar la guitarra, cantar y estar con mi familia. Un día me agarran y me obligan a luchar en la frontera contra los indios. En el ejército llevo una vida miserable. Después de tres años, no puedo aguantar más. Huyo y vuelvo a mi rancho. Encuentro que mis hijos se fueron y que mi mujer abandonó la casa para vivir con otro hombre. Me siento muy triste pero la perdono, porque para ella yo ya no existo. Ella sabe que los gauchos casi nunca vuelven de la frontera. No tiene dinero para vivir. Yo cambio de gaucho bueno a gaucho malo. Un día, otro gaucho me insulta mientras tomo una cerveza, y lo mato. La justicia siempre me persigue y tengo que huir constantemente. La vida de un gaucho es muy dura. No gana nada en la paz y es el primero en la guerra. Si aguanta la opresión es un gaucho bueno, si no aguanta es un gaucho malo.

C. Translate the English words in parentheses.

1. María es *(a nurse).* **2.** *(Women)* son más inteligentes que *(men, say the women).* **3.** *(The soul)* es invisible. **4.** Tengo sed porque *(it is very warm).*
5. *(The Eagle)* y la serpiente es una novela de la revolución mexicana.
6. Siempre tiene *(many crises)* en su vida. **7.** Salió *(without a hat).* **8.** No tengo *(a pencil).* **9.** Tengo *(one pencil).* **10.** Tomamos *(milk)* todos los días.

---

*An Argentinian *cowboy* who improvised songs.

Vocabulary

aburrir to bore
agarrar to seize
aguantar to tolerate, stand
apresuradamente hurriedly
asegurar to assure
bajo short
bastón *m.* cane
beso kiss; besito little kiss
bolsillo pocket
burlón joking, mocking
caber *(irreg.)* to fit
cerveza beer
comedia play (in theater)
contentamente gladly
cortés polite
cumbre *f.* peak
cumpleaños *m.* birthday
charla talk, chat
desarrollo development
desgraciado unfortunate
desilusionado disappointed
despedirse (i, i) (de) to say good-bye
  (to)
discutir to discuss; to argue
dramaturgo dramatist
duro hard
eficaz efficient
ejército army
encantador charming, enchanting
europeo European
feliz happy
feroz fierce, ferocious

flaco thin
gordo fat
hablador talkative
huir to flee
justicia justice; law
lento slow
luchar to fight
maleta suitcase
matar to kill
parecer (zc) to seem; to appear
pariente *m. f.* relative
paz *f.* peace
peligro danger
pelo hair
perseguir (i, i) to pursue
pino pine tree
prestar to lend
prometer to promise
próximo next
reconocer (zc) to recognize
regalo gift, present
repente: de— suddenly
ruidoso noisy
sí: para— to himself
tiempo time; weather;
  a— on time
tocar to play (an instrument)
tranquilamente calmly
único unique; only
valer *(irreg.)* to be worth
vivo lively, vivacious

Lesson 4

1 Possessive Adjectives

2 Possessive Pronouns

3 Demonstrative Adjectives

4 Demonstrative Pronouns

5 Idioms and Word Study

6 Compound Tenses

1

Possessive Adjectives

A. Possessive adjectives are placed before the nouns they modify and must agree in gender and number with the object possessed, not with the possessor.

1. The short forms of the possessive adjectives are:

mi, mis	*my*
tu, tus	*your (fam. sing.)*
su, sus	*his, her, its, your*
nuestro, -a, -os, -as	*our*
vuestro, -a, -os, -as	*your (fam. plur.)*
su, sus	*your, their*

Mi hermano y tus primos	*My brother and your cousins*
Nuestra escuela y nuestros profesores	*Our school and our teachers*
Mi casa es su casa.	*My house is your house.*
Su profesor es muy inteligente.	*His (her, your, their) teacher is very intelligent.*

From the classic Cuban song, *Siboney:*

Siboney, en tu boca	*Siboney, in your mouth*
la miel puso su dulzor.	*honey put its sweetness.*

2. Since **su** and **sus** mean *his, her, its, your* and *their,* the forms **de él, de ella, de Ud., de ellos, de ellas, de Uds.** may be added after the noun for clarity. The definite article is usually used instead of **su** or **sus.**

Tengo sus libros may be clarified by saying:

Tengo los libros de él.	*I have his books.*
Tengo los libros de ella.	*I have her books.*
Tengo los libros de Ud.	*I have your books.*
Tengo los libros de ellos.	*I have their (m.) books.*
Tengo los libros de ellas.	*I have their (f.) books.*
Tengo los libros de Uds.	*I have your (pl.) books.*

B. In addition to those already given, the possessive adjectives have stressed forms (also called "long" forms). The first and second persons plural, **nuestro** and **vuestro,** are the same as the short forms. Since the masculine singular of all stressed possessive adjectives ends in **-o,** each has four forms to show agreement in gender and number with the noun possessed.

mío, mía, míos, mías	*mine, my*
tuyo, tuya, tuyos, tuyas	*yours, your*
suyo, suya, suyos, suyas	*his, hers, her, its; yours, your*
nuestro, nuestra, nuestros, nuestras	*ours, our*
vuestro, vuestra, vuestros, vuestras	*yours, your*
suyo, suya, suyos, suyas	*theirs, their, yours, your*

The stressed forms are used:

1. After the verb **ser** to express possession.

Este coche es nuestro.	*This car is ours.*
Estos papeles son míos.	*These papers are mine.*

To emphasize possession, however, an article may be used after **ser.**

Estos papeles son los míos, no son (los) tuyos.	*These papers are **mine,** they are not **yours.***

2. After a noun to express *of mine, of yours*, etc.

Son amigos míos.   *They are friends of mine.*
Unos primos nuestros   *Some cousins of ours*

3. **Mío** and **nuestro** are often used after the noun in direct address.

Dios mío, ayúdame.   *My Lord, help me.*
Padre Nuestro, que estás en los   *Our Father, who art in heaven ...*
  cielos ...

From the song *Amapola:*†

Yo te quiero, amada niña mía,   *I love you, my beloved girl,*
igual que ama la flor la luz   *just as the flower loves the light*
  del día.   *of the day.*

4. The long forms are sometimes used in popular speech as a substitute for the simple short forms.

El coche tuyo ya no sirve.   *Your car is no good any more.*
¿Dónde puse el libro mío?   *Where did I put my book?*

EXERCISE 1

Fill in the blanks with the appropriate form of the possessive adjective, placing the short form before the noun and the long form after the noun. (The possessor will be the subject of the sentence.)

1. María está en _____ cuarto. **2.** Sé que ellos son _____ amigos. **3.** Ayer salimos con _____ padres. **4.** Amor _____, quiero darte un beso. **5.** Rosa siempre sale con ese amigo _____ . **6.** Juan pasaba todo el día en _____ oficina. **7.** ¿Escribían Uds. a _____ viejo profesor? **8.** El padre dio muchos regalos a _____ hijos. **9.** ¿No vendrás con _____ compañero de cuarto? **10.** ¿Sabéis quién es _____ mejor amigo?

2   Possessive Pronouns

A. The possessive pronouns are formed by placing the definite article before the long forms of the possessive adjectives when these stand in the place of nouns. The possessive pronouns also must agree with the object possessed, not the possessor.

el mío, la mía, los míos, las mías   *mine*
el tuyo, la tuya, los tuyos, las tuyas   *yours (fam. sing.)*
el suyo, la suya, los suyos, las suyas   *his, hers, its, yours*
el nuestro, la nuestra, los nuestros,   *ours*
  las nuestras

el vuestro, la vuestra, los vuestros, las vuestras	yours (fam. plur.)
el suyo, la suya, los suyos, las suyas	theirs, yours
Mi casa es igual que la suya.	My house is the same as his (yours, hers, theirs).
No encuentro mi lápiz, Ana, ¿puedo usar el tuyo?	I can't find my pencil, Ana, may I use yours?
Los nuestros son mejores que los suyos.	Ours are better than theirs.

From a popular Puerto Rican poem:

Cada cual con su derecho	Each one with his own right
y yo con el mío también;	and I with mine too;
lo mejor que Dios ha hecho	the best that God has made
es mi lindo Borinquén.	is my beautiful Borinquen (Puerto Rico).

B. Since the third person forms have many possible meanings, the following substitutions for **el suyo, la suya, los suyos, las suyas** may be used for clarity: **el, la, los,** or **las de él, de ella, de Ud., de ellos, de ellas, de Uds.**

| Tengo mis libros, pero ¿dónde están los de ella (los suyos)? | I have my books, but where are hers? |
| Esta clase es muy buena pero la de ellos (la suya) es mejor. | This class is very good but theirs is better. |

C. The neuter forms **lo mío, lo tuyo, lo suyo, lo nuestro, lo vuestro, lo suyo** have the meaning of *what is mine, what is yours,* etc.

| Lo mío es mío. | What is mine is mine. |
| No quiero lo tuyo. | I don't want what is yours. |

A popular *copla*:

Si quieres que yo te quiera,	If you want me to love you,
ha de ser con condición	it must be with the condition
que lo tuyo sea mío,	that what is yours be mine,
y lo mío tuyo no.	and what is mine not be yours.

EXERCISE 2

A. Substitute a possessive pronoun for the nouns and possessive adjectives.

1. De vez en cuando vamos en *mi coche.* **2.** *Mi casa y tu casa* están lejos de aquí. **3.** Juan vino en *su* (his) *coche.* **4.** Ésta es *mi pistola.* **5.** Llegamos tarde a *su* (their) *casa.* **6.** *Tu profesor y nuestro profesor* son buenos amigos.

7. Estos lápices son *mis lápices* y no sé dónde están *tus lápices.* **8.** Ya vendieron *el coche suyo* (her). **9.** Pedro me devolvió *mi dinero; ¿os* devolvió *vuestro dinero?* **10.** Envío *sus* (his) *cartas* y *mi carta* también.

B. Clarify the possession by using the prepositional forms of the third person possessive in sentences 3, 5, 8 and 10 above.

Demonstrative Adjectives

The demonstrative adjectives are:

este	esta	*this*	estos	estas	*these*
ese	esa	*that (nearby)*	esos	esas	*those (nearby)*
aquel	aquella	*that (over there)*	aquellos	aquellas	*those (over there)*

The forms **aquel, aquellos,** etc., usually refer to something distant or remote in space or time.

Estas cosas que tengo aquí son mías.	*These things I have here are mine.*
Dame **ese** vaso que tienes ahí.*	*Give me that glass that you have there.*
¿Ves allí **aquella** montaña cubierta de nieve?	*Do you see that mountain (over there) covered with snow?*

The opening lines of the popular Argentine tango, *Adiós muchachos,*† uses **aquellos** referring to a distant past.

Adiós muchachos, compañeros de mi vida,	*So long, pals, my lifelong companions,*
Barra querida de aquellos tiempos ...	*Beloved gang of those (good old) days ...*

NOTE: The demonstrative adjective precedes its noun. Occasionally, however, it may follow to provide a graphic, sometimes contemptuous feeling. **Ese, esa, esos, esas** are the forms most used in this construction.

No me gusta el tipo ese.	*I don't like that guy.*

EXERCISE 3

Write the appropriate forms of the demonstrative adjectives before each noun.

1. _____ mesa aquí **2.** _____ chico ahí **3.** _____ mapa aquí **4.** _____ mapas aquí **5.** _____ legumbres ahí **6.** _____ hombres aquí **7.** _____ montaña allí **8.** _____ barco de vela allí

*Aquí, *here,* ahí, *there (near you)* and allí, *there (more distant)* are used when place is indicated by **este, ese** and **aquel,** respectively.

4 Demonstrative Pronouns

A. The demonstrative pronoun takes the place of a noun, and is formed by placing a written accent over the **e** of the demonstrative adjectives.

éste, ésta, éstos, éstas	*this one, these*
ése, ésa, ésos, ésas	*that one, those (near you)*
aquél, aquélla, aquéllos, aquéllas	*that one, those (over there)*

No me gusta este libro; prefiero **ése**.
I don't like this book; I prefer that one.

Aquéllos son mejores que **éstos**.
Those (over there) are better than these.

Este chico y **ésos** son sinvergüenzas.
This boy and those are rascals.

Note that the pronoun agrees in gender and number with the noun it replaces.

B. Éste and **aquél** are also used to express *the latter* and *the former*.

María y Juanita son hermanas; **ésta** es baja y **aquélla** es alta.
Maria and Juanita are sisters; the latter is short and the former is tall.

Note that in Spanish *the latter* comes first and refers to the second one mentioned, *Juanita*.

C. The neuter demonstrative pronouns **esto, eso, aquello** do not refer to a specific thing, but rather to a general idea or situation. Note that these forms end in **o** and do not bear a written accent.

¿Qué es **esto**?	*What is this? (What's going on?)*
Esto es importante.	*This is important.*
Eso es.	*That's it. (That's right.)*
El profesor me dio una *F* y **eso** no me gustó.	*The teacher gave me an F, and I did not like that.*

D. Before **de** and **que** the definite articles **el, la, los, las** are used as demonstrative pronouns.

Estas maletas y las de Pedro
These suitcases and Pedro's (those of Pedro)

Esta corbata y la que compré ayer.
This tie and the one (that) I bought yesterday.

A popular Puerto Rican poem about characteristic popular expressions goes*:

Los que dicen, «Yes, my dear,»	*Those who say, "Yes, my dear,"*
ésos no son de aquí,	*they are not from here,*
Los que dicen, «chamaquito,»	*Those who say, "chamaquito,"*
ésos no son de aquí.	*they are not from here.*
Los que dicen, «adiós che,»	*Those who say, "adiós che,"*
ésos no son de aquí,	*they are not from here.*
Los que dicen, «¡ay, bendito!»	*Those who say, "ay, bendito,"*
ésos sí, ésos sí.	*they are, they are.*

EXERCISE 4

A. Write the appropriate form of the demonstrative pronoun by translating the English.

1. estos niños y *those* (ahí) **2.** esos retratos y *this one* **3.** aquellos árboles y *these* **4.** esa luz y *these* **5.** nuestra casa y *those* (ahí) **6.** estos pobres y *that one* (allí) **7.** esta camisa y *John's* **8.** esta manzana y *the one* que comí

B. Translate the demonstratives.

1. No me gusta *that.* **2.** ¿Dijeron *this* de mí? **3.** No lo metería en *this* bolsa. **4.** Su suéter y *these* son de Costa Rica. **5.** ¿Qué estás haciendo con *that* cuchillo? **6.** ¿Qué quiere decir *that*? **7.** El chico no es capaz de hacer *this.* **8.** No aceptaré tus explicaciones ni *those* de Pedro.

5

Idioms and Word Study

A. General Expressions.

¿Qué tiene Ud. (él, ella)?	*What is the matter with you (him, her)?*
¿Qué le pasa?	*What is the matter with you (him, her)?*
¿Qué pasa?	*What is the matter?*

de repente	*suddenly*
todo el mundo	*everybody*
todos los días	*every day*
todas las noches	*every night*
otra vez	*again*

*Line one, of course, refers to the United States. **Chamaquito** is Mexican for *boy.* **Che** is a typical Argentinian expression used to attract the attention of someone familiar to the speaker. One of the leaders of the Castro revolution in Cuba was Ernesto "Che" Guevara from Argentina. **¡Ay, bendito!** is a very popular Puerto Rican exclamation, denoting almost any emotion.

de vez en cuando	*from time to time*
ahora mismo	*right now*
aquí mismo	*right here*

B. Expressions with **tener**.

tener celos	*to be jealous*
tener cuidado	*to be careful*
tener en cuenta	*to bear in mind; to take into account*
tener éxito	*to be successful*
tener ganas (de)	*to feel like (doing something)*
tener la culpa	*to be to blame*
tener lugar	*to take place*
tener vergüenza	*to be ashamed*

C. Expressions of Obligation.

| hay que | *must, to have to* |
| tener que | |

Hay que + *infinitive* is used when the subject is impersonal, that is, when it does not refer to anyone in particular. **Tener que** + *infinitive* is used when the subject is a specific person or persons. Both denote obligation or necessity to perform an action.

Hay que estudiar para aprender.	*One (We) must study in order to learn.*
Tienes que estudiar más, Juan.	*You have to study more, Juan.*
Tenemos que estudiar esta noche.	*We must study tonight.*

EXERCISE 5

Select the sentence in each group that makes sense.

A. 1. ¿Qué tiene Juan? —Es guapo.
   2. De repente se cayó en la calle.
   3. Todo el mundo duerme con los ojos abiertos.
B. 1. Hay que respirar para vivir.
   2. Debemos dormir en una nube.
   3. El pobre se murió otra vez.
C. 1. Mario tiene que levantarse para dormir.
   2. Debemos enterrarnos ahora mismo.
   3. Estamos cansados de vez en cuando.
D. 1. ¿Cuándo terminó la primera guerra mundial? —Ahora mismo.
   2. ¿Qué te pasa? —Me hice daño.
   3. Los hombres tienen que casarse todos los días.
E. 1. Hay que comer para besar bien.
   2. ¿Cuándo te acostaste? —Aquí mismo.
   3. ¿Qué pasó? —Me caí.

F. 1. María tiene celos de su novio cuando le da un regalo.
    2. Debemos tener cuidado al cruzar la calle.
    3. El partido de fútbol tendrá lugar en la piscina.
G. 1. Nadie tiene ganas de ser millonario.
    2. Debemos tener vergüenza si salimos bien en un examen.
    3. Debemos tener en cuenta que hay que estudiar para aprender.
H. 1. Si salimos mal en los exámenes, los profesores siempre tienen la culpa.
    2. A todo el mundo le gusta tener éxito.
    3. Hay que tener frío para nadar.

Compound Tenses

As in English, compound tenses are formed by using an auxiliary verb plus an invariable past participle. The auxiliary verb in Spanish is **haber,** *to have.* The compound tenses generally correspond in usage in both languages.

A. Formation of the past participle.

1. The past participle of regular verbs is formed by dropping the infinitive ending **-ar** of the first conjugation verbs and adding **-ado: tomar—tomado.** In the second and third conjugations the infinitive ending **-er** or **-ir** is replaced by **-ido: comer—comido; recibir—recibido.**

2. Second and third conjugation verbs whose stem ends in a strong vowel (**a, e** or **o**) require a written accent over the **i** of the ending: **creer—creído; traer—traído; oír—oído.**

3. The following verbs have irregular past participles:

abrir	abierto	*opened*
cubrir	cubierto	*covered*
describir	descrito	*described*
escribir	escrito	*written*
freír	frito	*fried*
morir	muerto	*dead*
poner	puesto	*put*
romper	roto	*broken*
ver	visto	*seen*
volver	vuelto	*returned*

Note that all of the above past participles end in **-to.** The past participles of two important irregular verbs end in **-cho.**

decir	dicho	*said*
hacer	hecho	*done*

Dicho y hecho.   *No sooner said than done. (lit. Said and done.)*

Del dicho al hecho, hay gran
   trecho. (Proverb)

*There's many a slip 'twixt the cup
   and the lip. (lit. From said to
   done, there is a great stretch.)*

4. A past participle may be used as an adjective, in which case it agrees
with the noun it modifies in gender and number.

Enterraron al perro muerto.
Las ventanas están cerradas.

*They buried the dead dog.
The windows are closed.*

B. The present perfect tense.

The present perfect tense is formed by using the present tense of **haber** and
the past participle. It corresponds to English *have* or *has* plus the past
participle.

comprar	comer	vivir
he comprado	he comido	he vivido
has comprado	has comido	has vivido
ha comprado	ha comido	ha vivido
hemos comprado	hemos comido	hemos vivido
habéis comprado	habéis comido	habéis vivido
han comprado	han comido	han vivido

to buy	to eat	to live
I have bought *you have bought, etc.*	*I have eaten* *you have eaten, etc.*	*I have lived* *you have lived, etc.*

He estudiado las reglas pero todavía
   no he escrito los ejercicios.
¿Qué has hecho?

*I have studied the rules, but I have
   not yet written the exercises.
What have you done?*

Two popular sayings:

Quien no ha visto Sevilla
no ha visto maravilla.

*He who has not seen Seville
has not seen a marvel.*

Quien no ha visto Granada
no ha visto nada.

*He who has not seen Granada
has not seen anything.*

From the popular Cuban student song, *Vals del estudiante:*†

Yo por ti he vuelto a la escuela,	*Because of you I have returned to school,*
Yo por ti he vuelto a estudiar ...	*Because of you I have returned to studying . . .*

C. The past perfect tense.

The past perfect tense refers to a past action or event completed before another past action or event. It is formed by using the imperfect of **haber** plus the past participle. It corresponds to English *had* plus the past participle.

salir *to leave*		
había salido habías salido había salido	*I had left* *you had left, etc.*	habíamos salido habíais salido habían salido

Ya había comprado el regalo cuando ella llamó.	*I had already bought the present when she called.*
Volvimos a las cuatro pero ya habían salido.	*We returned at four o'clock but they had already left.*
Nos dijo que ya había leído este libro.	*He told us that he had already read this book.*

D. The future perfect tense.

The future perfect tense (*shall have* or *will have* plus past participle) is of rather limited use in English and in Spanish. It refers to a future action that will be completed before another future action takes place. It is formed by using the future of **haber** plus the past participle.

salir *to leave*		
habré salido habrás salido habrá salido	*I will have left, etc.*	habremos salido habréis salido habrán salido

Habremos terminado este libro para el miércoles.	*We shall (will) have finished this book by Wednesday.*

The future perfect tense may be used to indicate conjecture or probability of a past action.

Habrán salido.	*They must have left.*
¿Adónde habrán ido?	*I wonder where they have gone.*

E. The conditional perfect (past conditional) tense.

The conditional perfect (*would have* + *past participle*) is formed in Spanish by using the conditional of **haber** plus the past participle.

tomar *to take*		
habría tomado habrías tomado habría tomado	*I would have taken, etc.*	habríamos tomado habríais tomado habrían tomado

Usage in both languages generally corresponds.

Yo nunca habría hecho tal cosa.	*I never would have done such a thing.*
No te dije nada porque te habrías enojado.	*I did not say anything to you because you would have gotten angry.*

The conditional perfect may also be used to express past probability or conjecture. It is of rather infrequent use.

Cuando no contestaron, pensamos que habrían salido.	*When they did not answer, we thought they had probably gone out.*

The main use of the conditional perfect is in contrary-to-fact sentences in past time. It is treated in Lesson 7, Section 5.

F. The preterite perfect (past anterior) tense.

The preterite perfect tense is equivalent in translation to the past perfect but is rarely employed. It is formed by the preterite of **haber** plus the *past participle*.

comer *to eat*		
hube comido hubiste comido hubo comido	*I had eaten, etc.*	hubimos comido hubisteis comido hubieron comido

This tense is presented for recognitional purposes only and should not be used by the student. In literature or in elegant language it may appear after certain conjunctions of time, such as **cuando,** *when;* **después que,** *after;* **en cuanto, luego que, así que,** *as soon as;* etc. to express a past action immediately prior to another past action. Normally it is replaced by the simple preterite.

En cuanto hubo entrado (*or* entró) todos salieron.	*As soon as he had entered (**or** entered) they all left.*

Después de que lo hubo visto   *After she had seen (or saw) him*
(or vio) decidió irse a casa.   *she decided to go home.*

EXERCISE 6

Change the verbs to the corresponding compound tenses. (Remember that the simple preterite **hablé** is not replaced by the preterite perfect *[hube hablado]* but by the past perfect *[había hablado]*.)

1. No decimos nada. **2.** ¿Qué le escribías? **3.** Lo terminaremos para el jueves. **4.** No vi a nadie. **5.** No aprendían nada. **6.** Ana abrió la ventana. **7.** Le traigo un vestido nuevo. **8.** ¿Qué hacéis? **9.** ¿Llegas ahora mismo? **10.** ¿Qué les pasará?

Basic Class Exercises

1

I. A. Eduardo and Elvira are your brother and sister. Answer the following questions regarding your imagined family using a possessive adjective in your response.

EXAMPLE: ¿Cómo es el novio de Elvira?
                      Su novio es feo pero simpático.

1. ¿Cuál es vuestro apellido? **2.** ¿Viven con vosotros vuestros abuelos? **3.** ¿Cuántas personas viven en tu casa (o apartamento)? **4.** ¿Cuál es la diversión favorita de tus padres? **5.** ¿Te llevas bien con tus hermanos? **6.** ¿Te ayuda Elvira con tus tareas? **7.** ¿Te gusta llevar la ropa de Eduardo/Elvira? **8.** ¿Cómo es la novia de Eduardo? **9.** ¿Cómo son los amigos de Elvira? **10.** ¿Cómo se llama la escuela a la cual asisten Elvira y Eduardo?

B. Identify each item with a possessive adjective and underline the logical answer.

EXAMPLE: ¿Qué llevará Roberto a la fiesta?
                      (su)   perro   maletas   caballo   discos
                      su perro   sus maletas   su caballo   <u>sus discos</u>

1. ¿Qué llevarán María y Ana a la escuela?
(su)   casa   enemigos   gato   libros
2. ¿Qué te pondrás si hace frío?
(mi)   paraguas   suéter   corbata   vasos
3. ¿Uds. irán a la casa de Elena en qué cosa?
(nuestro)   piscina   motocicleta   perro   amigos
4. ¿Con quiénes voy a celebrar mi cumpleaños?
(tu)   ratón   compañeros   maridos   elefantes

2

II. A. Rewrite the phrase, clarifying the possessive as indicated.

EXAMPLE: mi amigo y el suyo *(hers)*
                      mi amigo y el de ella

1. tus amigos y los suyos *(hers)* **2.** nuestro profesor y el suyo *(theirs)*
3. vuestra madre y la suya *(his)* **4.** mi suegro y los suyos *(theirs f.)*
5. mis clases y las suyas *(his)*

B. Complete the following sentences using a possessive pronoun.

EXAMPLE: Yo me casé con mi novia pero Ramón no se casó _____ .
             Yo me casé con mi novia pero Ramón no se casó con la suya.

1. Quédate tú en tu casa y yo me quedaré en _____ . **2.** Yo no peleo nunca
con mi suegra pero mi hermana de vez en cuando pelea con _____ . **3.** Yo
vine con mis padres y David vino con _____ . **4.** Yo conocí a mi marido en un
baile. ¿Dónde conoció Ud. _____ ? **5.** Yo nunca toco lo suyo y él nunca toca
_____ . **6.** Ellos compraron su coche muy barato pero nosotros pagamos
_____ muy caro. **7.** Ana ha escrito a sus tíos y yo he escrito a _____ .
8. Tengo que pintar mi casa otra vez. ¿Tienes tú que pintar _____ ?

III. A. *"An old girlfriend."* Fill in the blanks with the appropriate form of **ese** or
aquel.

EXAMPLE: _____ coche (nearby) es de mi padre.
             Ese coche es de mi padre.

1. _____ chica (nearby) fue mi novia. **2.** Vive en _____ casa blanca (distant).
3. _____ años (distant) cuando éramos novios fueron muy felices. **4.** Ella me
dejó por _____ hombre (nearby) a su lado. **5.** _____ niños (distant) que
juegan delante de su casa son suyos; desgraciadamente no son míos.

B. Answer the questions using a form of **este** or **ese**. Pretend that the teacher is
asking them in the classroom.

EXAMPLE: ¿De qué color son estos lápices?
             Esos lápices son azules.

1. ¿De qué color son estas pizarras? **2.** ¿De quién es este libro que tengo en
la mano? **3.** ¿De quién son esos libros ahí? **4.** ¿Cómo se llama ese chico?
5. ¿Quién escribió en este cuaderno en mi mesa?

IV. Translate the English.

EXAMPLE: ¿Cuál de aquellas muchachas es tu prima? *(that one)*
             Aquélla.

1. ¿Qué corbata prefiere? (this one) **2.** ¿Sabes lo que dijeron de ti? (That does
not interest me.) **3.** ¿Cuáles de esos papeles son vuestros? (these) **4.** Quiero
hablarte de tu examen. (I prefer to forget this.) **5.** ¿De quién es este examen?
(That one is mine.) **6.** Pierre y Margaret son amigos míos. (The latter is English
and the former is French.) **7.** ¿Qué vestido prefieres? (The one I bought
yesterday.) **8.** ¿Qué tienes en las manos? (My watch and Mary's.)

V. A. Ask another student the following questions.

1. si tiene cuidado cuando cruza la calle **2.** cuándo tiene celos de su
novio (-a) **3.** si tiene ganas de ir al cine contigo **4.** quién tiene la culpa si tú

no tienes éxito en este curso **5.** si tiene vergüenza porque llega tarde todos los días **6.** qué hay que hacer para aprender bien el español

B. *"Why some teachers retire early!"* Translate the following passage.

1. —¿Qué está pasando?—dijo el profesor al entrar en la clase y al recibir un borrador en la cara. **2.** —Nada, estábamos estudiando aquí mismo la velocidad de los borradores comparada con la de las tizas. **3.** —Uds. tienen que comportarse bien cuando no estoy en la clase. **4.** De repente, otro borrador vuela por el aire y golpea al profesor en la cabeza. **5.** —Sinvergüenzas, ahora mismo los castigaré. **6.** ¿Qué tienen Uds.? Todo el mundo está loco.
7. Otra vez vuela un borrador, y otro, y otro, y otro. **8.** —Hay que tener paciencia,—grita el profesor mientras huye de la clase. **9.** —Todos los días es la misma historia. **10.** Ahora mismo salgo de este infierno para siempre.
11. Adiós muchachos y ¡buena suerte!

VI. A. Write the appropriate form of one of the compound tenses. (No conjecture or probability unless so indicated.)

EXAMPLE: Dice que lo (terminar)_____ ahora mismo.
Dice que lo ha terminado ahora mismo.

1. Dijo que lo (llevar)_____ ayer. **2.** Dice que lo (escribir)_____ para el lunes. **3.** ¿A qué hora (salir)_____ ella? (conjecture) **4.** Creían que nosotros lo (hacer)_____ de repente. **5.** ¿A qué hora (llegar)_____ tú esta mañana?

B. *"Why mothers get gray!"* Rewrite this story in the past. The first sentence would be: **Nunca había visto tal desorden.**

1. Nunca he visto tal desorden. **2.** Otra vez parece que ha entrado un ciclón en el cuarto. **3.** Cuando veo a mi hijo le pregunto por qué está así su cuarto.
4. Me contesta que ha estudiado mucho y que lo pondrá todo en orden mañana. (*Change to* al día siguiente.) **5.** Dice que ha tenido que salir para hablar con su amigo Pedro. **6.** Yo sé que «el amigo» se llama Dolores y que el estudio habrá sido una carta de amor, pero no digo nada. **7.** Los hijos adolescentes siempre tienen problemas de amor y no he querido aumentarlos. **8.** Sin embargo, más tarde el pobre ha limpiado su cuarto y lo ha preparado para el próximo ciclón.

Elective Exercises

VII. Translate the following sentences paying particular attention to the tense of the verbs and their subjects.

1. ¿Qué has hecho hoy? **2.** Vi a María pero no me dijo nada. **3.** ¿A qué hora vendrás a mi casa? **4.** No habíamos asistido a ese baile. **5.** ¿Llevaste ese vestido anoche? **6.** Peleé con mi novio y le devolví la sortija que me había dado. **7.** Nos divertíamos mucho cuando nos visitabas todos los días. **8.** Escribí a mis padres y me contestaron que me enviarían el dinero que les pedí.

VIII. Translate.

1. My love, what's mine is mine and what's yours will be mine, and so *(así)* we'll live happily. **2.** One must have patience to be a father, mother, daughter, or son. **3.** That son of yours *(fam. sing.)* must have been very bright in school since he is now president of his bank. **4.** Yes, the one that my husband established. **5.** This building and that one are hers; the others are theirs. **6.** He said he would have married me, but I didn't have enough money to support him.

IX. Answer the following questions.

1. ¿Has estudiado mucho para la lección de hoy? **2.** ¿Han leído Uds. esta revista? **3.** ¿Cuántas veces has comido hoy? **4.** ¿Había salido tu padre antes de las siete? **5.** ¿Ha explicado bien este punto tu profesor? **6.** ¿Quién ha mirado ese programa en la televisión? **7.** ¿Habrían ido Uds. al cine sin mí? **8.** ¿Cuándo habremos terminado nuestro texto?

X. Answer the questions related to the pictures.

1. ¿Cómo ha llegado Juan a la fiesta?

2. ¿Qué voy a ponerme cuando hace frío?

3. ¿Dónde están nadando José y Pedro?

4. ¿Qué vuela rápido en el mar cuando hace viento?

5. ¿Qué está haciendo el perro con su hueso?

6. ¿Dónde ha vivido siempre el diablo?

XI. Review of Lesson 3.

A. Translate the words in parentheses into Spanish.

1. Mi amiga (is from Spain). **2.** Tenemos que estudiar (some very difficult lessons). **3.** (There is no strong man here). **4.** Viviremos (happily). *(two ways)* **5.** Mi hermano (is a doctor). **6.** El Presidente llegó con (his charming wife). **7.** ¿Dónde (are the green dresses and the blue ones)? **8.** María y Ana (are intelligent and pretty). **9.** La sopa (is warm). **10.** Hablan (clearly).

B. Change the sentences to the past.

EXAMPLE: Saben que vendremos temprano.
             Sabían que vendríamos temprano.

1. Mario dice que hará un papel importante en mi vida. **2.** Me contesta que saldrá en seguida. **3.** No saben lo que dicen. **4.** Cree que vendrás a verme a menudo. **5.** Piensan que ya no volverán a visitarnos. **6.** Prometemos al profesor que estudiaremos más. **7.** Dice que el reloj valdrá cien dólares. **8.** Sabe que no iré con él.

Vocabulary

apellido surname
asistir (a) to attend
bendito blessed
borrador *m.* eraser
capaz capable
compañero companion;
  —**de cuarto** roommate
comportarse to behave
cruzar to cross
cuenta account, check
  (restaurant)
  darse—(de) to realize
cuento story
dejar to leave, abandon
diablo devil
enterrar (ie) to bury
golpear to hit
gozar (de) to enjoy
guardar to keep
infierno hell
joya jewel
llevar to wear
  — **se bien** to get along with

mar *m.* sea
meter to put (into)
motocicleta motorcycle
mundial world *(adj.)*
nube *f.* cloud
para siempre forever
pelear(se) to argue; to fight
película film
piscina swimming pool
recobrar to regain
regalo gift
respirar to breathe
revista magazine
rubio blonde
salud *f.* health
seguida: en— at once
siempre: para— forever
sinvergüenza *m.f.* scoundrel
sortija ring
suéter *m.* sweater
vestido dress
volver a (jugar) (to play) again

Lesson 5

1

Subject and Prepositional Pronouns

A. The subject pronouns are:

yo *I*	nosotros (-as) *we*
tú *you (fam.)*	vosotros (-as) *you (fam.)*
él *he*	ellos *they (m.)*
ella *she*	ellas *they (f.)*
usted *you*	ustedes *you*

The subject pronouns,* except **usted** and **ustedes**, are usually not expressed with verbs, unless needed for emphasis or clarity. **Usted** and **ustedes** are sometimes omitted, but are normally retained for politeness.

*The use of subject pronouns is discussed in Lesson 1, Section 4.B, in the treatment of the present tense.

Él miraba la televisión mientras ella estudiaba.	He was watching television while she was studying.
¿Quién es? Soy yo.	Who is it? It is I.
Tú y yo sabemos la verdad.	You and I know the truth.
Sabes que no podemos venir.	You know that we cannot come.
¿Quién lo tiene? Yo.	Who has it? I (do).
¿Qué van a hacer Uds.?	What are you going to do?

B. Prepositional Forms.

The pronouns used after prepositions *(for me, with him, against us, from her, etc.)* are the same as the subject forms in Spanish, except for the first and second persons singular and the reflexive **sí.** The prepositional forms are:

mí	*me*	mí	*myself*
ti	*you (fam.)*	ti	*yourself*
él	*him, it (m.)*	sí	*himself*
ella	*her, it (f.)*	sí	*herself*
Ud.	*you*	sí	*yourself*
nosotros (-as)	*us*	nosotros (-as)	*ourselves*
vosotros (-as)	*you (fam.)*	vosotros (-as)	*yourselves*
ellos	*them*	sí	*themselves*
ellas	*them*	sí	*themselves*
Uds.	*you*	sí	*yourselves*

Estas cartas son para mí, no para ti.	These letters are for me, not for you.
Vivimos con ella.	We live with her.
No hablamos de él.	We are not talking about him.
Trabaja para sí.	He works for himself.
Lo hizo por mí.	He did it for me.
¿Mi carro? Mejor no hablar de él.	My car? Better not to talk about it.

Mismo is often added to the reflexive prepositional pronoun for greater emphasis.

Siempre piensa en sí misma.	She is always thinking about herself.

When **mí, ti, sí** are used with **con,** they become **conmigo, contigo** and **consigo.**

Vino conmigo.	He came with me.
Lo llevaron consigo.	They took it with them(selves).

The following popular *copla* by the Spanish poet Ventura Ruiz Aguilera (1820–1881) contains several examples of prepositional pronouns.

Ni contigo ni sin ti	Neither with you nor without
mis penas tienen remedio;	you does my anguish have a cure;

contigo porque me matas,
y sin ti porque me muero.

with you because you slay me,
and without you because I die.

The first stanza of the popular romantic song, *Amor:*†

Amor, amor, amor,
nació de ti, nació de mí,
de la esperanza ...

Love, love, love,
was born of you, was born of me,
of hope . . .

EXCEPTION: The prepositions **entre, menos, excepto** and **según** are, however, followed by the subject pronoun forms.

Entre tú y yo ...
Todos menos yo ...
Según él ...

Between you and me . . .
All except for me . . .
According to him . . .

EXERCISE 1

A. Substitute a pronoun for the noun in italics.

1. *Los profesores* siempre tienen razón. **2.** Siempre tenía miedo de *María*.
3. Mi amigo me ayudó con *la tarea*. **4.** No me lo dijo a mí sino a *José*. **5.** Salió
sin *el paraguas*. **6.** Ni *Carlos* ni *Rosa* querrá(n) venir conmigo.

B. Translate the English word or words in parentheses into Spanish. (Use familiar forms when a first name is used.)

1. Me dijo que no quería salir (with me) al día siguiente. **2.** Entre (you and me),
Carlos, nunca habrá secretos. **3.** A ella le gusta hablar de (herself). **4.** ¿Tu
ensayo? No me acuerdo de (it). **5.** Estos mapas no son para (them). **6.** Me
mataré por (you) ahora mismo, amor mío, si no me dejas ir (with you). **7.** Recibí las
cartas pero me olvidé de (them) en seguida. **8.** No estoy satisfecho de (myself).

2 Object Pronouns

A. The indirect and direct object pronouns have the same forms in the first and second persons, singular and plural.

Indirect		Direct	
me	*(to) me*	me	*me*
te	*(to) you (fam.)*	te	*you (fam.)*
le	*(to) him, (to) her,*	le*	*him, you (m.)*
	(to) you (pol.), (to) it	lo	*him, you (m.), it (m.)*
		la	*her, you (f.) it (f.)*

*As a direct object referring to a male person, **le** is generally preferred in Spain, **lo** in Spanish America.

Indirect		Direct	
nos	*(to) us*	nos	*us*
os	*(to) you (fam.)*	os	*you (fam.)*
les	*(to) you, (to) them*	los	*them, you (m.)*
		las	*them, you (f.)*

It or *them* referring to things is almost always a direct object, rarely an indirect.

B. Position of object pronouns with conjugated verbs.

In the sentence *He gives the book to the boy* or *He gives the boy the book*, *the book* is the direct object of the verb *gives* and *the boy* or *to the boy* is the indirect object. In Spanish we would say: **Da el libro al muchacho.**

If we substitute the direct object pronoun in English the sentence would be *He gives it to the boy.* The object pronoun *it* follows the verb in English, but in Spanish the object pronoun (direct or indirect) precedes the conjugated verb: **Lo da al muchacho.**

If we replace *the boy* with an indirect object pronoun (**le**) the English sentence would be *He gives the book to him* or *He gives him the book.* In Spanish: **Le da el libro.**

Other examples:

Me vio y me dio el mensaje.	*He saw me and gave me the message.*
No la conozco personalmente, pero le he hablado por teléfono.	*I don't know her personally, but I have spoken to her by phone.*

C. The third person indirect object pronoun *may* be used to anticipate a noun indirect object referring to a person. This pronoun is redundant and is not to be translated into English. For example, *He gives the book to the boy* may also be expressed as: **Le da el libro al muchacho**.

D. The indirect object pronoun is used for persons with verbs like **pedir,** *to ask for;* **quitar,** *to take away;* **robar,** *to steal from*.

Siempre me piden dinero.	*They always ask me for money.*
Le quitaron sus libros.	*They took his (her) books away from him/her.*
Les robó todo lo que tenían.	*He robbed them of everything they had.*

E. The indirect object pronoun is also used as a dative (indirect object) of reference indicating the person concerned or affected by the action.

Le lavó la cara.	*She washed his face.*
¿Quieres plancharme esta camisa?	*Will you iron this shirt for me?*

F. The neuter direct object **lo** is used with **ser** and **estar** to refer to a predicate adjective or noun or a previously expressed idea.

Parecen ricos pero no lo son.	*They seem rich but they are not.*
¿Estás cansada, María? —Si, lo estoy.	*Are you tired, María? —Yes, I am.*

G. Double object pronouns.

The indirect object pronoun precedes the direct.

Me lo dio ayer.	*He gave it to me yesterday.*
Nos lo mandaron.	*They sent it to us.*

If both object pronouns are in the third person, the indirect **le** or **les** is replaced by **se**. In the example *He gives the book to the boy* (**Da el libro al muchacho**), if we replace both nouns with pronouns, we have in English *He gives it* (**lo**) *to him* (**le**). Since **le** and **lo** are both third person forms, the **le** is changed to **se**, hence: **Se lo da.**

H. Since **se** may mean *to him, to her, to you, to them,* we may clarify the reference by adding **a** plus the prepositional form.

Se lo da
{ a él.
a ella.
a Ud.
a ellos.
a ellas.
a Uds. }

He gives it
{ *to him.*
to her.
to you.
to them (m.).
to them (f.).
to you. }

The prepositional forms may also be added to give emphasis or contrast in any person.

Me los mandó.	*He sent them to me.*
Me los mandó a mí, no a Ud.	*He sent them to **me**, not to **you**.*
No le gusta a ella, pero me gusta a mí.	*She does not like it, but I do.*
No nos importa a nosotros.	*It doesn't matter to **us**.*

Examples of double object pronouns are found in the popular Mexican song, *Allá en el rancho grande.*†

Te voy a hacer tus calzones	*I am going to make your riding pants*
como los usa el ranchero;	*the way a rancher wears them;*
te los comienzo de lana,	*I'll begin them for you with wool,*
te los acabo de cuero.	*I'll finish them off with leather.*

From the Mexican greeting song, *Las mañanitas:*[†]

Estas son las mañanitas	*These are the morning songs*
que cantaba el rey David,	*which King David used to sing,*
a las muchachas bonitas	*to the pretty girls*
se las cantamos aquí.	*we sing them here.*

I. Position of object pronouns with infinitive or present participle.

The object pronoun must be attached to an infinitive or present participle, when it is not used with an auxiliary verb.

Antes de hacerlo ...	*Before doing it . . .*
Sin decírnoslo ...	*Without telling it to us . . .*
No conseguirás nada hablándole así.	*You will not gain anything by speaking to him (her) that way.*

If an auxiliary verb is used with the infinitive or present participle, the object pronouns may either be attached, as in the above examples, or they may be placed before the auxiliary verb.

No quiero verlos *or* No los quiero ver.	*I do not want to see them.*
Estaba hablándoles *or* Les estaba hablando.	*He was talking to them.*

J. Position of object pronouns with commands.

Object pronouns are also attached to *affirmative* commands, but precede *negative* commands. (See Lesson 6, Section 2, for a fuller treatment of commands.)

Dígame (Ud.) la verdad.	*Tell me the truth.*
No me diga (Ud.) nada.	*Don't tell me anything.*
Dígamela (Ud.).	*Tell it to me.*
No me la diga (Ud.).	*Don't tell it to me.*
Tómalo (tú).	*Take it.*
No lo tomes (tú).	*Don't take it.*

K. In the following cases a written accent is needed when object pronouns are added, in order to retain the stress on the syllable originally stressed. (See also Appendix D.)

1. When a double object pronoun is added:

Dámelo.	*Give it to me. (familiar command)*
Sin decírnoslo ...	*Without telling it to us . . .*
Leyéndoselo ...	*Reading it to them . . .*

2. When a single object pronoun is added to a present participle:

Está bebiéndolo.	*He is drinking it.*
Están siguiéndola.	*They are following her.*

3. When a single object pronoun is added to a command, unless the command is a monosyllable or a **vosotros** form.*

Mándelo (Ud.) por avión.	*Send it by plane.*
Escríbalas (Ud.) claramente.	*Write them clearly.*

as opposed to:

Dilo (tú) en seguida.	*Say it at once.*
Dame (tú) la pata.	*Give me your paw.*
Hacedlo (vosotros) ahora.	*Do it now.*

EXERCISE 2

Rewrite the sentences, substituting a pronoun for the italicized words. (Remember to add a written accent when necessary.)

1. Queremos hacer *la maleta.* **2.** ¿Habéis visto *a su marido*? **3.** Digan *al marido* que su mujer está buscándolo. **4.** Ya lo dije *al marido.* **5.** No coja Ud. *el cuchillo.* **6.** Guillermo Tell no dio en la manzana y su hijo se comió *la manzana.* **7.** Aceptó *la sortija* pero al día siguiente la devolvió *a su novio.* **8.** ¿Os escribió *las cartas* el Presidente? **9.** Los ladrones robaron mucho dinero *a José.* **10.** Quítale *la chaqueta al niño.*

Reflexive Pronouns and Verbs

A. The reflexive pronouns are the same as the direct or indirect object forms in the first and second persons, singular and plural. The third person singular and plural form is **se**.

Reflexive pronouns

me	*myself*	nos	*ourselves*
te	*yourself*	os	*yourselves*
se	*himself, herself, yourself, itself*	se	*themselves, yourselves*

A verb is reflexive in Spanish when the subject receives the action of the verb, that is, the subject and the object are the same person. The verbs in the English sentence *He gets up, washes, shaves and dresses* are reflexive in Spanish: **Se levanta, se lava, se afeita** y **se viste.**

Transitive verbs (**lavar,** to wash; **levantar,** to raise) may be made reflexive (**lavarse,** to wash oneself, to get washed; **levantarse,** to raise oneself, to get up) by placing the reflexive pronoun before the conjugated verb forms.

---

*Third conjugation reflexive **vosotros** commands require a written accent over the -i when the reflexive pronoun is added. **Vestíos.** *Get dressed.*

lavarse *to wash (oneself)*		
me lavo	*I wash (myself)*	
te lavas	*you wash (yourself)*	
se lava	*he washes (himself)*	
	she washes (herself)	
	you wash (yourself)	

nos lavamos	*we wash (ourselves)*
os laváis	*you wash (yourselves)*
se lavan	*they wash (themselves)*
	you wash (yourselves)

B. Many transitive verbs may logically be made reflexive. Here are a few
   examples.

acostar *to put to bed*	**acostarse** *to go to bed*
afeitar *to shave*	**afeitarse** *to shave (oneself)*
divertir *to amuse*	**divertirse** *to have a good time*
llamar *to call*	**llamarse** *to be named*
sentar *to seat*	**sentarse** *to sit down*
vestir *to dress*	**vestirse** *to get dressed*

La madre acostó a los niños a las ocho y ella se acostó a las diez.	*The mother put the children to bed at eight and she went to bed at ten.*
Llamé a Juan.	*I called Juan.*
¿Cómo se llama Ud.?	*What is your name?*
Me llamo José.	*My name is José.*

C. Some verbs assume a somewhat different meaning when reflexive.

A few examples are:

comer *to eat*	**comerse** *to eat up*
ir *to go*	**irse** *to go away*
llevar *to carry*	**llevarse** *to carry away*
dormir *to sleep*	**dormirse** *to fall asleep*
quitar *to take away*	**quitarse** *to take off (clothing)*

Se quitó la ropa.	*He took off his clothing.*
Se durmió en seguida.	*He fell asleep at once.*
Se comió todo el pastel.	*He ate up the whole pie.*
Lo que el viento se llevó.	*Gone with the wind. (What the wind carried away.)*

From the second stanza of the popular Argentinian tango *Adiós muchachos:*[†]

Adiós muchachos, ya me voy y me resigno ...	*Good-bye, fellows, I am going away and am resigned . . .*

Rubén Darío (1867–1916), born in Nicaragua, introduced modernism in Hispanic poetry. The refrain from one of his finest poems, *Canción de otoño en primavera:*

Juventud, divino tesoro,	*Youth, divine treasure,*
ya te vas para no volver.	*you are going away never to return.*
Cuando quiero llorar no lloro,	*When I want to cry, I don't cry,*
y, a veces, lloro sin querer.	*and, at times, I cry without wanting to.*

D. Some verbs may be reflexive or non-reflexive with little change in meaning.

caer(se) *to fall (down)*   **morir(se)** *to die*
callar(se) *to be quiet*   **quedar(se)** *to remain*

¡Cállate!	*Be quiet!*
Quien calla otorga. *(Proverb)*	*Silence gives consent.*
Decidimos quedarnos aquí.	*We decided to stay here.*
Nadie creía que iba a morirse cuando se cayó la semana pasada.	*Nobody thought that he was going to die when he fell last week.*

From the classic Cuban song, *Siboney:*

Siboney, yo te quiero,	*Siboney, I love you,*
yo me muero por tu amor ...	*I am dying for your love . . .*

E. Some verbs are always reflexive in Spanish.

arrepentirse *to repent*   **jactarse** *to boast*
atreverse *to dare*   **quejarse** *to complain*
                                  suicidarse *to commit suicide*

Quien no se atreve no pasa la mar. *(Proverb)*	*He who does not dare (take chances) does not cross the sea. (Nothing ventured, nothing gained.)*
Se queja de que no se acuerda de nada.	*He complains that he does not remember anything.*

F. Several verbs combine the reflexive and indirect object pronoun (dative of interest) to indicate the person affected by an unexpected action.

Se le perdieron los mapas.	*He lost the maps.*
Se me murió el caballo.	*My horse died "on me."*
Se nos escapó.	*He (she, it) got away from us.*

Certain verbs such as **olvidar, ocurrir, figurar,** etc. are often used in this way.

No se me ocurrió.	*It didn't occur to me.*
Se nos olvidó llamarle.	*We forgot to call him.*
Se me trabó la lengua.	*My tongue got twisted.*

G. The reflexive may be used in the plural to express a reciprocal action, either direct or indirect. **Uno a otro (el uno al otro)** may be added for clarity.

No nos vemos mucho, pero nos escribimos todas las semanas.	*We don't see each other often but we write (to one another) every week.*
Se miraron uno a otro.	*They looked at each other.*

H. The reflexive **se** is used to express the English indefinite *one, they, you, people, etc.*

Se cree que es tonto.	*People think he is a fool.*
Se dice que tiene mucho dinero.	*It is said that he has a lot of money.*
Se come bien aquí.	*One eats well here.*
¿Por dónde se sale?	*Where is the exit? (Through where does one leave?)*
Se habla español en muchos países.	*Spanish is spoken in many countries.*
Se prohibe fumar en clase.	*It is forbidden to smoke in class.*
Se alquila.	*For rent (it rents itself).*

EXERCISE 3

Insert the reflexive pronoun in the blank space, if necessary.

1. Según el letrero del escaparate, _____ habla español en esta tienda.
2. Mi novia _____ llama Juana. **3.** ¿A qué hora _____ acuestas? **4.** ¿_____ acuerdan Uds. de mí a menudo? **5.** La madre está lavando _____ el niño.
6. Pablo y Ana _____ quieren mucho.

Idioms and Word Study

A. General Expressions.

a lo lejos	*in the distance*
a propósito	*by the way*
cuanto antes	*as soon as possible*
darse cuenta (de)	*to realize (mentally)*
dar un paseo	*to take a walk (a ride)*

B. To become.

hacerse	*to become (through one's own efforts), usually referring to a trade or profession*

llegar a ser	*to become (get to be as a result of a series of circumstances)*
ponerse	*to become (used with adjectives usually referring to health or emotion)*
ser de	*to become of (happen)*
volverse	*to become (radical change, such as with **loco**)*

Su hijo se hizo médico.	*His son became a doctor.*
Su primo llegó a ser presidente.	*His cousin became (got to be) president.*
María se puso pálida.	*María became pale.*
Pablo se puso enfermo.	*Pablo became sick.*
Don Quijote se volvió loco porque leyó muchos libros de caballerías.	*Don Quijote went mad because he read many books of chivalry.*
¿Qué ha sido de Roberto?	*What has become of Roberto?*

C. Useful Expressions: Health inquiries.

¿Cómo está Ud.?	*How are you?*
No me siento (muy) bien.	*I'm not feeling (very) well.*
Lo siento mucho.	*I'm very sorry.*
Cuídese.	*Take care of yourself.*
Espero que se mejore pronto.	*I hope you feel better soon.*
¿Cómo está la familia?	*How is the family?*
Muy bien, gracias, ¿y la suya?	*Very well, thank you, and yours?*
Regular; así, así.	*Fair; so, so.*

EXERCISE 4

Fill in the blanks with an idiom or word from this section.

1. El mejor candidato _____ presidente. **2.** Los novios prefieren _____ por el parque. **3.** Ella _____ que esto es difícil. **4.** _____ , ¿qué hora es? **5.** Al ver que pegaban al caballo, Eduardo _____ furioso. **6.** Mi hermano está estudiando para _____ ingeniero. **7.** Si tienes prisa, lo haré _____ .
8. _____ se veían las montañas. **9.** Cuando los niños gritan yo _____ loco.

The Passive Voice

A. The true passive construction (the subject *receives* the action) is the same in English and Spanish.

Estas novelas fueron escritas por Juan Valera.	*These novels were written by Juan Valera.*
La puerta fue cerrada por el profesor.	*The door was closed by the teacher.*

The verb *to be* is **ser** in this construction, and the past participle must agree with the subject in gender and number. The agent is usually introduced by **por,** but **de** is generally used when the verb denotes mental action.

Es respetado de todos.	*He is respected by everyone.*

B. If, however, we are describing a state or condition, **estar** plus the past participle must be used.

La puerta estaba cerrada cuando llegamos.	*The door was closed when we arrived.*

C. If the agent (the one by whom the action is performed) is not expressed, Spanish often uses the reflexive to render the English passive. The verb agrees with the Spanish subject, which generally follows the verb.

De repente se abrió la puerta.	*Suddenly the door was opened.*
Se construyó esta casa en 1960.	*This house was built in 1960.*
A lo lejos se ven las montañas cubiertas de nieve.	*In the distance the mountains covered with snow are seen.*

D. Just as in English, the indefinite third person plural is often used in place of the passive when the agent is not indicated. The *they* does not refer to anyone in particular. Hence the sentence **Se construyó esta casa en 1960** may be stated: **Construyeron esta casa en 1960.** *They built this house in 1960.*

Other examples of this type:

Dicen que es millonario.	*It is said (They say) he is a millionaire.*
¿Dónde lo hallaron?	*Where was he found? (Where did they find him?)*
Hablan portugués en el Brasil.	*Portuguese is spoken (They speak Portuguese) in Brazil.*

Recapitulating, the passive may be expressed in the following ways if no agent is expressed.

La casa fue pintada.	
Se pintó la casa.	} The house was painted.
Pintaron la casa.	

If an agent is expressed, only the **ser** construction is used.

La casa ha sido pintada por Pedro.	*The house has been painted by Pedro.*

E. All the above passive sentences refer to things. When the subject (the receiver of the action) is a person, however, that person becomes the object of the reflexive verb. The verb then always remains in the singular.

Se eligió al presidente.	*The president was elected.*
	(One elected the president.)
Se nombró a los miembros del gabinete.	*The members of the cabinet were appointed.*

The other ways of expressing the passive for persons are the same as for things.

El presidente fue elegido.	*The president was elected.*
Los miembros del gabinete fueron nombrados.	*The members of the cabinet were appointed.*
Eligieron al presidente.	*The president was elected. (They elected the president.)*
Nombraron a los miembros del gabinete.	*The members of the cabinet were appointed. (They appointed the members of the cabinet.)*

EXERCISE 5

A. Express the same idea using the **se** construction.

1. La ventana fue abierta. **2.** Las luces serán encendidas más tarde. **3.** La lección ha sido terminada. **4.** Las puertas fueron cerradas. **5.** El cuarto es limpiado a menudo. **6.** El coche ya ha sido lavado.

B. Express the same idea as in the above sentences by using the third person plural verb construction.

C. Fill in the blank spaces with the proper form of **ser** or **estar.**

1. No podemos entrar porque la puerta ya _____ cerrada. **2.** Esa profesora _____ admirada de sus estudiantes. **3.** La novela _____ escrita por Cervantes en el siglo diez y siete. **4.** Las cartas _____ recibidas mañana. **5.** Los libros _____ abiertos *(open)* ahora. **6.** El jefe _____ nombrado por el presidente el mes pasado.

The Progressive Tenses

A. The simple present tense in Spanish (**hablo, como**) may be the equivalent of the English simple present *(I speak, I eat)* or the progressive *(I am speaking, I am eating).* Likewise the imperfect (**hablaba, comía**) may be translated as *I was speaking, I was eating.* The verb **estar** plus present participle is an equivalent of the English progressive *(to be* plus the present participle). The progressive tense is more vivid than the simple tense and is used mainly to emphasize or to intensify an action that is in progress at a particular time.

Juan habla inglés y español; ahora está hablando español.	Juan speaks English and Spanish; he is speaking Spanish now.
Comemos tres veces al día, pero no estamos comiendo ahora.	We eat three times a day but we are not eating now.
¿Qué estabas haciendo?	What were you doing?
Estaba estudiándolo.	I was studying it.

B. The present participle is formed by adding **-ando** to the stem of the infinitive of first conjugation verbs, and **-iendo** to the stem of the infinitive of second and third conjugation verbs.

mirar	mirando	*looking*
comer	comiendo	*eating*
escribir	escribiendo	*writing*

The forms of the present participle of all first conjugation verbs are regular. Second conjugation verbs whose stem ends in a vowel require the ending -yendo rather than -iendo. This occurs because an unaccented i between two vowels becomes a y.

| caer | cayendo | leer | leyendo |

The verb **oír** also follows this pattern: **oyendo**

First and second conjugation stem-changing verbs do not have a change in the stem.

pensar > pensando   **volver** > volviendo

Third conjugation stem-changing verbs change e of the stem to i, and o to u.

| pedir | pidiendo | dormir | durmiendo |
| sentir | sintiendo | morir | muriendo |

NOTE ALSO: **decir** > diciendo; **poder** > pudiendo.

The verbs **ir** (**yendo**) and **venir** (**viniendo**) are rarely used in the progressive tenses.

The following is a paradigm for all verbs:

estudiar *to study*		
estoy		I am	
estás		you are	
está	estudiando	he, she is; you are	studying
estamos		we are	
estáis		you are	
están		they, you are	

C. An object pronoun can be attached to the present participle or placed before the auxiliary verb.

Estoy explicándoselo *or* Se lo estoy explicando.	*I am explaining it to you.*
Yo estaba afeitándome *or* Yo me estaba afeitando.	*I was shaving.*
Están lavándose *or* Se están lavando.	*They are washing (themselves).*

D. The verbs **ir, venir, andar,** and **seguir** are sometimes used instead of **estar** as the auxiliary verb in the progressive construction. When used, these verbs retain something of their original meaning.

Va anocheciendo.	*It is growing dark.*
Siguen molestándonos.	*They keep on bothering us.*
Andan buscándolos por todas partes.	*They go around looking for them everywhere.*

From the popular song, *Cielito lindo:*[†]

De la Sierra Morena,	*From the Sierra Morena,*
cielito lindo,	*my darling,*
viene bajando	*down comes*
un par de ojitos negros,	*a pair of dark eyes,*
cielito lindo,	*my darling,*
de contrabando.	*stealthily.*

For the use of the present participle without an auxiliary verb, see Lesson 9, Section 4.B.

EXERCISE 6

A. Write the present participle of the following verbs.

1. tomar **2.** escribir **3.** decir **4.** tener **5.** dormir **6.** pedir **7.** volver
8. acostarse **9.** salir **10.** vestirse

B. Change the main verb to the corresponding progressive tense.

1. Mario se pone viejo. **2.** Dábamos un paseo cuando empezó a llover.
3. Llueve. **4.** Nos vestíamos cuando sonó el teléfono. **5.** ¿Qué hacéis?
6. Lo llamo por teléfono. **7.** ¿Qué dices? **8.** Me levanto ahora mismo.

Basic Class Exercises

1

I. Answer the following questions using a pronoun wherever possible.

EXAMPLE: ¿Pensabas mucho en mí?
Sí, yo pensaba mucho en ti.

1. ¿Quieres ir al cine conmigo? **2.** ¿Se olvidaron Uds. de Juan y María?
3. ¿Pelean Uds. mucho entre sí? **4.** ¿Podrías venir a mi casa sin tu hermano?
5. ¿Puedo ir al teatro contigo? **6.** ¿Preguntaban ellos por nosotros? **7.** Entre
tú y Miguel, ¿tenéis bastante dinero?

2

II. A. Replace the italicized nouns with the nouns indicated, then replace the
nouns with pronouns.

EXAMPLE: No encontré *a Gloria.*
No la encontré.

1. No encontré *a Marta.*
  a. a Juan **b.** a mis amigos **c.** a mis amigas **d.** la maleta
2. Estoy escribiendo *a Carlos.*
  a. a Elena **b.** a mis padres **c.** a la profesora **d.** a sus hermanas
3. Va a servir *la comida a los invitados.*
  a. el café a su marido **b.** la carne a los perros **c.** las legumbres a la niña
  d. los garbanzos a sus compañeras

B. Change the affirmative commands to negative ones.

EXAMPLE: Háblenles.
No les hablen.

1. Dénmelo Uds. **2.** Lávenla. **3.** Déjelo. **4.** Quítenselo. **5.** Escribámosles.

C. *"A Son In Love."* Fill in the blanks with pronouns to replace the italicized
nouns.

EXAMPLE: ¿Quieres mucho a esa chica?
Sí, la quiero mucho.

1. ¿Cuándo conociste a *Dolores*? _____ conocí hace un mes. **2.** ¿Has
conocido a *sus padres*? Todavía no _____ he conocido. **3.** ¿Hablaste a *Dolores*
de matrimonio? No, pero voy a hablar _____ de eso mañana. **4.** ¿Vas a pedirla
a *sus padres*? No _____ voy a pedir. Eso ya no se hace. **5.** ¿Vas a dejar a *tus
otras amigas* para siempre? ¿Es posible? Sí, mamá, _____ voy a dejar porque
estoy locamente enamorado. **6.** ¿Qué dirás a *las otras amigas*? No _____ diré
nada. Voy a desaparecer de sus vidas. **7.** ¿Has dado *una sortija* a *Dolores*? No
_____ he dado todavía. **8.** ¿Quieres *mi bendición,* hijo? Sí, mamá, _____
necesitaré porque el matrimonio es una cosa muy seria.

3

III. A. *"A Sad Story."* Read the following passage, then retell it in the third person singular about your friend Juan.

> Ayer trabajé mucho y anoche me acosté temprano porque me dormí mientras miraba la televisión. Durante la noche soñé que estaba trabajando en mi fábrica. Cuando me desperté vi que era la hora de levantarme y por poco me muero* al darme cuenta de que tenía que ir a trabajar.
> —Levántate, vago—dijo mi madre, entrando en mi cuarto.—Durmiendo no se gana nada.

B. Translate the following sentences. Remember **se** may have several meanings (**le, les,** *each other,* etc.)

1. No se lo dije. **2.** Nos lavamos. **3.** Se me olvidó el reloj. **4.** Nos escribimos a menudo. **5.** Están durmiéndose. **6.** Voy a pedírselo. **7.** No se acuestan tarde. **8.** Me la comí. **9.** Se le murió el caballo. **10.** Me la dio. **11.** Vamos a casarnos. **12.** Se vendieron las casas.

4

IV. Translate the English word(s) in parentheses.

1. No sé (what has become of them). **2.** Al oír la noticia (she became ill). **3.** Si estudias demasiado (you will become mad). **4.** Mi cuñado (became) ingeniero. **5.** Después de veinte años (he became) director de la compañía. **6.** (In the distance) se veían los rascacielos del puerto. **7.** Por la tarde (we shall take a walk) por el parque. **8.** (We did not realize) que estaba tan grave. **9.** Lo haré (as soon as possible). **10.** (By the way), ¿sabes qué hora es?

5

V. A. Fill in the blanks with the appropriate form of **ser** or **estar** and, where necessary, with **por** or **de**.

1. La puerta _____ abierta por Carlos pero ahora _____ cerrada. **2.** La profesora Blanco _____ estimada _____ todos. **3.** El agua _____ convertida en hielo _____ la máquina. **4.** Juan se enamoró de una muchacha pero desgraciadamente ya _____ casada. **5.** El asunto _____ discutido acaloradamente _____ los políticos ayer. **6.** Los autores _____ aplaudidos _____ el público.

B. *"Life in my college."* Answer the following questions related to your college using the reflexive as a passive construction.

EXAMPLE: ¿Dónde sirven las comidas?
Se sirven las comidas en la cafetería.

1. ¿Estudian mucho en su universidad? **2.** ¿Celebran muchas fiestas? **3.** ¿Dónde juegan los partidos de fútbol? **4.** Por lo general, ¿obedecen los reglamentos universitarios? **5.** ¿Respetan mucho a los profesores? **6.** ¿Fuman cigarrillos en las clases? **7.** ¿Hablan español mucho en la clase de español? **8.** ¿Terminarán el año estudiantil en junio?

*Por poco me muero *(I almost died).* **Por poco** meaning *almost* is followed by the present tense even though the action is past.

VI. A. Write the appropriate form of the present tense of the verb and translate the sentence.

1. Ellos siempre (andar) _____ diciendo disparates. **2.** ¿De qué (estar) _____ hablando Ud.? **3.** Mi mujer (seguir) _____ durmiendo. **4.** Esto (venir) _____ haciéndose más difícil. **5.** Nosotros (estar) _____ acostándonos.

B. Answer the following questions using the progressive form of the tense used in the question.

EXAMPLE: ¿Jugaban Uds. al tenis?
            Sí, estábamos jugando al tenis.

1. ¿Dices la verdad? **2.** ¿Vuelven Uds. solos? **3.** ¿Hablaba yo demasiado?
4. ¿Escribías a tu madre? **5.** ¿Te sientes mejor? **6.** ¿Aprendéis bien el español?

Elective Exercises

VII. *"Who needs the money more urgently?"* Translate the following passage.

1. Hello, John! By the way, I was looking for you. **2.** When are you going to give me back the money you owe me? **3.** I will give it to you in September. **4.** I am taking a trip to Mexico and I need it. **5.** So do I! (I too) I need it as soon as possible because I am going to get married. **6.** That's not a good reason; I am studying to be a teacher of Spanish and I must go to a country where Spanish is spoken. **7.** Go *(Ve)* to your sweetheart and tell *(di)* her you can get married in September.

VIII. Review of Lesson 4.

A. *"A Hard Day's Work."* Fill in the blanks with the appropriate compound tense.

1. (trabajar) Hoy nosotros _____ mucho. **2.** (dar) El jefe nos _____ mucho trabajo. **3.** (ser) _____ un trabajo difícil. **4.** (decir) El jefe _____ que no sería fácil. **5.** (terminar) Dijo que debíamos terminarlo antes del domingo pero nosotros lo _____ para *(by)* el sábado. **6.** (hacer) Nosotros lo _____ rápidamente porque esperamos recibir una recompensa.

B. Rewrite the following sentences, translating the words in parentheses into Spanish.

1. El perro enterró el hueso en (their garden). **2.** (These) chicos trataron de huir de (their school). **3.** Él dijo que era capaz de bajar al infierno por (a little kiss of mine). **4.** Para guardar (her beauty) ella era capaz de bajar al infierno.
5. (That hell) estará lleno de locos. **6.** Mis hijos y (yours) Elena, se comportan bien cuando duermen. **7.** Esta motocicleta y (that one) son (ours). **8.** De repente (a friend of theirs) apareció a lo lejos. **9.** De vez en cuando (her boyfriends) le dan piedras preciosas. **10.** Yo la llamaba a menudo pero (she did not like that).

Vocabulary

acaloradamente hotly
acordarse (ue) (de) to remember
asunto matter, subject
cubierto (de) covered (with)
cuchillo knife
cuñado brother-in-law
desgraciadamente unfortunately
discutir to discuss; to argue
disparate *m.* nonsense
encender (ie) to light
ensayo essay
escaparate *m.* shop window
estudiantil scholastic
fábrica factory
fumar to smoke
ganar to gain, earn
garbanzo chick pea
guante *m.* glove
hielo ice

hueso bone
ingeniero engineer
invitado guest
jefe *m. or f.* chief, head
letrero sign
llover (ue) to rain
nieve *f.* snow
partido game (match)
pegar to strike
piedra stone
político politician
puerto port
rascacielos *m.* skyscraper
recompensa reward
reglamento rule
soñar (ue) (con) to dream (about)
tienda store
vago lazy

Lesson 6

1 **Formation of the Present Tense of the Subjunctive Mood**

2 **Commands**

3 **Idioms and Word Study**

4 **The Subjunctive in Noun Clauses**

1

Formation of the Present Tense of the Subjunctive Mood

A. All regular and almost all irregular verbs base the present subjunctive on the first person singular **(yo)** of the present indicative. They drop the **-o** ending and first conjugation verbs add **-e, -es, -e, -emos, -éis, -en;** second and third conjugation verbs add **-a, -as, -a, -amos, -áis, -an.**

tomar	comer	vivir	hacer	poner	ver	conocer
tome	coma	viva	haga	ponga	vea	conozca
tomes	comas	vivas	hagas	pongas	veas	conozcas
tome	coma	viva	haga	ponga	vea	conozca
tomemos	comamos	vivamos	hagamos	pongamos	veamos	conozcamos
toméis	comáis	viváis	hagáis	pongáis	veáis	conozcáis
tomen	coman	vivan	hagan	pongan	vean	conozcan

The following irregular verbs are the only ones that do not use the first person of the indicative as a stem for the subjunctive since their first person does not end in -o:

104

dar	dé, des, dé, demos, deis, den
estar	esté, estés, esté, estemos, estéis, estén
ir	vaya, vayas, vaya, vayamos, vayáis, vayan
saber	sepa, sepas, sepa, sepamos, sepáis, sepan
ser	sea, seas, sea, seamos, seáis, sean

Note also the auxiliary verb **haber:** haya, hayas, haya, hayamos, hayáis, hayan. These forms of **haber** are used mainly to form the present perfect subjunctive.

B. Stem-changing verbs of the first and second conjugations have the same changes as the indicative (**e > ie** or **o > ue**).

pensar	entender	mostrar	volver
piense	entienda	muestre	vuelva
pienses	entiendas	muestres	vuelvas
piense	entienda	muestre	vuelva
pensemos	entendamos	mostremos	volvamos
penséis	entendáis	mostréis	volváis
piensen	entiendan	muestren	vuelvan

Stem-changing verbs of the third conjugation also have the same changes as the indicative (**e > ie** or **e > i**). In addition, these verbs have a change of **e > i** in the first and second persons plural.

sentir	pedir
sienta	pida
sientas	pidas
sienta	pida
sintamos	pidamos
sintáis	pidáis
sientan	pidan

Two verbs, **dormir** and **morir,** change **o > ue** in the singular and third person plural, **o > u** in the first and second persons plural.

dormir	morir
duerma	muera
duermas	mueras
duerma	muera
durmamos	muramos
durmáis	muráis
duerman	mueran

C. Orthographic-changing verbs ending in **-car, -gar** and **-zar** change their spelling in order to keep the original sound of the infinitive. (See Appendix D.)

buscar	pagar	rezar
busque	pague	rece
busques	pagues	reces
busque	pague	rece
busquemos	paguemos	recemos
busquéis	paguéis	recéis
busquen	paguen	recen

Verbs such as **coger** *(to catch)* and **seguir** *(to follow)* and their compounds (e.g. **escoger, conseguir,** etc.) use the first person singular of the present indicative as a stem (**cojo, sigo**) in accordance with the basic rule, and become:

coger   coja, cojas, coja, cojamos, cojáis, cojan
seguir   siga, sigas, siga, sigamos, sigáis, sigan

EXERCISE 1

Write the present subjunctive forms of the following verbs.

1. yo: romper/escribir/pensar/hacer/decir   **2.** ellos: acostarse/coger/aprender/pedir/discutir   **3.** tú: charlar/sacar/seguir/volver/perder   **4.** nosotros: sentir/dormirse/entender/devolver/empezar   **5.** Ud.: gozar/pagar/poner/conocer/caer   **6.** vosotros: traer/buscar/llegar/traducir/quedarse   **7.** yo: ser/ir/haber/saber/estar

Commands

A. All commands, except for the affirmative **tú** and **vosotros,** use the present subjunctive forms.

The polite forms (**Ud.** and **Uds.**) use the subjunctive forms in both the affirmative and negative commands.

Tome (Ud.). *Take.*
No tome (Ud.). *Don't take.*

Escriba (Ud.). *Write.*
No escriba (Ud.). *Don't write.*

Salga (Ud.). *Leave.*
No salga (Ud.). *Don't leave.*

Tomen (Uds.). *Take.*
No tomen (Uds.). *Don't take.*

Escriban (Uds.). *Write.*
No escriban (Uds.). *Don't write.*

Salgan (Uds.). *Leave.*
No salgan (Uds.). *Don't leave.*

B. The familiar singular (**tú**) command uses the third person singular of the present indicative for the affirmative command and the second person singular of the subjunctive for the negative command.

Toma (tú). *Take.*
No tomes (tú). *Don't take.*

Escribe (tú). *Write.*
No escribas (tú). *Don't write.*

NOTE: The subject pronouns **Ud.** and **Uds.** are usually used for politeness. **Tú** is normally not used except for emphasis.

C. The following common verbs have an irregular command form in the affirmative familiar singular form. The negative uses the subjunctive, as is normal.

decir	Di.	*Say, tell.*	No digas.	*Don't say, tell.*
hacer	Haz.	*Do, make.*	No hagas.	*Don't do, make.*
ir	Ve.	*Go.*	No vayas.	*Don't go.*
poner	Pon.	*Put.*	No pongas.	*Don't put.*
salir	Sal.	*Leave.*	No salgas.	*Don't leave.*
ser	Sé.	*Be.*	No seas.	*Don't be.*
tener	Ten.	*Have.*	No tengas.	*Don't have.*
venir	Ven.	*Come.*	No vengas.	*Don't come.*

Here are some examples of familiar commands in song and poetry. A popular *copla:*

Toma esta canasta
llenita de flores.
No las desparrames,
que son mis amores.

Take this basket
nicely filled with flowers.
Don't spill them,
for they are my loves.

The refrain of the popular Mexican song *Cielito lindo:*[†]

Ay, ay, ay, ay,
Canta y no llores ...

Ay, ay, ay, ay,
Sing and don't cry ...

D. The familiar plural form (**vosotros**) affirmative command for all verbs is formed by changing the **-r** ending of the infinitive to **-d**. As with all the other persons, the negative forms use the subjunctive.

hablar	hablad (vosotros)	no habléis (vosotros)
escoger	escoged (vosotros)	no escojáis (vosotros)
escribir	escribid (vosotros)	no escribáis (vosotros)
decir	decid (vosotros)	no digáis (vosotros)
ir	id (vosotros)	no vayáis (vosotros)

The pronoun **vosotros** is usually omitted except when needed for emphasis.

E. In the following table the verbs **tomar, vender** and **abrir** are used to illustrate the command forms discussed in sections A–D.

tome	(Ud.)	no tome	(Ud.)
tomen	(Uds.)	no tomen	(Uds.)
toma	(tú)	no tomes	(tú)
tomad	(vosotros)	no toméis	(vosotros)
venda	(Ud.)	no venda	(Ud.)
vendan	(Uds.)	no vendan	(Uds.)
vende	(tú)	no vendas	(tú)
vended	(vosotros)	no vendáis	(vosotros)
abra	(Ud.)	no abra	(Ud.)
abran	(Uds.)	no abran	(Uds.)
abre	(tú)	no abras	(tú)
abrid	(vosotros)	no abráis	(vosotros)

NOTE: The **vosotros** command forms are not used in Spanish America, but are widely used in Spain. (See Lesson I, 4, B.)

F. Position of Object Pronouns with Commands.

All object pronouns, whether direct, indirect, or reflexive, are attached to the *affirmative* command but always precede the *negative* command. (See Lesson 5, Section 2. K, for use of written accents with command forms when pronouns are added.)

Hábleme (Ud.).	*Speak to me.*	No me hable (Ud.).	*Don't speak to me.*
Dígamelo (Ud.).	*Tell it to me.*	No me lo diga (Ud.).	*Do not tell it to me.*
Siéntese (Ud.).	*Sit down.*	No se siente (Ud.).	*Do not sit down.*
Háblenme (Uds.).	*Speak to me.*	No me hablen (Uds.).	*Do not speak to me.*
Díganmelo (Uds.).	*Tell it to me.*	No me lo digan (Uds.).	*Do not tell it to me.*
Siéntense (Uds.).	*Sit down.*	No se sienten (Uds.).	*Do not sit down.*
Dámelo (tú).	*Give it to me.*	No me lo des (tú).	*Do not give it to me.*
Siéntate (tú).	*Sit down.*	No te sientes (tú).	*Do not sit down.*
Vete (tú).	*Go away.*	No te vayas (tú).	*Do not go away.*
Escuchadme (vosotros).	*Listen to me.*	No me escuchéis (vosotros).	*Do not listen to me.*
Mandádmelo (vosotros).	*Send it to me.*	No me lo mandéis (vosotros).	*Do not send it to me.*

In the affirmative reflexive form of **vosotros** commands, the final **-d** of the verb form (**sentad**) is dropped before the reflexive pronoun os is added.

Sentaos (vosotros). *Sit down.*

No os sentéis (vosotros).
Do not sit down.

Vestíos (vosotros). *Get dressed.*

No os vistáis (vosotros).
Do not get dressed.

EXCEPTION: Idos (vosotros).

Go away.

But the negative is regular.

No os vayáis (vosotros).

Do not go away.

Here are examples in song and poetry to illustrate the construction of commands with object pronouns.
From the popular Mexican song, *Cielito lindo:*[†]

Ese lunar que tienes, Cielito lindo,

That beauty mark that you have, my heavenly love,

junto a la boca,

next to your mouth;

No se lo des a nadie, Cielito lindo,

Don't give it to anyone, my heavenly love,

que a mí me toca.

for it belongs to me.

The young Cuban exile, José María Heredia (1803–1839), inspired by the Niagara Falls, begins his *Oda a Niágara* with the following words, using the poetic *vosotros* form.

Templad mi lira, dádmela ...

Tune my lyre, give it to me ...

G. Third Person (Indirect) Commands.

To express a command in the third person in English it is necessary to use an expression such as "let him ...", "have him ..." In Spanish we use the subjunctive introduced by **que**... Note that if a subject is expressed it follows the verb.

Que pase él.

Let (have) him come in.

Que vengan en seguida.

Let (have) them come at once.

Que lo haga Jorge.

Let George do it.

Que no lo vuelvan a hacer.

Let them not do it again.

With the verbs **vivir** and **morir** the **que** is often omitted.

¡Viva Zapata!

Long live Zapata!

¡Mueran los traidores!

Death to the traitors!

In poetry the **que** is often omitted in the third person command. The most beautiful elegy in the Spanish language, Jorge Manrique's (1440–1479) *Coplas por la muerte de su padre,* contains three commands of this type in the first two lines. The translation is by Henry Wadsworth Longfellow.

Recuerde el alma dormida,   *Oh, let the soul her slumbers*
                                             break,
avive el seso y despierte ...   *Let thought be quickened and*
                                             awake ...

Santa Teresa de Jesús (1515–1582) was one of Spain's great mystic authors in prose and verse. A short poem expressing her implicit faith was found in her breviary after her death. The opening lines are:

Nada te turbe,   *Let nothing disturb thee,*
nada te espante ...   *let nothing frighten thee ...*

NOTE: The third person reflexive form is often used to give instructions of an impersonal nature:

Tradúzcanse al español las   *Translate (let be translated) into*
  frases siguientes.   *Spanish the following sentences.*
Véase la página 45.   *See page 45.*

H. First Person Plural Commands.

Spanish uses the subjunctive for the first person plural command expressed in English by *Let's (let us) do something.*

Cantemos y bailemos.   *Let's sing and dance.*
No volvamos todavía.   *Let's not return yet.*
No nos sentemos aquí.   *Let's not sit down here.*

The final -s is dropped before **-nos** and **-se.**

Sentémonos.   *Let's sit down.*
Démoselo.   *Let's give it to him.*

A popular *seguidilla* (seven-line poem) of the 15th century contains an example of the first person plural command as well as a number of other uses of the subjunctive.

No me mires, que miran   *Do not look at me, for they see*
que nos miramos,   *that we are looking at one another,*
y verán en tus ojos   *and they will see in your eyes*

que nos amamos.	that we love one another.
No nos miremos,	Let us not look at one another,
que cuando no nos miren	for when they are not looking at us,
nos miraremos.	we shall look at one another.

An alternative and popular way of expressing the first person plural command construction in the affirmative is **Vamos a** + *infinitive*. The negative always uses the subjunctive.

Vamos a cantarlo *or* Cantémoslo.	Let's sing it.
No lo cantemos.	Let's not sing it.
Vamos a levantarnos *or* Levantémonos.	Let's get up.
No nos levantemos.	Let's not get up.

The inspiring short poem, *Solidaridad,* by Amado Nervo (1870–1919), one of Mexico's popular writers, begins as follows:

Alondra, ¡vamos a cantar!	Lark, let us sing!
Cascada, ¡vamos a saltar!	Waterfall, let us leap!
Riachuelo, ¡vamos a correr!	Stream, let us run!
Diamante, ¡vamos a brillar!	Diamond, let us shine!
Águila, ¡vamos a volar!	Eagle, let us fly!
Aurora, ¡vamos a nacer!	Dawn, let us be born!

NOTE: *Let us go* in the affirmative is **vamos,** rather than the subjunctive form. **No vayamos** is used to express the negative.

Vamos a casa.	Let's go home. (**or,** We are going home.)
Vámonos.	Let's go (away).
No nos vayamos.	Let's not go (away).

EXERCISE 2

A. Write the negative form of the following affirmative commands. Remember that object and reflexive pronouns are placed before a negative command.

1. Volved temprano. **2.** Acuéstense Uds. **3.** Dame un beso. **4.** Díganselo Uds. **5.** Come tú ahora. **6.** Que se acuesten los niños. **7.** Levantémonos a las seis. **8.** Váyanse Uds. **9.** Pídale Ud. dinero a su padre. **10.** Acostaos. **11.** Levántate. **12.** Hazlo.

B. Write the affirmative of the following familiar commands.

1. No contestes tú esas preguntas. **2.** No vuelvas temprano. **3.** No escribas la lección. **4.** No digáis eso. **5.** No te pongas el abrigo. **6.** No sigas hablando. **7.** No le des tu rubí. **8.** No os levantéis temprano. **9.** No le vendas tu casa. **10.** No te acuestes ahora. **11.** No lo saquéis. **12.** No salgas de tu cuarto.

C. Express the same command using the subjunctive in place of the infinitive.

1. Vamos a dar un paseo. **2.** Vamos a acostarnos. **3.** Vamos a decírselo. **4.** Vamos a sacar el dinero.

3

Idioms and Word Study

A. General Expressions.

acabar (present) de + *infinitive*	*to have just + past participle*
acabar (imperfect) de + *infinitive*	*had just + past participle*
en cambio	*on the other hand*
en (por) todas partes	*everywhere*
hoy día, hoy en día	*nowadays*
ir de compras	*to go shopping*
la semana que viene	*next week*
para siempre	*forever*
por aquí	*this way, through here*

Acaban de dormirse.	*They have just fallen asleep.*
Acababan de dormirse cuando el teléfono los despertó.	*They had just fallen asleep when the phone woke them up.*

B. Pedir and **preguntar.**

pedir	*to ask (request) someone to do something, to ask for something*
preguntar	*to ask a question*
preguntar por	*to ask for (about) someone*

Me pide que le haga un favor.	*He asks me to do him a favor.*
Pedro me pidió diez dólares.	*Pedro asked me for ten dollars.*
El profesor me preguntó: «¿Qué hizo Ud. anoche?»	*The teacher asked me, "What did you do last night?"*
Pregunté por Ana pero no estaba en casa.	*I asked for Ana but she wasn't home.*

C. Useful Expressions: Basic social amenities.

Con permiso.	*Excuse me (when taking leave of a person or persons).*
Perdone; perdóneme.	*Excuse me (for interrupting, bumping against someone, etc.).*
(Muchas) gracias.	*Thank you (very much).*
No hay de qué. (De nada.)	*You're welcome.*
No vale la pena.	*It's not worth the trouble.*

No se preocupe (por eso).	*Don't worry (about that).*
No se moleste.	*Don't go to the trouble.*
No es ninguna molestia.	*It's no trouble at all.*
Es Ud. muy amable.	*You're very kind.*

EXERCISE 3

Fill in the blanks by selecting **a, b,** or **c.**

1. Los novios juraron amarse _____.
   a. diez años   **b.** hasta el divorcio   **c.** para siempre
2. Supimos que acababan de _____.
   a. volver a casa   **b.** comer claveles   **c.** hablar con Cervantes
3. Cuando llegué a casa de Carlos, _____ por él.
   a. pedí   **b.** pregunté   **c.** me maté
4. Hoy en día muchos jóvenes esperan varios años antes de _____.
   a. dar un paseo   **b.** tener sueño   **c.** casarse
5. _____ , muchísimas parejas se casan muy jóvenes.
   a. En el cielo   **b.** En cambio   **c.** En la luna
6. Daniel me _____ veinte dólares para la fiesta de la semana que viene.
   a. preguntó   **b.** pidió   **c.** rompió
7. Acaban de _____.
   a. llegar   **b.** hacer sol   **c.** estrangularse
8. Hay gente mala _____.
   a. sólo en el norte   **b.** en el paraíso   **c.** en todas partes

The Subjunctive in Noun Clauses

In Spanish, the subjunctive, which is introduced by **que** in noun clauses, is used when the verb in the main clause expresses volition, doubt or emotion. It is also used after most impersonal expressions.

It should be noted that English also has a subjunctive, as in *I insist that he go* or *It is important that she be here.* Whenever the subjunctive is used in English it must be used in Spanish. It is, however, less frequent in English than in Spanish.

A. After verbs of volition (wish, want, request, permission, etc.).

1. As we have seen, the subjunctive is used to express a command.

Hable (Ud.).	*Speak.*
Salgan (Uds.).	*Leave.*

If we were to use a complete sentence in English to express the same idea, we could say *I want you to speak (that you speak)* or *I want you to leave (that you leave)*.

While English normally uses an infinitive, Spanish must use the subjunctive when one person wants another person to do something. The most common verbs in this construction are **querer, desear,** and **preferir.**

Quiero que Ud. hable.	*I want you to speak.*
Desean que lleguemos a tiempo.	*They want us to arrive on time.*
Prefiero que él lo haga.	*I prefer that he do it.*

After the verb *prefer* (as in the last example above) English uses the subjunctive construction also *(that he do it)*; this is exactly the way Spanish expresses the idea. It may be helpful to convert the English sentence *I want him to do it* into *I want that he do it* (**Quiero que él lo haga**).

If there is no change in subject, however, these verbs are followed by an infinitive in Spanish, as in English.

	No quiero hacerlo.	*I don't want to do it.*
BUT:	No quiero que Ud. lo haga.	*I don't want you to do it.*

The opening lines of the popular romantic song *Te lo juro* has several subjunctives following **querer.**

Yo no quiero que me digas
  tus amores,
	*I don't want you to tell me
	  about your love affairs,*

Ni tampoco que me cuentes
  tu pasado,
	*Nor that you recount your
	  past to me,*

Pues la historia del ayer no
  me interesa,
	*For yesterday's history does not
	  interest me,*

Yo te amo y sólo quiero que
  me quieras.
	*I love you and only want you to
	  love me.*

2. The following verbs expressing volition, when followed by **que**, require a subjunctive in the noun clause.

aconsejar	*to advise*
dejar	*to allow*
desear	*to want*
exigir	*to demand*
hacer	*to make (someone do something)*
impedir	*to prevent*
insistir (en)	*to insist (on)*
mandar	*to order*
pedir	*to ask, request*

permitir	*to permit*
preferir	*to prefer*
prohibir	*to prohibit, forbid*
querer	*to want*
recomendar	*to recommend*
rogar	*to beg*
sugerir	*to suggest*
suplicar	*to beg*

Les aconseja a sus primos que no acepten la oferta.	*He advises his cousins not to accept the offer.*
Sugiero que ella la escriba a máquina.	*I suggest that she type it.*
María insiste en que su hermano vaya con él.	*María insists that her brother go with him.*

3. Of the above verbs, **hacer, mandar, dejar, permitir, aconsejar, impedir** and **prohibir** may be followed by an infinitive in Spanish, even if the subject changes, especially when the subject of the second clause is a pronoun.*

No nos permiten fumar. *or* No permiten que fumemos.	*They don't allow us to smoke.*
Le mando salir. *or* Mando que él salga.	*I order him to leave.*
Nos manda volver temprano. *or* (Nos) manda que volvamos temprano.	*He orders us to return early.*

4. **Decir** and other verbs of communication are followed by the subjunctive when they express a command, but by the indicative if they make a statement.

Me dice que venga a las tres.	*She tells (orders) me to come at three o'clock.*
Me dice que viene a las tres.	*She tells (informs) me that she is coming at three o'clock.*
Me escribe que vuelva.	*He writes (orders) to me to return.*
Me escribe que vuelve.	*He writes (informs) to me that he is returning.*

The following lines are from a Spanish poem by the great Portuguese poet and dramatist Gil Vicente (1470–1539). The heroine replies to a marriage suggestion.

Dicen que me case yo.	*They tell me to get married.*
¡No quiero marido, no!	*I don't want a husband, no!*

*The acronym CPA (command, permission, prohibition, advice) may help the student to remember these verbs.

B. After verbs of doubt or denial.

1. One of the basic functions of the subjunctive is to convey doubt or uncertainty. It is used, therefore, after **dudar** *(to doubt)* and **negar** *(to deny)*. The negative of these verbs, however, is usually followed by the indicative.

Dudamos que lo sepa.	*We doubt that he knows it.*
Niego que me conozcan.	*I deny that they know me.*
No duda que lo tengo.	*He doesn't doubt that I have it.*
No niego que lo hiciste bien.	*I don't deny that you did it well.*

2. Verbs of thinking and believing, **pensar** and **creer,** in the affirmative are followed by the indicative. When they are negative they are normally followed by the subjunctive. When they are in the interrogative, they may be followed by the indicative or the subjunctive.

Creo que tiene razón.	*I believe she is right.*
Pienso que vendrá pronto.	*I think he will come soon.*
No creemos que tenga razón.	*We don't believe he is right.*
¿Piensas que $\begin{cases} \text{vendrá} \\ \text{venga} \end{cases}$ pronto?	*Do you think he will come soon?*

C. After verbs of emotion.

1. The subjunctive is used after verbs of emotion.

alegrarse (de) *to be glad*	sentir *to regret, be sorry*
esperar *to hope*	temer *to fear*
gustar *to please*	tener miedo (de) *to be afraid*

Nos alegramos de que Uds. estén aquí.	*We are glad that you are here.*
Espero que vuelvan pronto.	*I hope you return soon.*
Siente que sufran tanto.	*He is sorry that they are suffering so much.*
Temo que nos dé un examen.	*I am afraid that he will (may) give us an exam.*

2. As noted in Section A, if there is no change in subject the infinitive is normally used.

Se alegran de estar aquí.	*They are glad to be here.*
Espero volver pronto.	*I hope to return soon.*
Siento no poder venir.	*I am sorry that I cannot come.*
Temo haberlo perdido.	*I am afraid that I have lost it.*

3. The verbs **esperar** and **temer** may be followed by the indicative when there is a feeling of certainty in the mind of the speaker.

Espero que estará (esté) aquí pronto.	*I expect (hope) that he will be (may be) here soon.*
Temo que ya ha (haya) muerto.	*I think (fear) that he has (may have) already died.*

D. The subjunctive after impersonal expressions.

1. The subjunctive is used after almost all impersonal expressions *(It is+ adjective)*. If there is no dependent clause the infinitive is used.

Es imposible hacerlo hoy.	*It is impossible to do it today.*
Es imposible que lo hagan hoy.	*It is impossible for them to do it today.*
Es necesario trabajar para vivir.	*It is necessary to work in order to live.*
Es necesario que trabajemos para vivir.	*It is necessary for us to work in order to live.*

The most common impersonal expressions which require a subjunctive in the dependent clause are:

Es posible	*It is possible*
Es imposible	*It is impossible*
Es probable	*It is probable*
Es importante	*It is important*
Es necesario	*It is necessary*
Es menester	*It is necessary*
Es preciso	*It is necessary*
Es urgente	*It is urgent*
Es natural	*It is natural*
Es justo	*It is fitting*
Es interesante	*It is interesting*
Es mejor	*It is better*
Es (una) lástima	*It is a pity*
Basta	*It is enough*
Conviene	*It is suitable*
Importa	*It is important*
Parece mentira	*It is hard to believe*

No es posible que lo tenga.	*It is not possible that he has it.*
Es probable que llueva.	*It is probable that it will rain.*
Será importante que estén aquí.	*It will be important for them to be here (that they be here).*
Es interesante que nadie la conozca.	*It is interesting that nobody knows her.*

2. The following impersonal expressions denoting certainty take the indicative when affirmative. When negative or interrogative they usually take the subjunctive.

Es cierto	*It is certain*
Es seguro	*It is sure*
Es evidente	*It is evident*
Es verdad	*It is true*
Es (está) claro	*It is clear*

Es verdad que lo han expulsado.	*It is true that they have expelled him.*
Es evidente que lo ha escrito.	*It is evident that he has written it.*
No es cierto que nos lo devuelvan.	*It is not sure that they will return it to us.*

EXERCISE 4

A. Change the sentence using the noun or pronoun indicated as subject of a subordinate clause.

1. Será necesario estudiar (nosotros). **2.** Tengo miedo de no casarme (mi hija). **3.** Creo haberla visto (tú). **4.** Conviene ir de compras ahora (Uds.). **5.** Se alegran de poder venir mañana (yo). **6.** No creo equivocarme (ellos).

B. Write the present indicative or present subjunctive of the verb indicated.

1. Me pedirán que les (devolver) _____ el dinero. **2.** Sabe que yo ya no lo (tener) _____ . **3.** Es natural que ella (pensar) _____ así. **4.** Dicen que (ser) _____ tarde. **5.** Les recomiendo que (pasar) _____ por aquí. **6.** Es verdad que no lo (saber) _____ él. **7.** Te ruego que me lo (explicar) _____ en seguida.

Basic Class Exercises

I. Substitute the appropriate form of the present subjunctive.

1. No quiero que lo *hagas* tú.
  a. escribir **b.** tomar **c.** decir **d.** coger **e.** traer
2. Preferimos que *vengan* a las ocho.
  a. llegar **b.** llamar **c.** acostarse **d.** comer **e.** empezar
3. Nos pide que *escribamos* las frases.
  a. traducir **b.** sacar **c.** aprender **d.** leer **e.** decir
4. No será necesario que *pague* Ud.
  a. irse **b.** ser **c.** venir **d.** salir **e.** estar

II. A. Miss González is telling her class what to do and what not to do for the umpteenth time. Use the *Uds.* command form.

What to do: **1.** llegar a clase a tiempo **2.** hacer bien la tarea **3.** escribir claramente siempre

What not to do: **1.** no ser malos **2.** no comer en clase **3.** no hablar sin permiso

Juanito, however, merits a little special attention. Use the familiar (**tú**) command.

What to do: **1.** venir a clase todos los días **2.** hacer bien la tarea siempre **3.** limpiarse los zapatos

What not to do: **1.** no tirar del pelo a Rosa **2.** no pelear con Roberto **3.** no hacer tanto ruido

B. Tell a fellow student to perform the commands indicated. He/she will perform the act, then say in Spanish what he/she has done. Use **Ud.** in sentences 1–5 and **tú** in 6–10.

1. Open the door. **2.** Close the window. **3.** Stand up. **4.** Sit down. **5.** Go to the blackboard. **6.** Write on the blackboard and return to his/her seat. **7.** Say a sentence in Spanish. **8.** Pick up a book and put it on the desk. **9.** Count to ten. **10.** Close his/her eyes.

C. Make commands of the following.

EXAMPLE: Juan viene mañana. *Que venga Juan mañana.*
             Empezamos a leerlo. *Empecemos a leerlo.*

1. Nos acostamos ahora. **2.** Juan se lo dice. **3.** El mozo nos trae la comida. **4.** Pedro no vuelve temprano. **5.** No le decimos nada.

3

III. A. Answer the following questions.

1. ¿Te gusta ir de compras? ¿Con quién vas? ¿Adónde vas? **2.** ¿Acabas de llegar a la escuela? **3.** ¿Te preguntó algo el profesor cuando te sentaste? **4.** Si te pido que salgas conmigo la semana que viene, ¿qué dirás? **5.** Si necesitas dinero, ¿a quién se lo pides? ¿Te lo da?

B. Translate the English part of the following sentences.

1. Mi profesora *has just* darme una *A,* lo cual me dejó muy asombrada. **2.** *They had just gone out* cuando empezó a tronar y relampaguear. **3.** Si no le ves, *ask for him.* **4.** *Nowadays* no es costumbre levantarse cuando entra el profesor.

4

IV. A. Translate the following sentences.

1. Es (una) lástima que no estés casado. **2.** No quiero que te hagas daño. **3.** Duda que acaben de hacerlo. **4.** Les diré que dejen de molestarla. **5.** No es verdad que vengan mañana. **6.** Esperamos que Ud. no tenga frío.

B. Replace the subordinate clause with an infinitive.

EXAMPLE: Impiden que yo salga.
             Me impiden salir.

1. Manda que yo trabaje mucho. **2.** No dejan que hagamos la maleta. **3.** Mi mujer prohibe que yo mire la televisión. **4.** Hace que yo lave los platos. **5.** He permitido que duermas hasta las diez. **6.** Aconsejan que abandonéis el país.

C. Replace the main verb with the verbs indicated, changing the second verb if necessary.

1. *Sentimos* que sea así.
    a. alegrarse de **b.** saber **c.** querer **d.** temer
2. *Es necesario* que lo hagas mañana.
    a. Es verdad **b.** Es probable **c.** Es mejor **d.** Basta
3. Nos *pedirá* que vengamos temprano.
    a. rogar **b.** prohibir **c.** mandar **d.** recomendar

D. *"A Day in Class."* Write the appropriate form of the verb indicated.

1. El profesor prohibe que nosotros (dormir) _____ en clase. **2.** Queremos que él nos (dejar) _____ en paz. **3.** Le ha dicho a Juan que (venir) _____ (Juan) a verle la semana que viene. **4.** El profesor me pide que (hacer) _____ el papel de Romeo. **5.** Me doy cuenta de que eso (ser) _____ difícil. **6.** Será mejor que yo (aceptar) _____ si quiero recibir una buena nota.

E. Translate the following sentences.

1. We ask them to leave. **2.** We order them to leave. **3.** It is necessary for us to remain. **4.** We insist that he stay home. **5.** I am sorry he will come too.

F. Marta and Carlos exchange prenuptial thoughts and preferences. Write the appropriate form of the verb indicated. (Use **tú** for *you*.)

Marta: **1.** (ayudar) Quiero que me _____ a lavar los platos. **2.** (salir) Es necesario que nosotros _____ a bailar todos los sábados. **3.** (volver) Insisto en que _____ del trabajo temprano. **4.** (fumar) Prefiero que no _____ en casa.

Carlos: **1.** (salir) Prohibo que _____ con otro hombre. **2.** (venir) Temo que tu madre _____ a vivir con nosotros. **3.** (gastar) Espero que no _____ mucho dinero. **4.** (ser) Sé que nosotros _____ felices si no peleamos mucho.

Elective Exercises

V. *"Making Plans for the Afternoon."* Answer the following questions.

1. ¿Qué quieres que hagamos esta tarde? **2.** ¿Será posible que vayamos al cine? **3.** ¿Prefieres que yo conduzca o que tomemos el tren? **4.** ¿Insisten tus padres en que estudies mucho esta noche? **5.** ¿Es necesario que vuelvas a casa temprano?

VI. *"Parents and Children—What to Do?"* Translate the following story.

1. Get up *(fam.)*, Dolores. I want you to go shopping. **2.** Don't wake me up, Mom, I'm still sleeping. **3.** Nowadays the kids don't want to do anything. **4.** You ask them to do something and they refuse. **5.** You forbid them to go out and they go out. **6.** On the other hand, they study more and are more successful than we are. **7.** If you ask me, it's better for us to leave them alone *(tranquilos)* and hope they will change. **8.** Parents insist that their children do everything they ask.

VII. Answer the following questions basing the answer on the picture. Use a noun clause in the response.

EXAMPLE: ¿Qué quiere Lola de su novio?
Lola quiere que su novio le dé una sortija.

1. ¿Qué pedirá Juanito a su papá?

2. ¿Qué le manda la madre a su hija?

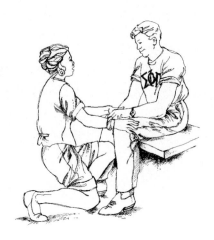

3. ¿Qué ruega el novio a su novia?

4. ¿Qué ruega la novia a su novio?

5. ¿De qué tiene miedo el niño?

6. ¿Qué dice la madre a su hijo?

7. ¿Qué piensa la profesora de la estudiante?　　**8.** ¿Qué duda la cajera?

VIII. Review of Lesson 5.

A. Answer the following questions using a pronoun where possible.

EXAMPLE:　　¿Quieres comprarme esa joyita?
　　　　　　No, no quiero comprártela hoy.

1. ¿Entregaron Uds. la tarea a la profesora?　**2.** ¿Enviaste el paquete a tu madre?　**3.** ¿Hablarás con Luisa y le dirás la verdad?　**4.** ¿Cuándo vas a devolver el dinero a tus padres?　**5.** ¿Es cierto que Pablo estará contigo mañana y que te devolverá los libros?

B. Change the following sentences to the **se** form of the passive.

EXAMPLE:　　Encendieron la luz.
　　　　　　Se encendió la luz.

1. Estudian demasiado en esta universidad.　**2.** Han pintado la casa.　**3.** Hablan español en México.　**4.** Las cartas fueron escritas.　**5.** Eligieron al presidente.　**6.** Han empezado el trabajo.

Vocabulary

abandonar to abandon, leave
abogado lawyer
aconsejar to advise
asombrado astonished
cajera cashier
cielo heaven; sky
clavel *m.* carnation
conducir (zc) to drive (a vehicle)
convenir *(irreg.)* to be suitable
costumbre; es— it is customary
devolver (ue) to return (give back)
equivocarse to be mistaken
estrangularse to strangle oneself
impedir (i, i) to prevent
joyita (dim. of joya) little jewel

jurar to swear
llegar a tiempo to arrive on time
mentir (ie, i) to lie
molestar to bother, annoy
mozo waiter
nube *f.* cloud
paquete *m.* package
paraíso paradise
pareja pair, couple
paz *f.* peace
pescar to fish
relampaguear to flash (lightning)
rubí *m.* ruby
taquilla box office
tronar (ue) to thunder

Review of Lessons 1–6

I. Change to the plural.

1. La trama del drama es muy interesante. **2.** Este lápiz amarillo escribe muy bien. **3.** Me gusta estudiar el idioma. **4.** El niño tenía la mano sucia. **5.** Esa casa grande es mía. **6.** La chica inglesa vino a los Estados Unidos con su madre.

II. Insert the definite article, then change the phrase to the plural.

1. _____ canción portuguesa **2.** _____ luz roja **3.** _____ problema difícil **4.** _____ flor azul **5.** _____ jardín lindo **6.** _____ pared verde
7. _____ examen fácil **8.** _____ viejo profesor **9.** _____ primer bailarín
10. _____ buen pianista

III. Translate.

1. their house and mine **2.** these lessons and those (two ways) **3.** our university and his **4.** her papers and yours (fam. sing.) **5.** my first chapter and this one **6.** that tree (over there) and these **7.** his father and yours (fam. pl.)
8. a friend of mine

IV. Fill in the blanks with the appropriate form of **ser** or **estar**.

1. Cuando llegué a casa _____ las siete y media. **2.** Hoy el cielo _____ gris.
3. Mi reloj no _____ de oro. **4.** Su padre _____ médico. **5.** La nieve _____ blanca pero a los tres días _____ casi negra. **6.** Mi novia _____ de Chile, pero ahora _____ en el Canadá. **7.** Mi coche _____ en malas condiciones.
8. Mi profesora _____ simpática. **9.** La casa _____ sucia porque yo _____ enferma por tres días. **10.** Nuestro profesor _____ amable pero hoy _____ enojado.

V. Answer the following questions.

1. ¿A qué hora vuelves a casa? **2.** ¿Por qué no quieres salir conmigo?
3. ¿A quién te diriges con tus problemas? **4.** ¿Piensan Uds. ir a España este año? **5.** ¿Qué te pones cuando llueve? **6.** ¿Por qué no querías hacer el

trabajo? **7.** ¿A qué hora os acostabais cuando erais niños? **8.** ¿Qué hacías cuando estabas de vacaciones en el campo durante el verano? **9.** ¿Cuándo supiste que nosotros teníamos tu llave? **10.** ¿Con quién viniste a la universidad hoy? **11.** ¿Se divirtieron Uds. en la fiesta anoche? **12.** ¿Tocaste el piano ayer? **13.** ¿Quién sirvió la comida, tú o tu madre? **14.** ¿Qué hiciste cuando te lo dijeron? **15.** ¿Cuándo empezaste a estudiar español? **16.** Si necesitas dinero, ¿se lo pedirás a tu padre? **17.** ¿Con quién vendrás a la reunión? **18.** ¿Harán Uds. la tarea sin ayuda? **19.** ¿Qué harías con un millón de dólares? **20.** ¿Qué hora sería cuando llegaron?

VI. Change the following sentences to the past, using the preterite tense in the main clause.

1. Dice que han llegado. **2.** Sabe que lo tendremos a tiempo. **3.** Les escriben que se lo darán. **4.** Me doy cuenta de que no ha venido todavía. **5.** Me dicen que no lo habéis hecho. **6.** Me pregunto qué edad tendrás.

VII. Change the following summary of a famous 19th-century novel to the past, using the appropriate tense.

María vive en Sevilla con su marido Fritz Stein. Ella llega a ser una gran cantante porque tiene una voz lindísima. Fritz es un gran cirujano y quiere mucho a su mujer. Sin embargo ella se enamora de un torero famoso, Pepe Vero. En Madrid empieza relaciones amorosas con Pepe y descuida a su marido. Éste, cuando se entera de la aventura de su mujer, se va para Cuba donde muere. María ahora es muy célebre pero sólo piensa en su amor por Pepe. Un día, aunque está enferma, va a la plaza para ver torear a Pepe. El toro embiste a Pepe y éste cae mortalmente herido. María, enferma y abandonada, pierde la voz y vuelve a su pueblo. Allí se casa con el barbero que siempre ha desdeñado.

ADAPTED FROM *LA GAVIOTA* BY FERNÁN CABALLERO, PSEUDONYM OF CECILIA BÖHL DE FABER (1796 – 1877)

VIII. Rewrite the sentences, replacing the italicized nouns with pronouns.

1. Vamos a pedir *permiso a la maestra* ahora mismo. **2.** Estábamos haciendo *las maletas*. **3.** El camarero sirve bien *a los clientes*. **4.** No pudimos abrir *la puerta*. **5.** Volveremos a visitar *a nuestros tíos* a menudo. **6.** Entre tú y yo, podremos prestarle *el dinero*.

IX. Change the following sentences to the passive construction using **se**.

1. La casa fue pintada. **2.** Leyeron muchas novelas en la clase. **3.** Alfredo fue elegido. **4.** Todas las noches toman mucho vino. **5.** En el Brasil hablan portugués. **6.** La conferencia ha sido aplazada.

X. Complete using command forms.

1. Déselo Ud. a él, no _____ a ella. **2.** Háblenles Uds. en español, no _____ en inglés. **3.** Llama tú a Eduardo, no _____ a Rosa. **4.** Prestad vosotros atención a la profesora, no _____ atención a los chicos. **5.** No vuelva Ud. hoy,

_____ mañana. **6.** No te acuestes ahora, _____ más tarde. **7.** No nos sentemos aquí, _____ allí. **8.** No me lo preguntes a mí, _____ a ellos.

XI. Fill in the blanks with the appropriate form of the verb in parentheses.

1. Es (una) lástima que (hacer) _____ tanto frío. **2.** Prefiero que María y Luisa (recoger) _____ los papeles. **3.** Saben que esto me (hacer) _____ daño. **4.** No dudamos que (hacer) _____ buen tiempo mañana. **5.** Me piden que lo (decir) _____ yo. **6.** Será mejor que nosotros no (volver) _____ juntos. **7.** El profesor no permite que nosotros (fumar) _____ en clase. **8.** ¿Dudas que lo (saber) _____ ellos? **9.** Nos dijeron que la conferencia (tener) _____ lugar en el teatro. **10.** Es imposible que ellos (llegar) _____ a tiempo.

Lesson 7

1 The Present Perfect Subjunctive

A. Formation of the Present Perfect Subjunctive.

Just as the *present perfect indicative* is formed by using the present tense of the auxiliary verb **haber** (**he, has, ha, hemos, habéis, han**) + *the past participle*, so the *present perfect subjunctive* uses the present subjunctive of **haber** + *the past participle*.

$$\left.\begin{array}{l} \text{haya} \\ \text{hayas} \\ \text{haya} \\ \text{hayamos} \\ \text{hayáis} \\ \text{hayan} \end{array}\right\} \text{tomado, comido, venido}$$

B. Use of the Present Perfect Subjunctive.

The present perfect subjunctive is used when the verb in the main clause requires the subjunctive and the present perfect is called for in the dependent clause.

    Compare the sentences.

Sabemos que han llegado.	*We know that they have arrived.*
Dudamos que **hayan llegado.**	*We doubt that they (may) have arrived.*
Acabo de saber que ha mentido.	*I have just learned that he has lied.*
Siento que **haya mentido.**	*I am sorry that he has (may have) lied.*

EXERCISE 1

Complete the sentence, changing the verb in the dependent clause to the subjunctive.

1. Creemos que han tenido mucho éxito. Esperamos que _____. **2.** Me escriben que Elena se ha hecho daño. Sentimos que _____. **3.** Sé que has vuelto a verla. Me alegro de que _____. **4.** Es verdad que me he enfermado. No es verdad que _____. **5.** No dudo que lo han dicho Uds. Dudo que _____. **6.** Está claro que habéis querido hacerlo. Es probable que _____.

The Imperfect Subjunctive

A. Formation of the Imperfect Subjunctive.

All verbs, *without exception,* form the imperfect subjunctive by taking the **ellos** form of the preterite tense (**hablaron**), dropping the **-ron** ending, and adding either of the following sets of endings:

-ra,	-ras,	-ra,	⁻ramos,	-rais,	-ran
-se,	-ses,	-se,	⁻semos,	-seis,	-sen

tomar:	tomara, tomaras, tomara, tomáramos, tomarais, tomaran
(tomaron)	tomase, tomases, tomase, tomásemos, tomaseis, tomasen
vender:	vendiera, vendieras, vendiera, vendiéramos, vendierais, vendieran
(vendieron)	vendiese, vendieses, vendiese, vendiésemos, vendieseis, vendiesen

servir:	sirviera, sirvieras, sirviera, sirviéramos, sirvierais, sirvieran
(sirvieron)	sirviese, sirvieses, sirviese, sirviésemos, sirvieseis, sirviesen

hacer:	hiciera, hicieras, hiciera, hiciéramos, hicierais, hicieran
(hicieron)	hiciese, hicieses, hiciese, hiciésemos, hicieseis, hiciesen

NOTE: Only the first person plural has a written accent. In almost all cases, either the **-ra** or **-se** form may be used interchangeably. There is, however, a preference for the **-ra*** form in Spanish America.

B. Use of the Imperfect Subjunctive.

The imperfect subjunctive is used when the verb in the main clause requiring a subjunctive expresses an action that happened in the past (imperfect, preterite, past perfect or conditional tense). Compare the sentences.

Quieren que yo lo haga.	*They want me to do it.*
Querían que yo lo hiciera.	*They wanted me to do it.*

Dudo que lo tenga.	*I doubt that he has it.*
Dudaba que lo tuviera.	*I doubted that he had it.*

Será necesario que aparezcan.	*It will be necessary for them to appear.*
Sería necesario que aparecieran.	*It would be necessary for them to appear.*

Siento que no esté aquí.	*I am sorry that he is not here.*
Sentía que no estuviera aquí.	*I was sorry that he was not here.*

Me piden que se lo diga a ellos.	*They ask me to tell it to them.*
Me pidieron que se lo dijera a ellos.	*They asked me to tell it to them.*

EXERCISE 2

Write the imperfect subjunctive of the infinitives in parentheses.

1. Insistieron en que nosotros _____ (salir, traducir, volver). **2.** Era una lástima que tú no _____ (darse cuenta, vencer, seguir). **3.** Dudábamos que ellos_____ hacerlo. (saber, poder, alegrarse de) **4.** Recomendaría que Ud. se lo _____ (decir, enviar, vender). **5.** Habían sugerido que yo _____ temprano. (levantarse, irse, empezar) **6.** Nos alegramos de que vosotros _____ (divertirse, venir, acostarse).

*The **-ra** form is also sometimes used as a substitute for the conditional. In the song *Aurora*, **diera** is used in place of **daría**:

Si tú fueras más sincera,	*If you were more sincere,*
¡ay, ay, ay, ay, Aurora!	*Oh, oh, oh, oh, Aurora!*
Cuántas cosas yo te diera,	*How many things I would give you,*
¡ay, ay, ay, ay, Aurora!	*Oh, oh, oh, oh, Aurora!*

The Past Perfect Subjunctive

A. Formation of the Past Perfect Subjunctive.

The past perfect subjunctive is formed by using the imperfect subjunctive of **haber** (**hubiera** or **hubiese**) + *the past participle*.

hubiera, hubieras, hubiera,
   hubiéramos, hubierais,
   hubieran
hubiese, hubieses, hubiese,
   hubiésemos, hubieseis,
   hubiesen
} tomado, comido, venido

B. Use of the Past Perfect Subjunctive.

The past perfect subjunctive is used when the main verb requires the subjunctive and the past perfect is called for in the dependent clause.

Dudábamos que lo hubiesen hecho.	*We doubted that they had (might have) done it.*
Era posible que hubieran salido.	*It was possible that they had (might have) left.*
Sus padres se alegraban de que se hubiese casado con Ana.	*His parents were glad that he had married Ana.*

EXERCISE 3

Complete the sentence, changing the verb in the dependent clause to the past perfect subjunctive.

1. Sabían que habías vuelto a hacerlo. Temían que _____. **2.** No negó que había sucedido así. Negó que _____. **3.** Supieron que se lo habías dado tú. Esperaban que _____. **4.** Creíamos que lo habían dicho ellos. No creíamos que _____. **5.** Era evidente que no habían estado de acuerdo. No era evidente que _____.

Sequence of Tenses

A. Normally, if the main verb is in the present, future, or present perfect indicative, the subordinate verb is in the present or present perfect subjunctive.

The command form is followed only by the present subjunctive.
   If the main verb is in a past or conditional tense, an imperfect or past perfect subjunctive is called for. The most common combinations follow.

Main clause (indicative)		Dependent clause (subjunctive)

Present: Siente
Future: Sentirá } que { llegues tarde.
Pres. perf.: Ha sentido } { hayas llegado tarde.

Command: Dígale   que   llegue temprano.

Preterite: Sintió
Imperfect: Sentía } que { llegaras (llegases) tarde.
Past Perf.: Había sentido } { hubieras (hubieses) llegado tarde.
Conditional: Sentiría }

Espero que lo sepan.	*I hope they (may) know it.*
Les diré que se vayan.	*I will tell them to leave.*
Es probable que lo hayas encontrado.	*It is probable that you have found it.*
Le he pedido que lo pague.	*I have asked him to pay for it.*
Le dije que se fuera.	*I told him to leave.*
Sentíamos que no hubieran venido.	*We were sorry they had not come.*

B. The imperfect or the past perfect subjunctive may be used after a present tense, however, if logically called for.

Algunos eruditos niegan que Colón descubriera el Nuevo Mundo.	*Some scholars deny that Columbus discovered the New World.*
Dicen que es posible que marineros de otro país hubieran llegado antes.	*They say that it is possible that sailors from another country had (might have) arrived earlier.*

EXERCISE 4

Write the proper form, indicative or subjunctive, of the verb in parentheses.

1. Los novios me rogaron que no (encender) _____ la luz. **2.** Dicen que Mario (realizar) _____ su ambición. **3.** Prefiero que María le (dar) _____ las gracias. **4.** Nos pidieron que (volver) _____ al día siguiente. **5.** Han sugerido que nosotros (escoger) _____ las mejores cerezas. **6.** Era una lástima que ellos nunca (estar) _____ de acuerdo. **7.** Se había dado cuenta de que su futuro marido (ser) _____ un vago. **8.** Será posible que vosotros (poder) _____ hacerlo.

5

Conditional Sentences (If-Clauses)

A. The subjunctive after **si.**

1. To express a condition contrary to fact in the present time, Spanish uses the conditional in the main clause and the imperfect subjunctive in the si clause.

Luis nos ayudaría si estuviera (estuviese) aquí ahora.	*Luis would help us if he were here now.*
Irían a España si tuvieran (tuviesen) el dinero.	*They would go to Spain if they had the money.*
Si yo fuera (fuese) Ud., no diría eso.	*If I were you, I would not say that.*

From the romantic song *Cuatro vidas*:

Si tuviera cuatro vidas cuatro vidas serían para ti.	*If I had four lives my four lives would be for you.*

2. To express a condition contrary to fact in the past, Spanish uses the past conditional *(would have + past participle)* in the main clause, and the past perfect subjunctive in the **si** clause. The past perfect subjunctive **-ra** form (**hubiera** + *past participle*) may be used as a substitute for the past conditional in the main clause.

Nos habría (hubiera) ayudado si hubiera (hubiese) estado aquí.	*He would have helped us if he had been here.*
Habrían (hubieran) ido a España el año pasado si hubieran (hubiesen) tenido el dinero.	*They would have gone to Spain last year if they had had the money.*

3. Other combinations are possible if logically called for.

Si hubieran (hubiesen) estudiado antes no tendrían problemas ahora.	*If they had studied before, they would not have problems now.*
Nos habría acompañado si no tuviera (tuviese) que trabajar hoy.	*He would have accompanied us if he did not have to work today.*

B. The indicative after **si**.

The most frequent combination is the present indicative in the **si** clause and the future in the main clause, but other tenses may be used if called for. The indicative is used in **si** clauses unless a conditional or past conditional is used in the main clause.

Si llueve esta tarde, no iremos a la playa.	*If it rains this afternoon, we won't go to the beach.*
Si trabaja, gana bastante dinero.	*If he works he earns enough money.*
No le des nada si no termina a tiempo.	*Don't give him anything if he doesn't finish on time.*
Si él tenía dinero, yo no lo sabía.	*If he had money, I did not know it.*

From a popular *copla:*

Si duermo, sueño contigo,	*If I sleep I dream of you,*
Si despierto, pienso en ti ...	*If I awake, I think of you . . .*

C. After **como si,** the imperfect or past perfect subjunctive must be used, as it expresses an untrue or hypothetical situation.

Gastan dinero como si tuvieran un millón de dólares.	*They spend money as if they had a million dollars.*
Habla francés como si hubiera pasado varios años en Francia.	*She speaks French as if she had spent several years in France.*

From the all-time favorite song, *Bésame:*†

Bésame, bésame mucho,	*Kiss me, kiss me a lot,*
Como si fuera esta noche	*As if tonight were the*
la última vez ...	*last time . . .*

EXERCISE 5

Write the proper form, indicative or subjunctive, of the verb in parentheses.

1. Si nosotros (tener) _____ dinero, habríamos hecho el viaje a Buenos Aires. **2.** Si (hacer) _____ mucho calor la semana que viene, nos quedaremos en casa. **3.** Lo haría con mucho gusto si Ud. me (dar) _____ el permiso. **4.** Por lo general, mi novio y yo (ir) _____ al cine si hacía frío. **5.** La maestra lo miró como si (ser) _____ un burro. **6.** Si yo lo hubiera sabido, se lo (decir) _____ .

Uses of the Subjunctive in a Main Clause

A. The **-ra** form of the imperfect subjunctive is used with **deber, querer** and **poder** in a main clause to make a polite or softened statement.

Uds. debieran estudiar más.	*You really ought to study more.*
Quisiéramos ir con Uds.	*We would like to go with you.*
¿Pudiera Ud. ayudarme?	*Could you help me?*

The refrain from the sentimental Mexican song *Canción mixteca:*†

Quisiera llorar, quisiera	*I would like to cry, I would like*
morir de sentimiento ...	*to die from grief . . .*

B. The subjunctive is always used after the word **¡ojalá (que) ... !** variously translated as *would that . . . , if only . . . , I hope (that) . . . , I wish (that) . . .* The present subjunctive is used with reference to something that may happen in the future; the imperfect and past perfect subjunctives are used for contrary to fact situations in present and past times, respectively.

¡Ojalá que lleguen pronto!	*I hope they arrive soon!*
¡Ojalá que estuviera aquí!	*Would that he were here!*
	(If only he were here!)
¡Ojalá que nunca la hubiera conocido!	*I wish I had never known her!*

Ojalá standing alone may mean *I hope so, I wish it were so.*

—¿Sabes que el profesor no viene hoy? —Ojalá.	*—Do you know the teacher is not coming today? —I hope so.*
—Estoy seguro de que ya lo sabes de memoria. —Ojalá.	*—I am sure you already know it by heart. —I wish it were so.*

C. The subjunctive is usually used after the Spanish equivalents of *maybe, perhaps:* **acaso, quizá(s), tal vez**.

No te preocupes; quizás venga en el próximo vuelo.	*Don't worry; perhaps he'll come on the next flight.*
Tal vez no lo saben (sepan) todavía.	*Perhaps they don't (may not) know it yet.*

EXERCISE 6

A. Make the following statements softer, more polite, by substituting a subjunctive for the italicized verb.

1. *Quiero* un vaso de agua. **2.** ¿*Puedes* prestarme cien dólares? **3.** *Queremos* llevarte al teatro. **4.** *Debemos* hacer menos ruido. **5.** ¿*Pueden* Uds. acompañarnos?

B. Express the same feeling using sentences starting with the words indicated.

1. Espero que vengan mañana. Ojalá que _____. **2.** Sé que lo harán. Quizás _____. **3.** Dudo que lo hagan. Quizás _____. **4.** Temo que llueva mañana. Tal vez _____. **5.** Espero que me dé una A. Ojalá _____. **6.** Estoy seguro de que lo hizo ella. Tal vez _____.

C. Translate, using **ojalá (que), quizás,** or **tal vez**.

1. I wish it were possible! **2.** Would (I wish) that it had been so! **3.** Perhaps he may do it. **4.** Perhaps he said it. **5.** I hope it doesn't rain. **6.** He said that? I hope so.

Idioms and Word Study

A. General Expressions.

al contrario	*on the contrary*
dar las gracias	*to thank*
estar de acuerdo	*to agree, be in agreement*
llevar una vida	*to lead a life*
¿Qué tal?	*How goes it?*
¿Qué tal (le) parece ... ? *or*	*How do (you) like . . . ?*
¿Qué (le) parece ... ?	*What do (you) think of . . . ?*
tener que ver con	*to have to do with*
no tener nada que ver con	*to have nothing to do with*

B. To realize.

realizar	*to realize (carry out, fulfill)*
darse cuenta (de)	*to realize (become aware of)*
Realizó su sueño de hacerse rico.	*He realized his dream to become rich.*
Me doy cuenta de que debo trabajar más.	*I realize that I should work more.*

C. Useful Expressions: Travel.

¿Cuándo es el próximo vuelo para Barcelona?	*When is the next flight to Barcelona?*
¿Hay que cambiar?	*Is it necessary to change?*
¿Cuánto es un billete (boleto *Sp. Amer.*) de ida y vuelta (sencillo)?	*How much is a round-trip (one-way) ticket?*
¿Dónde está la parada del autobús?	*Where is the bus stop?*
¿Dónde se puede alquilar un automóvil (carro, coche)?	*Where can one rent an automobile (car)?*

EXERCISE 7

Fill in the blanks with one of the idioms or words in Section 7.

1. María _____ su ambición de ser abogada. **2.** Desde que se divorció, Elena _____ muy tranquila. **3.** Nosotros no _____ de las dificultades que íbamos a encontrar. **4.** ¿ _____ la novela? **5.** Yo _____ ese asunto. **6.** Cuando le dio el regalo Ana, Juan le _____ efusivamente. **7.** No pelean nunca; siempre _____.

Basic Class Exercises

1

I. Combine the sentences, making all necessary changes.

EXAMPLE: Ha muerto su padre. Es una lástima _____ .
Es una lástima que haya muerto su padre.

1. Ha llegado su novio. Se alegra de _____.   **2.** Han andado cinco kilómetros. Les sorprende _____.   **3.** Me he levantado tarde. Es verdad _____.   **4.** El profesor ha exigido mucho trabajo. No nos alegramos de _____.   **5.** Habéis vuelto temprano. Es mejor _____.   **6.** Lo hemos terminado. Les gusta _____.   **7.** Has mentido. Está claro _____.   **8.** Te has puesto gordo. Es una lástima _____.

2

II. A. Change the dependent verb to correspond to the subjects indicated.

1. Dudaron que lo *hiciéramos nosotros*.
  a. tú   **b.** ella   **c.** vosotros   **d.** Juan y Pablo
2. Quería que *yo me acostara* temprano.
  a. nosotros   **b.** Uds.   **c.** tú   **d.** Elena
3. No había permitido que *ellos entrasen*.
  a. nosotros   **b.** Juan   **c.** tú   **d.** yo
4. Convenía que lo *escribieses tú*.
  a. ellas   **b.** Ud.   **c.** vosotros   **d.** yo

B. Change the sentences to the past.

EXAMPLE: Es importante que vengas temprano.
Era (fue) importante que vinieras temprano.

1. Quiero que lo hagas tú.   **2.** Es necesario que hagan las maletas.   **3.** Prefiero que vayan de compras ellos.   **4.** Le recomienda a Juan que estudie más.   **5.** Saben que llegaré cuanto antes.   **6.** Dudan que sepamos hacerlo.   **7.** Es mejor que lo traduzcáis vosotros.   **8.** Le pide a Carlos que toque el piano.

C. Use the appropriate form of the verb in parentheses.

1. Quiero que ella _____ (cantar).   **2.** Quería que ella _____ (cantar).
3. Prohiben que yo _____ (salir).   **4.** Prohibieron que yo _____ (salir).
5. Es imposible que ellos lo _____ (hacer).   **6.** Era importante que ellos lo _____ (traducir).

3

III. Rewrite the sentences beginning with the verb in parentheses.

EXAMPLE: Se lo había dicho él. (Sentían)
Sentían que se lo hubiera dicho él.

1. Me había quedado solo. (Temían)   **2.** Se habían enojado mucho. (Era cierto)
3. Había tenido éxito. (Se alegraron)   **4.** Nos habíamos divertido. (Esperaban)
5. Habías tenido mucha suerte. (Dudaron)   **6.** Habíamos sido felices. (Se dieron cuenta)

4

IV. A. *"A Wallflower Blooms."* Fill in the blanks with the appropriate form of the verbs in parentheses.

1. Pablo era un muchacho bastante feo. Le habría gustado que una muchacha (enamorarse) _____ de él, pero no (suceder) _____ así. **2.** Pidió a unas muchachas que (ir) _____ al cine con él, pero ninguna (decir) _____ que sí. **3.** —Es verdad que yo no (ser) _____ guapo, —(decir) _____ Pablo, —pero no soy malo y soy capaz de hacer que alguna chica (divertirse) _____ saliendo conmigo. **4.** Su madre le decía que (salir) _____ y (ir) _____ a un baile. Allí habría muchas chicas. **5.** —Es necesario que tú (salir) _____ , —decía ella. **6.** —En casa no (encontrar) _____ a nadie. **7.** Pablo sabía que su madre lo (querer) _____ mucho y que se lo (decir) _____ por su bien. **8.** Al día siguiente fue a un baile y allí vio a una muchacha no muy linda, sentada en un rincón. Tímidamente le pidió que (bailar) _____ con él y le sorprendió que ella (aceptar) _____ en seguida. **9.** Esa noche Pablo volvió a casa muy contento. Cuando vio a su madre le dijo, —Me alegro mucho de que me (decir) _____ ayer que (ir) _____ al baile. **10.** Creo que (ser) _____ la mejor madre del mundo.

B. Translate.

1. They were glad we were coming. **2.** They are sorry we did not come. **3.** They order us to work harder. **4.** They ordered us to work harder. **5.** They recommended that we do it. **6.** They are afraid that she will come.

5

V. A. Ask another student what he / she would do in the following circumstances.

1. if he / she were sick **2.** if he / she needed money **3.** if a thief asked him / her for his / her money **4.** if a teacher had given him / her an *F* **5.** if a teacher had given him / her an *A* **6.** if his / her uncle left him / her a million dollars

B. Ask another student:

1. Qué hace si llueve. **2.** Qué hace si tiene mucho tiempo libre. **3.** Qué hacía si necesitaba dinero. **4.** Qué hacía si llovía. **5.** Qué hace si su novio(-a) no quiere salir.

C. Complete the sentences.

1. Me mira como si _____. **2.** Yo llevaba una vida como si _____.
3. Él trabajaba como si _____. **4.** Comíamos como si _____.

6

VI. A. *"Asking politely for a date."* Use the softened form (imperfect subjunctive) of the verb indicated.

1. —¿ _____ (poder—tú) salir conmigo esta noche? **2.** —_____ (querer) salir contigo, pero _____ (deber) estudiar para un examen que tengo mañana. **3.** —¿ _____ (poder—nosotros) cambiar la cita para el sábado? Tendría mucho gusto en salir contigo. **4.** —Perfecto. _____ (querer) ver una buena película, si fuera posible.

B. Express a thought related to the sentence.

EXAMPLE: El bote está hundiéndose. ¡Ojalá que _____ !
                    ¡Ojalá que supiera nadar!

1. Mi madre está enferma. ¡Ojalá _____ !   **2.** Necesito dinero. Quizás _____ .
3. Estoy esperando ansioso(-a) a mi novia(-o). ¡Ojalá que _____ !   **4.** Tengo
que llevar este paquete muy pesado pero no puedo. ¡Ojalá que_____ !

VII. Answer the following questions.

1. ¿Qué clase de vida lleva Ud.?   **2.** Si alguien le diera a Ud. diez mil dólares,
¿le daría Ud. las gracias?   **3.** ¿Qué tiene que ver el estudio del español con su
vida?   **4.** ¿Cuál es la ambición que Ud. desea realizar?   **5.** ¿Se ha dado Ud.
cuenta de lo difícil que es aprender a hablar un idioma?   **6.** ¿Qué le parece la
idea de hacer un viaje a un país hispano para aprender a hablar español?
7. ¿Está Ud. de acuerdo que es mejor estudiar una lengua extranjera antes de ir
al país extranjero?   **8.** ¿Prefiere Ud. estudiar mucho o, al contrario, estudiar lo
menos posible?

Elective Exercises

VIII. Translate.

A. 1. I would like you to do me a favor.   **2.** He looked at me as if I were asking
for the moon.   **3.** I asked him to take me home.   **4.** He realized afterwards that I
meant my house, not his.

B. 1. Here is *(aquí tienes)* the hat (that) I just bought. What do you think of it?
2. If you like it, wear it.   **3.** Would that I had the courage to say what I think!
4. It was better for me to keep quiet.

IX. Answer the following questions, basing the answer on the picture. Use a noun
clause in the response.

EXAMPLE: ¿Qué le pidió el hombre al camarero?
                    Le pidió que le trajera una cerveza.

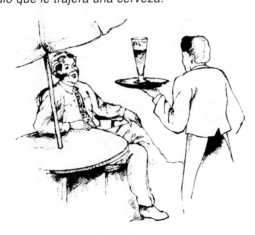

1. ¿Qué quería la niña?

2. ¿Qué duda la chica?

3. ¿Qué grita la madre a su hijo desde la ventana?

4. ¿De qué tenía miedo el hombre?

5. ¿Qué le dijo el padre a su hijo?

6. ¿Qué dijo el padre de su hijo?

7. ¿Qué mandó la madre que hiciera su hija?

8. ¿Qué es evidente?

X. Review of Lesson 6.

A. Make commands of the following. (Use familiar commands with first names.)

EXAMPLE: Juan no habla mucho.
Juan, no hables mucho.

1. El profesor Gómez me da el libro. **2.** Juanito no se hace daño con el cuchillo. **3.** Los chicos no se levantan tarde. **4.** Mario va de compras. **5.** El señor Blanco pregunta por Ana. **6.** Pablo y Elena escriben la tarea. **7.** Isabel lo come. **8.** El señor González y el señor Rivera se divierten.

B. Write the appropriate form of the verb in parentheses.

1. No quiero que lo (hacer) _____ tú. **2.** Dudan que ellos (tener) _____ éxito. **3.** Supieron que nosotros (acabar) _____ de llegar. **4.** Es una lástima que tú no (poder) _____ ayudarme. **5.** Le piden a Elena que (llamar) _____ más tarde. **6.** Es evidente que uno (entrar) _____ por aquí. **7.** Dicen que hoy día los jóvenes (tener) _____ más libertad. **8.** Es mejor que (cantar) _____ tú y no yo.

C. Translate.

1. I want him to come with me. **2.** They advise me to stay home. **3.** I am sorry you cannot come. **4.** I beg her to marry me. **5.** They prevent us from doing it.

Vocabulary

abajo down
andar to walk
ansioso anxious
arriba up
asombrar to surprise
asunto matter
bastante enough, quite
bastar to be enough
belleza beauty
bobo fool, "dummy"
bote *m.* boat
cereza cherry
cerveza beer
colina hill
cumpleaños *m.* birthday
choque *m.* collision
efusivamente effusively
exigir to demand

éxito success
extranjero foreign
feo ugly
general: por lo— in general
helado ice cream
hundir to sink
idioma *m.* language
mente *f.* mind
pesado heavy
rincón *m.* corner
rogar (ue) to beg
ruido noise
salir bien (mejor) to do well (better);
    —bien en un examen to pass an
    exam
suceder to happen
sugerir (ie, i) to suggest

Lesson 8

1 **The Subjunctive in Adjective Clauses**

2 **The Subjunctive in Adverbial Clauses**

3 **Idioms and Word Study**

---

1 **The Subjunctive in Adjective Clauses**

A. An adjective clause is a phrase containing a conjugated verb that functions as an adjective. In the sentence *I am looking for a book that is interesting, that is interesting* describes the word *book* and is an adjective clause. The subjunctive is used in adjective (or relative) clauses when the antecedent (noun or pronoun) in the main clause is indefinite or negative (nonexistent).

Tengo un libro que explica bien el subjuntivo. *(Definite)*	*I have a book that explains the subjunctive well.*
Necesito un libro que explique bien el subjuntivo. *(Indefinite)*	*I need a book that explains the subjunctive well.*
Conozco a un hombre que habla griego. *(Definite person, no subjunctive)*	*I know a man who speaks Greek.*
Busco un hombre que hable griego. *(Indefinite)*	*I am looking for a man who speaks Greek.*
¿Conoce Ud. a alguien que hable griego? *(Indefinite)*	*Do you know anyone who speaks Greek?*
No hay nadie aquí que hable griego. *(Negative)*	*There is no one here who speaks Greek.*

Buscábamos a alguien que hablase griego. *(Indefinite)*

Había mucha gente allí que lo conocía. *(Definite)*

No había nadie allí que lo conociera. *(Negative)*

No hay mal que por bien no venga. *(Indefinite; Proverb)*

We were looking for someone who spoke Greek.

There were many people there who knew him.

There was no one there who knew him.

There is no evil that does not come for some good. (It's an ill wind that blows nobody any good.)

The following *copla* contains the subjunctive in lines 1 and 2 because the antecedent is nonexistent.

No soy bonita que asombre,
ni fea que cause miedo;
soy morenita y con gracia,

y así me quiere mi dueño.

I am not a beauty who dazzles,
nor so ugly as to frighten;
I am a cute brunette with sparkle,

and that's the way my boyfriend likes me.

B. The subjunctive may sometimes be used after a superlative when it implies some possible reservation on the part of the speaker.

Es el hombre más generoso que yo haya conocido.

He is the most generous man I (may) have ever known.

C. The subjunctive is used after **el que (la que, los que, las que)** and **lo que** when indefiniteness is involved; otherwise, the indicative is used.

Los que dijeron eso mintieron.
(Definite, no subjunctive)

Los que digan eso mentirán.
(Indefinite, subjunctive)

Haré todo lo que Ud. quiere.
(Definite, no subjunctive)

Haré todo lo que Ud. quiera.
(Indefinite, subjunctive)

Those who said that lied.

Those who (may) say that will be lying.

I shall do everything you wish. (You've told me what you want.)

I shall do everything you (may) wish. (I do not yet know what you want.)

From the song *Salud, dinero y amor:*

El que tenga un amor, que lo cuide, que lo cuide ...
(Indefinite, subjunctive)

He who has (may have) a love, let him take care of it, let him take care of it . . .

D. The subjunctive is used after indefinites, such as **cualquiera*,
quienquiera** and **dondequiera,** if there is uncertainty.

Quienquiera que sea, no quiero
  verlo.

*Whoever he may be, I don't want
  to see him.*

Cualquier ventaja que le ofrezcas,
  no te la agradecerá.

*Whatever advantage you (may) offer
  him, he will not be grateful to you.*

The indicative is used if there is no uncertainty.

Quienquiera que conocía a ese
  sinvergüenza, lo odiaba.

*Whoever knew that scoundrel
  hated him.*

E. The expression **por (más)** + *adjective or adverb* + **que,** or **por mucho
que,** is followed by the subjunctive unless certainty is expressed.

Por (más) rico que sea, nunca
  será feliz.

*No matter how rich he may be (or
  becomes), he will never be happy.*

Por (más) rico que es, no es feliz.

*No matter how rich he is, he is not
  happy. (He is known to be rich.)*

Por mucho que estudien, no lo
  aprenderán perfectamente.

*No matter how much they (may)
  study, they will not learn it
  perfectly.*

Por mucho que estudian, no lo
  aprenden perfectamente.

*No matter how much they study,
  they do not learn it perfectly.
  (They do indeed study.)*

EXERCISE 1

A. Change the sentence to make the antecedent indefinite.

1. ¿Conoces a la secretaria que habla español? **2.** ¿Buscáis al chico que toca
la guitarra? **3.** Espero casarme con el hombre que se enamoró perdidamente
de mí. **4.** ¿Dónde tienes el televisor que funciona bien? **5.** Llame al abogado
que se especializa en divorcios.

B. Translate the following sentences, noting the use of the subjunctive.

1. El que llegue primero, bailará con la reina. **2.** Los que hicieron bien el
trabajo, salieron bien en los exámenes. **3.** Él no comprende lo que tú le dijiste
ayer. **4.** No comprenderá lo que tú le digas. **5.** Dondequiera que vayan Uds.,
no serán bien recibidos. **6.** Por mucho que él se esforzaba, no sacaba nada de
ello. **7.** Quienquiera que sea, no abriré la puerta.

---

*Cualquiera loses its final -a before a noun.

2

The Subjunctive in Adverbial Clauses

A. The subjunctive is always used in a clause after conjunctions denoting purpose, proviso, exception, etc. The most important conjunctions requiring this construction are:

para que	*in order that, so that*
a fin de que	*in order that, so that*
con tal (de) que	*provided that*
en caso (de) que	*in case, in the event that*
a menos que	*unless*
sin que	*without*

Lo repite varias veces para que la clase lo entienda bien.	*He repeats it several times so that the class will understand it well.*
Lo repitió para que la clase lo entendiera.	*He repeated it so that the class would understand it.*
Iremos contigo con tal de que no llueva.	*We will go with you provided it does not rain.*
Miraré la televisión a menos que haya un examen mañana.	*I shall watch television unless there is an exam tomorrow.*
Salid sin que nadie os vea.	*Leave without anyone's seeing you.*
Salieron sin que nadie los viera.	*They left without anyone's seeing them.*

NOTE: The sequence of tenses discussed in Lesson 7, Section 4.A, applies also to adverbial clauses, as in the above examples.

When there is no change of subject, the prepositions **para, a fin de, sin,** etc. + *infinitive* are normally used.

Lo repito varias veces para aprenderlo de memoria.	*I am repeating it several times in order to (so that I may) learn it by heart.*
Salid sin hablar con nadie.	*Leave without speaking to anyone.*

B. The conjunctions **de modo que** and **de manera que** take the subjunctive when purpose is intended, but the indicative when result is expressed.

Lo explicó de modo (manera) que lo comprendiéramos. *(Purpose)*	*He explained it so that (in order that) we might understand it.*
Lo explicó de modo (manera) que lo comprendimos bien. *(Result)*	*He explained it so that (with the result that) we understood it well.*

C. Aunque *(although, though, even though, even if)* takes the subjunctive when there is doubt, conjecture or uncertainty.

Aunque me lo pida de rodillas, no cambiaré su nota.	*Even if he begs me on his kness, I shall not change his grade.*
Aunque me lo pidió de rodillas, no cambié su nota.	*Although he begged me on his knees, I did not change his grade.*

La mona, aunque se vista de seda, mona se queda. *(Proverb)*

A monkey, although she may dress in silk, remains a monkey. (Clothes do not make the man.)

The following *copla* uses the subjunctive after **aunque** to indicate uncertainty.

Aunque tú no me quieras,
tengo el consuelo
de saber que tú sabes
que yo te quiero.

*Though you may not love me,
I have the consolation
of knowing that you know
that I love you.*

D. After Conjunctions of Time.

The subjunctive is used after conjunctions of time when future or subsequent time is implied. The most common time conjunctions are:

cuando *when*
hasta que *until*
después (de) que *after*
mientras (que) *while*

en cuanto *as soon as*
luego que *as soon as*
tan pronto como *as soon as*

NOTE: **Antes (de) que** *(before)* is *always* followed by the subjunctive.

En cuanto venga se lo diré.

As soon as he comes I shall tell it to him.

Esperen hasta que volvamos.

Wait until we return.

Me dijeron que esperarían hasta que viniera.

They told me they would wait until I came. ("I came" is future in relation to the rest of the sentence.)

Volvieron antes de que saliéramos.

They returned before we left.

If there is no change of subject, the prepositions **antes de, después de** and **hasta** are generally used with the infinitive, rather than the corresponding conjunction plus subjunctive.

Antes de condenarlo, debes escuchar su explicación.

Before condemning (you condemn) him, you should listen to his explanation.

Después de terminarlo, apagaré la luz.

After finishing it, I shall turn out the light.

If future or subsequent time is not implied, the indicative is used.

En cuanto vino se lo dije.

As soon as he came I told it to him.

Cuando se encuentran, siempre pelean.

When they meet, they always fight.

EXERCISE 2

Change the main verb from the present to past, and the future to the conditional, making all other necessary changes.

1. Aunque tenga tiempo, no iré contigo. **2.** Te doy ocho mil dólares para que te compres un coche. **3.** Te doy ocho mil dólares, de modo que puedes comprarte un coche. **4.** Dice que volverá cuando tenga más dinero. **5.** Siempre cuando viene, le ofrezco una taza de café. **6.** Lo haré con tal de que estemos de acuerdo. **7.** A veces salgo de casa sin que se den cuenta mis padres. **8.** Aunque no tiene la culpa, la castigan. **9.** Me lo dice antes de que yo se lo pida. **10.** No te lo diré a menos que prometas callarlo.

3 Idioms and Word Study

A. General Expressions.

a veces, algunas veces	sometimes
al principio	at first
dejar de	to stop (doing something)
de nuevo	again
(doblar) a la derecha	(to turn) to the right
(doblar) a la izquierda	(to turn) to the left
llamar la atención	to attract attention
(todo) derecho	straight ahead

B. The verb **pensar**.

pensar	to think, intend
pensar en	to think about (have on one's mind)
pensar de	to think of (to be one's opinion)
Pienso en mis amigos.	I think about my friends.
¿Qué piensas de mi tío?	What do you think of (What is your opinion of) my uncle?
Pienso hacer el viaje.	I intend to take the trip.
Déjalo. Está pensando.	Leave him alone. He is thinking.

C. Useful Expressions: Hotels.

Buscamos un hotel con precios módicos.	We are looking for a hotel with moderate prices.
Una habitación (un cuarto) para dos con baño.	A room for two with bath.
Está en el tercer piso.	It's on the third floor.
¿Cuánto es con (sin) pensión?	How much is it with (without) meals?
¿Tiene Ud. algo menos caro?	Do you have something less expensive?

EXERCISE 3

Fill in the blanks with one of the expressions from this section.

1. _____ me gusta ir al teatro solo. **2.** Todos los que fuman deben _____ fumar. **3.** Esa chica siempre _____ cuando anda por la calle. **4.** Para ir a su casa no sé si tengo que doblar _____ o _____. **5.** _____ después de la boda la vida conyugal es difícil. **6.** ¿Qué _____ vosotros _____ la situación económica? **7.** Empiezan _____ las mismas dificultades. **8.** En la clase de español, yo siempre _____ aquel muchacho colombiano. **9.** ¿Qué _____ (tú) hacer este verano?

Basic Class Exercises

1

I. A. Fill in the blanks with the appropriate form of the verb in parentheses.

1. ¿Conoce Ud. a alguien que (poder)_____ ayudarme? **2.** No, no conozco a nadie que (poder)_____ ayudarte. **3.** Sí, conozco a alguien que (poder)_____ ayudarte. **4.** ¿Qué quieres para tu cumpleaños? Quiero una sortija que (tener) _____ muchos diamantes y rubíes. **5.** ¿No te gustaría ésta que (tener)_____ esmeraldas y perlas? **6.** Cualquier cosa que tú (decir)_____, no te creeré.

B. Ask another student the following questions.

1. Does he / she know anyone who knows how to dance well? **2.** Is there anyone in the class who sings well? **3.** Is there anyone who studies a great deal? **4.** Describe the ideal woman / man that he / she would like to meet. **5.** Who is the best teacher of English he / she has known? **6.** Will he / she pass the exam no matter how little he / she studies?

2

II. A. *"A Modern Tragedy."* Fill in the blanks with the appropriate form of the verbs indicated.

1. Rosa y Luis, aunque no _____ (estar) casados vivían juntos. **2.** Pensaban casarse cuando (ellos) _____ (tener) bastante dinero para vivir bien. **3.** Un día Luis dijo:—Tan pronto como (yo) _____ (llegar) a ser el jefe de mi oficina nos casaremos. **4.** Rosa dijo:—Yo también trabajaré mucho para que _____ (poder) comprarnos una casa. **5.** Desgraciadamente cuando Luis _____ (llegar) a ser jefe ya _____ (estar) enamorado de otra mujer. **6.** Rosa se dio cuenta de lo que estaba pasando y le dijo a Luis:—Antes que tú me _____ (decir) que ya no me quieres, yo te digo que estás libre para hacer lo que tú _____ (querer). **7.** Luis dijo:—No me sentiré libre a menos que tú me _____ (perdonar). **8.** —Te perdono—contestó Rosa—con tal que tú _____ (salir) ahora mismo. **9.** Después que _____ (irse) Luis, Rosa quedó muy triste. **10.** Seis meses más tarde la otra mujer rompió sus relaciones con Luis, de modo que él también _____ (sentirse) muy triste pensando en la vida con Rosa que había perdido.

B. Combine the sentences using the conjunction in parentheses.

EXAMPLE: Dice que hará el viaje. Yo la acompañaré. *(con tal que)*
Dice que hará el viaje con tal que yo la acompañe.

1. Eduardo tomaba una copa de vino. Juanita tocaba la guitarra. (antes que) **2.** María siempre venía a mi casa. Se lo pedía. (cuando) **3.** Mi padre me dio quinientos dólares. Me compré una nevera. (para que) **4.** No me quedaré en casa. José vendrá mañana. (aunque) **5.** Dijeron que no vendrían conmigo. Ana vendría con Pedro. (a menos que) **6.** Escribieron que habían enviado un regalo. Se lo daré a mi madre. (para que) **7.** Nos saludaron. Nos vieron. (en cuanto) **8.** Se lo diré. Lo veré. (cuando)

C. *"Tell something about yourself."* Answer the following questions.

1. ¿Prefieres casarte con una mujer (un hombre) que trabaje o que se quede en casa? **2.** ¿Vienes siempre a la clase aunque llueva o nieve? **3.** ¿Vendrás aunque llueva mañana? **4.** Cuando entraste en la clase, ¿qué hacía el profesor? **5.** ¿Para qué te dan dinero tus padres? **6.** ¿Qué haces antes de que empiece la clase? **7.** Después de que termine el curso de español, ¿qué piensas hacer para no olvidarlo? **8.** ¿Te levantas por la mañana sin que nadie te despierte?

3 **III.** Read the following sentences. If a sentence is true say **sí**; if it is false say **no** and restate it to make it correct.

1. Los matrimonios se odian siempre al principio. **2.** En la clase de español nunca cometemos faltas. **3.** Una mujer bonita casi siempre llama la atención. **4.** Dondequiera que ande hay que tener sueño. **5.** *De nuevo* quiere decir *otra vez.* **6.** Para aprender bien un idioma hay que dejar de estudiar mucho. **7.** Para seguir una línea recta hay que ir a la izquierda o a la derecha. **8.** Los enamorados nunca piensan el uno en el otro. **9.** A veces caminamos por la calle sin tener cuidado. **10.** *¿Qué les parece esto?* quiere decir *¿Qué piensan Uds. de esto?*

Elective Exercises

IV. Rewrite the sentences using a conjunction to introduce the dependent clause as indicated.

EXAMPLE: Lo compré sin verlo. (sin que mi madre ...)
Lo compré sin que mi madre lo viera.

1. Vamos a España para conocer el país. (para que mi hijo ...) **2.** Nos quedaremos en un buen hotel con tal de tener bastante dinero. (con tal de que mis padres ...) **3.** No me gustaría viajar sin ver la capital. (sin que nosotros ...) **4.** No saldré de Madrid sin asistir a una zarzuela. (sin que mi marido y yo ...)

V. *"Did José enjoy his swim?"* Complete the following sentences based on the pictures.

1. José vio a una salvavidas que ...

2. Él pasó delante de ella sin que ella ...

3. Frustrado, José empezó a nadar aunque ...

4. De repente, José gritó—¡Socorro! ¡Socorro!—para que ella ...

5. La salvavidas le dijo a otro salvavidas que ...

6. José dejó de gritar y empezó a nadar hacia la playa cuando vio que ...

7. Cansado, mojado y triste, José le dijo—Adiós—a la salvavidas que ...

VI. *"Choosing a Profession."* Translate.

1. "Do you think a lot about your career?" **2.** "Of course. I have decided to become a nurse although my parents don't like it. **3.** They prefer that I study medicine so that I will earn a lot of money." **4.** "I think that is fine *(bien)*, provided that you like the profession. **5.** Whatever profession you choose, it should not be only to earn money." **6.** "What you say is true. **7.** I don't admire anyone who has chosen a career only for money. **8.** I selected mine before my parents had time to object *(para oponerse)*."

VII. Review of Lessons 6, 7, and 8.

A. Read the following story. Pick out the subjunctives and tell why they are used.

El libro talonario

En Rota, cerca de Cádiz, vivía un hortelano llamado Buscabeatas, aunque éste no era su nombre. Un año Buscabeatas había criado muchas calabazas magníficas. Las conocía tan bien que les dio nombres. Una mañana, con tristeza, dijo a sus queridas calabazas:

—Mañana voy al mercado de Cádiz y quiero que cuarenta de vosotras me acompañéis.

Al día siguiente cuando volvió para recogerlas, vio que alguien se las había robado. Empezó a calcular y comprendió que el ladrón no podía estar en Rota, pues sería imposible que las vendiera sin que él las reconociera.

—Están en Cádiz—se dijo de repente—y cuando llegue allí, cogeré al ladrón.

En Cádiz se paró delante de un puesto de verduras y dijo a un policía:

—Éstas son mis calabazas. ¡Prenda Ud. a ese hombre!

—No es verdad que sean las suyas—dijo el hombre—yo las he comprado.

—¿A quién ha comprado Ud. esas calabazas?

—Al tío Fulano, vecino de Rota—contestó el vendedor.

—Entonces es él quien me las robó—gritó Buscabeatas.

En ese momento llegó el vecino de Rota. El vendedor dijo:

—Me alegro de que haya venido Ud. Dígales que estas calabazas no han sido robadas.

—Sí, eran mías y las vendí—dijo el ladrón.

—¡Mentiroso! Son mías y voy a probárselo a todo el mundo!—exclamó Buscabeatas, desatando un saco que llevaba consigo. Uds. saben que en el libro talonario siempre queda un pedazo para probar si los recibos son falsos o no. Pues aquí traigo el libro talonario de mi huerta, los tallos a que estaban unidas estas calabazas antes de que me las robara el ladrón. Miren. Este tallo es de esta calabaza. Éste más ancho ... es de aquélla. Y éste de ésta ...

Y mientras que hablaba, iba pegando los tallos a las calabazas, uno por uno.

Todos se asombraron de que los tallos correspondieran perfectamente a las calabazas, y empezaron a reír y a gritar.

El ladrón fue a la cárcel y Buscabeatas a su casa, muy contento de haber hallado de nuevo a sus queridas calabazas.

ADAPTED FROM THE STORY BY
PEDRO ANTONIO DE ALARCÓN (1833–1891),
AUTHOR OF THE FAMOUS *EL SOMBRERO DE TRES PICOS*

B. Translate the English portion of the following.

1. No conviene (that they see us) juntos.   **2.** Me pidió (to tell it to him).
3. Siento que (they have not seen it).   **4.** ¡Ojalá que (I had never known her)!
5. Se lo diré (when they come back).   **6.** Entró sin que (anyone's seeing him).
7. (Even if he cries) no lo haré.   **8.** Buscaban una secretaria (who spoke French).   **9.** (If you had studied) el examen sería fácil.   **10.** (If he does not come) pronto, nos iremos sin él.

Vocabulary

asombrarse to wonder
boda wedding
calabaza pumpkin
callar to keep quiet
cárcel *f.* jail
cometer to commit
cómodo comfortable
conyugal conjugal
copa goblet, glass (for wine)
desatar to untie
dondequiera wherever
esforzarse (ue) (por) to strive (to)
esmeralda emerald
falta: hacer— to need;
  to be lacking
fulano so and so
hortelano vegetable farmer
huerta vegetable farm, garden
matrimonio married couple
mentiroso liar
mercado market
mojado wet
nevera refrigerator
pararse to stop

pedazo piece
pegar to stick, attach
perdidamente wildly, madly
prender to arrest
probar (ue) to prove: to taste
prueba proof
puesto de verduras vegetable stand
quienquiera whoever
recibo receipt
recoger to pick
recto straight
reina queen
rubí *m.* ruby
saco bag
salvavidas *m., f.* lifeguard
socorro help
soñar (ue) (con) to dream (about)
talonario: libro— stub book
tallo stalk
televisor *m.* television set
vecino neighbor; resident
vencer to win, overcome
verduras vegetables
zarzuela *zarzuela* (musical comedy)

Lesson 9

1 Prepositions

2 *Para* and *Por*

3 Idioms and Word Study

4 The Infinitive and the Present Participle

1 Prepositions

The use of prepositions in Spanish and English usually corresponds. There are, however, many cases where the constructions are not parallel and may cause difficulties for the student.

A. The use of prepositions with pronouns is discussed in Lesson 5, Section 1.B.

Me lo dio a mí, no a ti.　　　　　*He gave it to me, not to you.*
Entre nosotros, esto no es bueno　*Just between us, this is not good*
　para él.　　　　　　　　　　　*for him.*

B. Spanish uses the infinitive after all prepositions* whereas English uses a present participle after most prepositions.

Antes de regresar ...　　　　　*Before returning . . .*

*There is a rare use of **en** + *present participle*, rather archaic or literary, meaning "as soon as":

En nombrando al ruin de Roma,　*As soon as you mention the Evil One of Rome,*
　luego asoma. *(Proverb)*　　*he appears. (Speak of the devil and he appears.)*

156

Sin trabajar ...   *Without working . . .*
Después de sentarse ...   *After sitting down . . .*

C. Some verbs are followed directly by an infinitive; others require a preposition before the infinitive. We are including a rather complete list of these verbs for reference.

1. Verbs requiring no preposition before an infinitive are:

aconsejar	*to advise*	olvidar	*to forget*
conseguir	*to succeed in*	parecer	*to seem*
deber*	*ought, should*	pensar	*to plan, intend to*
decidir	*to decide*	permitir	*to permit*
dejar	*to let, allow*	poder	*to be able to*
desear	*to desire*	preferir	*to prefer*
esperar	*to hope, expect*	prohibir	*to forbid*
fingir	*to pretend*	prometer	*to promise*
hacer	*to make, do*	querer	*to want, wish, love*
impedir	*to prevent*	rehusar	*to refuse*
intentar	*to attempt*	resolver	*to resolve*
lograr	*to succeed in*	saber	*to know how to*
mandar	*to order*	sentir	*to regret, be sorry*
necesitar	*to need*	temer	*to fear*

Siento molestarlos.	*I am sorry to bother you.*
¿Quién puede ayudarle?	*Who can help him?*
No sabe nadar.	*He doesn't know how to swim.*
No consiguió convencernos.	*He did not succeed in convincing us.*
¿Qué piensas hacer?	*What do you intend to do?*
Decidieron salir juntos.	*They decided to leave together.*

2. Verbs requiring **a** before an infinitive include verbs of *beginning, motion, teaching,* and *learning* and a number of others.

acercarse a	*to approach*	decidirse a	*to decide to*
acostumbrarse a	*to become accustomed to*	detenerse a	*to stop to*
		echarse a	*to begin to*
acudir a	*to hasten, run (to help)*	empezar a	*to begin to*
		enseñar a	*to teach to*
aprender a	*to learn to*	incitar a	*to incite to*
apresurarse a	*to hasten to*	invitar a	*to invite to*
atreverse a	*to dare to*	ir a	*to go to*
ayudar a	*to help to*	negarse a	*to refuse to*
comenzar a	*to begin to*	obligar a	*to oblige to*
convidar a	*to invite to*	oponerse a	*to be opposed to*
correr a	*to run to*	persuadir a	*to persuade to*

*Deber may be followed by **de** to denote probability:

Deben (de) estar en casa.   *They must be at home.*

ponerse a	*to begin to*	venir a	*to come to*
prepararse a	*to prepare oneself*	volver a	*to return to; to do (something) again*
principiar a	*to begin to*		
resistirse a	*to resist*		
resolverse a	*to resolve to*		

Me ayudó a aprender a nadar.	*He helped me to learn to swim.*
Se pusieron a trabajar.	*They began to work.*
No me atrevo a criticarlo.	*I do not dare criticize it.*
La convidaron a comer.	*They invited her to eat.*
Van a enseñarnos a conducir.	*They are going to teach us to drive.*
Volvió a leerlo.	*He read it again.*

3. Verbs requiring **de** before an infinitive include:

acabar de	*to have just*	dejar de	*to stop; to fail to*
acordarse de	*to remember*	encargarse de	*to take charge of*
alegrarse de	*to be glad*	olvidarse de	*to forget*
arrepentirse de	*to repent*	quejarse de	*to complain*
cansarse de	*to tire*	tratar de	*to try to; to deal with*
cesar de	*to stop*	tratarse de	*to be a matter of*

¡Cuánto me alegro de verlo!	*How glad I am to see you!*
No dejes de llamarme.	*Don't fail to call me.*
Dejó de llamarme.	*He stopped calling me.*
Se arrepiente de haberlo hecho.	*He regrets having done it.*
Se trata de conseguir un préstamo.	*It's a matter of getting a loan.*
¡Traten de llegar a tiempo!	*Try to arrive on time!*

4. Verbs requiring **en** before an infinitive include:

consentir en	*to consent to*	insistir en	*to insist on*
consistir en	*to consist of*	persistir en	*to persist in*
empeñarse en	*to insist on*	quedar en	*to agree to*
equivocarse en	*to be mistaken in*	tardar en	*to be late in, take time to*

Se empeñó en pagar la cuenta.	*He insisted on paying the bill.*
No tardará en llegar.	*He won't be long in arriving.*
Quedamos en alquilarlo.	*We agreed to rent it.*
Ana consintió en casarse.	*Ana consented to get married.*

5. Two common verbs require **con** before an infinitive:

contar con	*to count on*	soñar con	*to dream of*

Cuento con verte a las nueve.	*I am counting on seeing you at nine.*
Soñamos con ir a la capital.	*We dream about going to the capital.*

D. Use of the preposition before nouns or pronouns.

1. Verbs that require a preposition in Spanish that differs from the usual translation in English are:

llegar a	*to arrive in (or at)*
oler a	*to smell of*
saber a	*to taste of*
depender de	*to depend on*
despedirse de	*to say good-bye to (to take leave of)*
enamorarse de	*to fall in love with*
llenar de	*to fill with*
reírse de	*to laugh at*
servir de	*to serve as*
tratar de	*to deal with*
consistir en	*to consist of*
pensar en	*to think of (about)*
apurarse por	*to worry about*
esforzarse por	*to strive to*
preocuparse por	*to worry about*
casarse con	*to get married to*
contar con	*to count on*
cumplir con	*to fulfill, keep one's promise*
encontrarse con	*to meet, run into*

José se enamoró de Ana, pero ella no quería casarse con él.	*José fell in love with Ana, but she did not want to marry him.*
¿En qué consiste la felicidad?	*What does happiness consist of?*
No te preocupes por eso.	*Don't worry about that.*
Cuenta conmigo.	*Count on me.*
¿De qué se trata?	*What is it about?*
El informe trata de los problemas del gobierno actual.	*The report deals with the problems of the present government.*
En casa de mi cuñado la sala huele a tabaco y la comida sabe a ajo.	*In my brother-in-law's house the living room smells of tobacco and the food tastes of garlic.*
—Parece que siempre piensas en tu novia.	*—It seems that you are always thinking about your girlfriend.*
—Es verdad. ¿Y qué piensas tú de ella?	*—That's true. And what do you think of her?*
Siempre cumple con su palabra.	*He always keeps his word.*

From a popular *copla:*

Si duermo sueño contigo,	*If I sleep I dream of you,*
si despierto pienso en ti ...	*if I awake I think of you . . .*

2. Some common Spanish verbs are equivalent to *English verb + preposition.*

buscar	*to look for*	mirar	*to look at*
escuchar	*to listen to*	pedir	*to ask for*
esperar	*to wait for*		

No me mires así.	*Don't look at me like that.*
Buscamos un método fácil.	*We are looking for an easy method.*
Escúchame; quiero que esperes a tu tía en la esquina y que no le pidas dinero.	*Listen to me; I want you to wait for your aunt at the corner and not to ask her for money.*

3. Some Spanish verbs require a preposition whereas the English verb takes a direct object.

acercarse a	*to approach*	fijarse en	*to notice*
acordarse de	*to remember*	gozar de	*to enjoy*
asistir a	*to attend*	jugar a	*to play (a game)*
disfrutar de	*to enjoy*	olvidarse de	*to forget*
entrar en	*to enter*	parecerse a	*to resemble*
fiarse de	*to trust*	salir de	*to leave (a place)*

¿Te fijaste en el vestido que llevaba?	*Did you notice the dress she was wearing?*
En vez de asistir a clase, juega al tenis.	*Instead of attending class she plays tennis.*
Siempre ha gozado de buena salud.	*He has always enjoyed good health.*

E. Personal **a**.

1. Spanish requires an **a** before a direct object that refers to a definite person or persons.

¿Han visto a mi hermana?	*Have you seen my sister?*
Veo a los niños.	*I see the children.*
¿Conoce Ud. a Pedro Gómez?	*Do you know Pedro Gómez?*
Busco al médico.	*I am looking for the doctor.*

BUT: If the object is not a definite person, the personal **a** is not used.

Busco un médico.	*I am looking for a doctor.*
Los Piratas buscan peloteros latinos en Miami.	*The Pirates are looking for Latin ballplayers in Miami.*

2. The personal **a** is generally used before a direct object when it refers to an intelligent animal (such as one's pet) or personified things.

Llamó a su perro.   *He called his dog.*
No temían a la muerte.   *They were not afraid of death.*

3. When referring to persons, the personal **a** is also used with:

interrogatives (**quién, quiénes, cuál, cuáles**)
relatives (**quien, quienes, el cual, el que,** etc.)
indefinites (**alguien, alguno, varios,** etc.)
negatives (**nadie, ninguno,** etc.)
demonstratives (**éste, ése,** etc.)

¿A quiénes vieron Uds.?   *Whom did you see?*
No conocemos a nadie aquí.   *We don't know anyone here.*
¿Esperas a alguien?   *Are you waiting for someone?*
¿A cuál conoces, a María o a   *Whom (which one) do you know,*
  su hermana?   *María or her sister?*

4. The personal **a** is normally not used after the verb **tener.**

Tienen tres hijos.   *They have three children.*

BUT: If **tener** does not mean *have* in the literal sense (possession), but rather *to be* or *to hold,* the personal **a** is used.

Tengo a mi padre enfermo en casa.   *I have my father ill at home.*
                                       (My father is ill at home.)
Tiene a la niña de la mano.   *She is holding the child by the hand.*

EXERCISE 1

A. Insert a preposition, if necessary.

1. Anoche soñé _____ un banquete suntuoso. **2.** Les pedí _____ dinero a mis padres. **3.** Insistieron _____ que diéramos un paseo. **4.** ¿ _____ qué te quejas? **5.** Estaban buscando _____ un paraguas. **6.** Ten cuidado si te enamoras _____ un marinero. **7.** Este pollo sabe _____ lana vieja. **8.** Dejen _____ hacer tanto ruido. **9.** Si me ayudases _____ hacer mi tarea, te daría un buen regalo. **10.** Por fin lograron _____ realizar sus sueños. **11.** No podemos depender _____ él. **12.** Quisiera servir _____ intérprete durante nuestro viaje. **13.** Esperaban _____ una respuesta pronto. **14.** Se arrepintieron _____ haberlo dicho. **15.** Tardarán mucho _____ llegar.

B. Insert the personal **a**, if necessary.

1. Buscaban _____ un chico que fuera fuerte. **2.** No vimos _____ nadie. **3.** Encontraron _____ la secretaria que hablaba griego. **4.** Al principio no quería ver _____ ningún hombre que se pareciera a su antiguo novio. **5.** No vieron _____ su amigo en la fiesta.

2 Para and Por

A. Para basically expresses:

1. *Purpose* (in order to), *direction toward*, *destination*, or *intended for.*

¿Para qué estudia tanto? Para poder ingresar en la Facultad de Medicina.	*Why (for what purpose) does he study so much? In order to be able to get into medical school.*
Quiere estudiar para cirujano.	*He wants to study to be a surgeon.*
Partieron para Barcelona.	*They left for Barcelona.*
Estas cartas son para ti.	*These letters are (intended) for you.*
¿Para qué sirve?	*What is it for?*
No sirve para nada.	*It is not good for anything.*
Compré tazas para té.	*I bought teacups.*

A stanza of the Mexican song of the Revolution, *La cucaracha*[†], mentions a Mexican city or state and what it is famous for.

Para sarapes, Saltillo,	*For serapes, Saltillo,*
Chihuahua para soldados,	*Chihuahua for soldiers,*
para mujeres, Jalisco,	*for women, Jalisco,*
para amar, toditos lados.	*for loving, everywhere.*

2. **Para** is also used to indicate a limit of time by which something is to be done.

Habremos terminado la novela para el martes.	*We shall have finished the novel by Tuesday.*

3. **Para** may mean *considering the fact that,* implying a comparison.

Para (un) profesor baila muy bien.	*For a teacher he dances very well.*

4. **Para** may mean *as for* or *to oneself.*

Para mí, eso no tiene importancia.	*As for me (as far as I am concerned), that has no importance.*
Lo dijo para sí.	*He said it to himself.*

B. Por has a wide variety of meanings and uses.

1. *Along* or *through.*

Evidentemente los ladrones entraron por la ventana y salieron por la puerta.	*Evidently the thieves entered through the window and left through the door.*
Pasan el verano viajando por España.	*They are spending the summer traveling through Spain.*
¿Por dónde se sale?	*Which way (through where) does one leave?*

From the Argentinian song, *Isabelita*,[†] the opening lines:

A las cinco por Florida,	*At five o'clock along Florida (street),*
muy bien vestida,	*very well dressed,*
pasa Isabel.	*passes Isabel.*

2. *For*, in the sense of during a period of time. (The word **por** is sometimes omitted in this construction.)

Vivieron allí (por) muchos años.	*They lived there (for) many years.*
Estudiamos en Buenos Aires (por) dos años.	*We studied in Buenos Aires for two years.*

3. *In exchange for.*

¿Cuánto pagaste por el mapa?	*How much did you pay for the map?*
Cambió su reloj por el mío.	*He exchanged his watch for mine.*
Ojo por ojo, diente por diente.	*An eye for an eye, a tooth for a tooth.*

4. *For*, as the object of an errand.

Mandaron por el médico.	*They sent for the doctor.*
Fue a la tienda por pan y queso.	*He went to the store for bread and cheese.*
Ir por lana y volver trasquilado. (*Proverb*)	*To go for wool and come back shorn.*

5. *For* (the sake of), *because of, on behalf of.*

Lo hizo por su familia.	*He did it for his family.*
No pudimos salir por el calor.	*We could not go out because of the heat.*
Madrid es conocido por sus museos.	*Madrid is famous for its museums.*

From the Cuban *Vals del estudiante*:[†]

Yo por ti no voy a la escuela,	*Because of you I don't go to school,*
Yo por ti no voy a estudiar,	*Because of you I am not going to study,*
Yo por ti no voy al colegio,	*Because of you I don't go to school,*
Y es por ti que no soy colegial.	*And it is because of you that I am not a student.*

6. **Por** equals the English *per* before units of measure.

El límite de velocidad es ochenta kilómetros por hora.	*The speed limit is 80 kilometers an hour.*
Diez por ciento de los alumnos fueron suspendidos.	*Ten percent of the students failed.*
Los huevos se venden por docena.	*Eggs are sold by the dozen.*
Pagamos cinco dólares por hora.	*We pay five dollars an hour.*

7. *Times* (multiplied by) in arithmetic.

Cuatro por cinco son veinte.	*Four times five is twenty.*

8. *By* (means of):

Deben mandar las cartas urgentes por avión.	*They should send the urgent letters by airmail.*
Muchos inmigrantes vinieron por barco.	*Many immigrants came by boat.*
Usó el lenguaje por señas para comunicarse con sus padres.	*She used sign language in order to communicate with her parents.*

9. *By* (the agent) in the passive construction.

Las novelas ejemplares fueron escritas por Cervantes.	*"The Exemplary Novels" were written by Cervantes.*

From the song *Isabelita:*[†]

Nadie ha conseguido ser preferido por Isabel.	*No one has succeeded in being preferred by Isabel.*

10. **Por** before an infinitive indicates that something remains to be done.

Todavía queda mucho por escribir.	*There is still a lot to be written.*
Más vale el mal conocido que el bien por conocer. *(Proverb)*	*The bad that you know is better than the good that may yet be known.*

11. **Por** is used in many idiomatic expressions. Some of the most common are:

por allí, por aquí	*around there, around here*
por casualidad	*by chance*
por consiguiente	*therefore, consequently*
¡por Dios!	*for Heaven's sake!*
por ejemplo	*for example*
por eso	*therefore, for that reason*
por el estilo	*of the sort, of the same kind*
por favor	*please*
por fin	*finally*

por la mañana*	*in the morning*
por la noche	*in the evening*
por la tarde	*in the afternoon*
por lo general	*in general*
por lo pronto	*for the time being*
por lo menos	*at least*
por lo tanto	*therefore*
por lo visto	*evidently*
por medio de	*by means of*
por primera vez	*for the first time*
por supuesto	*of course*
por todas partes	*everywhere*
por último	*finally*

EXERCISE 2

A. Tell why **por** or **para** is used in the following sentences.

1. Haré la tarea por ti. **2.** Para un viejo es muy ágil. **3.** Ten cuidado, este dinero no es para ti. **4.** ¿Han viajado Uds. por Chile? **5.** Ana, si quieres, te daré mi tocadiscos por el tuyo. **6.** Nos quedaremos allí por dos semanas. **7.** Terminarán el trabajo para el mes que viene. **8.** Mañana salimos para el Canadá. **9.** Mi padre me envió por vino. **10.** Dio su vida por nosotros. **11.** No salió bien en el examen por ser vago. **12.** Hice este traje por María para Elena porque María no sabía coser.

B. Use an idiom with **por** in the blank spaces.

1. No les gusta levantarse temprano _____. **2.** Juanito, no hagas eso ni otra cosa, _____. **3.** Me gustaría ganar _____ mil pesos por semana. **4.** Mi cuñado nos visita _____ a la hora de comer. **5.** La conoció _____ en Laredo. **6.** Estudió muchos años para médico y _____ realizó su ambición. **7.** Tu novia, _____, es rica si te da tantos regalos. **8.** _____ se encuentran locos. **9.** Hay mucha gente mala _____ . **10.** No digáis eso, ¡ _____!

Idioms and Word Study

A. General Expressions.

a (los dos días)	*after (two days)*
al otro día, al día siguiente	*the next day*
al poco rato	*after a while*
de ningún modo, de ninguna manera	*not at all (emphatic negative)*
estar para	*to be about to*

*En la mañana, etc. is the usual expression in Mexico and some other Spanish-American countries.

estar por	to be in favor of, (Sp. Am. to be about to)
No es para tanto.	It's not that important.
ponerse a (gritar)	to begin to (shout)
por poco (se desmaya)*	(He) almost (fainted).
tomar por	to (mis)take for (consider)

B. Conocer and encontrar.

conocer	to meet (become acquainted with)
encontrar	to find; to meet, come upon

Estaban para salir cuando llegó su amiga.	They were about to leave when their friend arrived.
Yo estoy por quedarnos aquí.	I am in favor of our staying here.
Me tomaron por tonto.	They took me for a fool.
Por poco me muero de miedo.	I almost died of fright.
La conocí en Londres.	I met (became acquainted with) her in London.
Encontré a mi sobrino en la calle.	I met my nephew on the street.

C. Useful Expressions: Food and restaurants.

¿A qué hora se sirve el desayuno (el almuerzo, la cena)?	At what time do you serve breakfast (lunch, dinner)?
¿Qué van a tomar?	What will you have?
Un jugo (zumo in Spain) de naranja.	An orange juice.
La cuenta, por favor.	The check, please.
¿Está incluido el servicio?	Is the service charge included?

EXERCISE 3

Translate the English words in parentheses using the words or idioms from this section.

1. (I took him for a) profesor pero resultó ser sacerdote. **2.** Viajando en avión, (he met her) en Nueva York y se enamoró de ella en Chicago. **3.** Resbaló en el hielo y (he almost broke) una pierna. **4.** El niño (began) gritar cuando vio partir a su mamá. **5.** (We were about to leave) cuando sonó el teléfono. **6.** ¿Perdiste tus guantes? No llores, (it's not that important). **7.** Querían venir a visitarme (the next day). **8.** Parecía una persona encantadora pero (after two hours) estábamos aburridos. **9.** (I met) a mi padre en la estación. **10.** (We were in favor of) quedarnos solteros. **11.** ¿Te molesta si la acompaño? (Not at all.) **12.** (After a short while) volvió a sentarse.

---

*Note that the present tense is used after **por poco** even though the action is in the past.

4 The Infinitive and the Present Participle

A. The infinitive can be used:

1. As the object of a verb or a preposition. As has been pointed out (Section 1.B of this lesson), Spanish regularly uses the infinitive after a preposition while English often uses a present participle.

Corrió a saludarnos.	*He ran to greet us.*
Decidieron devolverlo.	*They decided to return it.*
Antes de abrir la boca, debes pensar.	*Before opening your mouth, you should think.*

2. After a verb of perception (**ver, oír, sentir, escuchar**), the dependent infinitive is placed immediately after the main verb.

Vemos jugar a los niños en el parque.	*We see the children play (playing) in the park.*

A famous short poem by the Catalan poet, Joaquín María Bartrina (1850–1880), has an example of this construction in its opening words.

Oyendo hablar a un hombre, fácil es	*Hearing a man speak, one can easily*
acertar dónde vio la luz del sol:	*guess where he saw the light of day:*
si os alaba a Inglaterra, será inglés;	*if he praises England to you, he must be English;*
si os habla mal de Prusia, es un francés;	*if he speaks ill to you of Prussia, he is a Frenchman;*
y si habla mal de España, es español.	*and if he speaks ill of Spain, he is a Spaniard.*

3. The verbs **hacer** and **mandar** + *infinitive* have a causative effect (cause something to be done).

Hicimos lavar la ropa.	*We had the clothing washed.*
Mandaron construir una casa.	*They had a house built.*
Hizo venir al médico.	*He had the doctor come.*

4. **Al** + *infinitive* is equal to the English *on* or *upon* + *present participle*.

Al terminar la lección ...	*Upon finishing the lesson . . .*

5. As a noun.

The proverbs:

Ver es creer.	*Seeing is believing.*
Querer es poder.	*To want is to be able. (Where there's a will there's a way.)*

Comer y rascar, todo es empezar.	*Eating and scratching need only a beginning. (Appetite comes with eating.)*

The definite article **el** may sometimes be used before the infinitive when used as a noun.

(El) viajar mucho es interesante.	*Traveling a lot is interesting.*

6. As a command, especially to give instructions of an impersonal nature.

Traducir al español las palabras siguientes.	*Translate the following words into Spanish.*
No fumar.	*No smoking.*

B. The Present Participle.

The formation of the present participle and its use with **estar** and other verbs to form the progressive tense *(to be + -ing)* is discussed in Lesson 5, Section 6. B.

The present participle standing alone is equivalent to the English present participle standing alone, or preceded by *while, by, when, since,* etc.

Estando en Madrid, conocí a Enrique.	*While (being or while I was) in Madrid, I met Enrique.*
Durmiendo todo el día y jugando toda la noche, no vas a conquistar el mundo.	*(By) sleeping all day and playing all night, you're not going to conquer the world.*

The Chilean poet Gabriela Mistral (1889–1957) won the Nobel Prize for Literature in 1945. Many of her poems deal with motherhood, as does the excerpt from *Meciendo* (Rocking) which follows.

El mar sus millares de olas mece, divino. Oyendo a los mares amantes, mezo a mi niño.	*The sea its thousands of waves divinely rocks. Listening to the loving seas, I rock my child.*

The opening stanza of the Cuban *Vals del estudiante:*[†]

Yo tengo un amor que me tiene penando, por el que dejé de seguir estudiando. Dejando los libros y en vez de estudiar, con ansias me pongo a cantar ...	*I have a love that has me suffering, because of which I stopped studying. Leaving my books and instead of studying, with anxiety I begin to sing . . .*

EXERCISE 4

A. Translate the English words of the following sentences.

1. (By eating) demasiado, engordarás.   **2.** (Eating) demasiado es un vicio.
3. Después de (seeing) a su viejo amigo, se puso a llorar.   **4.** En la estación había un letrero que decía: (No smoking).   **5.** Al otro día (she kept on working).
6. Nos oyó (singing).   **7.** (On seeing) al policía el ladrón se escondió.   **8.** (By repeating) las palabras del profesor sacarás una *A*.   **9.** (Studying) mucho sin hacer ejercicio no es bueno para la salud.   **10.** (They went around saying) que yo era un tonto.

B. Replace the verb of the dependent clause with a present participle and make other changes if necessary.

1. Cuando íbamos al cine, encontramos a Juan.   **2.** Mientras la esperaba, pasé el tiempo leyendo.   **3.** Como es así, podemos charlar un rato más.   **4.** Cuando hablo contigo, tengo la impresión que el tiempo vuela.

Basic Class Exercises

1

I. *"A long courtship proves to be invaluable in this case."* Fill in the blanks with a preposition, if necessary.

1. Ernesto conoció _____ Alicia por primera vez hace dos años.   **2.** Soñaba _____ ella todas las noches y después de dos semanas estaba ya enamorado _____ ella.   **3.** Trataba _____ olvidarse _____ ella pero no podía.   **4.** La veía _____ salir con otros e iba poniéndose celoso.   **5.** Por fin logró _____ que ella consintiera _____ salir con él.   **6.** Pronto ella se dio cuenta _____ que Ernesto, aunque no era guapo, era bueno y simpático.   **7.** Pensaba mucho _____ él, y pronto quedó enamorada _____ él.   **8.** Un día Ernesto le pidió _____ Alicia que se casara con él.   **9.** Ella dijo:—No conozco _____ ninguna compañera que quiera casarse.   **10.** Nosotras, las jóvenes de hoy, somos libres y queremos gozar _____ la vida.   **11.** No quiero casarme _____ nadie.   **12.** Ernesto se vio obligado _____ hacer lo que ella quería.   **13.** La invitó _____ salir con él casi todas las noches.   **14.** Pasaron dos años y Ernesto y Alicia estaban muy enamorados ... pero _____ otras personas, y se separaron.   **15.** Dieron las gracias _____ Dios por no haberse casado.

2

II. Fill in the blanks with **por** or **para**.

1. Me mataría _____ ti, amor mío.   **2.** ¿Cuánto me das _____ este paraguas?
3. El cuchillo que tienes ahí no sirve _____ cortar pan.   **4.** Tú tienes la culpa _____ habérselo dicho.   **5.** _____ abogado no conoce bien esa ley.   **6.** A veces prefiere andar _____ la orilla del mar.   **7.** El avión partió _____ Buenos Aires.   **8.** Espero terminarlo _____ el veinte de abril.   **9.** Envió la carta _____ avión.   **10.** Lo hizo _____ fin.

3

III. Translate the following sentences.

1. Están para salir ahora mismo. **2.** Su madre se puso a gritar. **3.** Por poco me ahogo en el agua. **4.** La conocí por primera vez en casa de mi sobrino. **5.** Volveremos a los dos meses. **6.** De ningún modo. **7.** Se encontraron en la tienda a las ocho. **8.** Logré entrar porque me tomaron por un personaje importante. **9.** Tomaremos un refresco al poco rato. **10.** Al otro día supe la verdad.

4

IV. A. *"A Thief in Spite of Himself."* Fill in the blanks with the infinitive or present participle of the verbs indicated.

1. _____ (Andar) por la calle mientras (yo) miraba el cielo, choqué con un hombre. **2.** _____ (Pedirme) me perdón, el hombre echó a _____ (correr). **3.** _____ (Meter) la mano en el bolsillo, vi que no tenía mi cartera. **4.** En seguida empecé a correr, alcancé al hombre, y _____ (coger) lo por la garganta le dije:—Dame la cartera. **5.** Éste inmediatamente sacó la cartera, me la dio y huyó como si el diablo lo estuviera _____ (perseguir). **6.** _____ (Volver) a la oficina les conté la historia a mis compañeros, muy satisfecho de mí mismo. **7.** Me puse a _____ (trabajar) pero al _____ (abrir) un cajón, vi dentro mi cartera. **8.** _____ (Sacar), horrorizado, la otra cartera de mi bolsillo; me di cuenta de que ... ¡el ladrón había sido yo!

B. Write the equivalent infinitive command.

EXAMPLE: No fumen Uds.
　　　　　　 No fumar.

1. Traduzcan al español. **2.** Siéntense. **3.** No habléis en voz alta. **4.** Escribid una composición.

C. Complete the sentences using your imagination.

1. Volviendo a casa, vi _____. **2.** Después de graduarme, voy a _____. **3.** Comiendo mucho, uno _____. **4.** Hice venir al médico porque _____. **5.** El bostezar mucho indica que _____. **6.** Vine corriendo por la calle cuando por poco _____.

Elective Exercises

V. *"The Evils of Drinking."* Translate.

1. Anna met Paul for the first time eight months ago. **2.** He fell in love with her and she with him. **3.** He was handsome and charming, but he liked to drink. **4.** Drinking too much is a terrible habit. **5.** By marrying him, Anna thought she could make him change. **6.** At first he consented not to touch alcohol but, after four months, he began to take a drink from time to time. **7.** "Keep on drinking," said Anna, "I almost left you last week because of it *(eso).* **8.** If you don't stop drinking by next week, there will be a divorce." **9.** Paul tried to stop drinking for her sake, but he did not succeed in doing so *(lo).* **10.** They are now about to be divorced.

VI. Read the following story, then translate the italicized phrases.

Primer amor

La primera vez que (1) *yo me enamoré de una mujer* fue a los trece años. (2) *No estando mi tía en casa,* me gustaba registrar los cajones de su cómoda. Un día, encontré un retrato. Era de una joven lindísima (3) *que parecía sonreírme* y pedirme que me acercara. Pronto (4) *oí entrar a mi tía* y devolví el retrato a su sitio.

Desde aquel día (5) *yo sólo pensaba en aquella mujer* que me llamaba desde el cajón. (6) *Al salir mi tía,* yo sacaba el retrato y (7) *soñaba con ella.*

Un día, (8) *no pudiendo resistir más,* saqué del marco a la dama de mis sueños y le di un beso ardiente. (9) *Después de besar el retrato,* me conmoví tanto que me desvanecí.

Cuando volví en mí, vi a mi padre, mi madre y mi tía. (10) *Ésta se esforzaba por quitarme el retrato* que, aunque estaba desvanecido, no solté.

—Suelta, chiquillo—decía mi tía—no estropees el retrato. Lo quiero mucho (11) *por ser* el único recuerdo de mi juventud.

—¿Usted? ... ¿El retrato ... es usted?

—¿No te parezco tan guapa, chiquillo? Los veintiséis años son muy bonitos, ¿no crees?

Yo no pude contestar. (12) *Cerrando los ojos,* juré no registrar más los cajones de mi tía.

ADAPTED FROM THE STORY BY THE FAMOUS SPANISH
WRITER, EMILIA PARDO BAZÁN (1852 – 1921)

VII. Fill in the blanks with one of the idioms using **por**.

1. _____ María es muy inteligente. **2.** Andando por la calle, _____ encontré a Silvia. **3.** Trató de escribir una buena novela y _____ tuvo éxito. **4.** Tenía pocos amigos y _____ se sentía muy solo. **5.** ¿Os gustaría que os diera por lo menos cinco mil pesos? ¡ _____ !

VIII. *"If you were a rich man (or woman)!"* Answer in Spanish.

1. ¿Sueña Ud. con hacerse millonario(-a)? **2.** Si consiguiera serlo, ¿se olvidaría de sus amigos pobres? **3.** ¿Qué aconsejaría que hicieran sus amigos para llegar a ser ricos? **4.** ¿Trataría de ayudarlos? **5.** ¿Cómo los ayudaría a ganar dinero? **6.** ¿Consiste la verdadera felicidad en la riqueza? **7.** ¿Se arrepentiría de haberse hecho rico(-a)? **8.** ¿Vale la pena esforzarse mucho por ganar dinero? **9.** Siendo rico, ¿cómo gozaría de la vida? **10.** ¿Para qué sirve el dinero?

IX. Review of Lesson 8.

A. *"Her boyfriend has another girlfriend!"* Fill in the blanks with the appropriate form of the verb in parentheses.

1. Supe que mi novio (salir) _____ con otra chica. **2.** Es una lástima que los hombres (ser) _____ así. **3.** Si él (saber) _____ que yo lo sabía, no habría salido con ella. **4.** Insistiré en que él (escoger) _____ entre ella y yo. **5.** Sin duda me dirá que él no (tener) _____ la culpa. **6.** Cuando lo (ver) _____ , al principio fingiré no saber nada. **7.** A veces los hombres salen con otras para que sus novias (tener) _____ celos.

B. Translate.

1. I beg you to forget it. **2.** She asked me to help her. **3.** Before they came, we stopped cleaning the house. **4.** They advised us to stay home. **5.** I gave him money so that (in order that) he would be able to buy a house. **6.** I am glad they have come.

Vocabulary

ágil agile
ahogarse to drown
andar to go; to walk
ascender (ie) to go up
banquete *m.* banquet
bostezar to yawn
cajón *m.* drawer (of a chest)
celoso jealous
cómoda chest of drawers
conmoverse (ue) to be moved
coser to sew
culpa fault, blame
charlar to chat
desvanecerse to faint
engordar to get fat
enloquecer (zc) to go mad
ensayo essay
esconderse to hide oneself
esforzarse (por) to strive (to)
estropear to damage
felicidad happiness
fingir to pretend
gozar (de) to enjoy
griego Greek
hermosura beauty
hielo ice
jurar to swear
lana wool
letrero sign
libre free
lograr to succeed (in)
manejar to drive
marco frame

marinero sailor
obedecer (zc) to obey
orilla shore
parecer (zc) (-se) to seem (to resemble)
pierna leg
pollo chicken
quejarse (de) to complain (about)
quitar to take away
rango rank
rato little while, short time
recuerdo remembrance, souvenir
refresco soft drink
regalo gift
registrar to search
resbalar to slip
resultar to turn out
saber (a) to taste (of)
sacerdote *m.* priest
sitio place
soltar (ue) to let go; to loosen
soltero bachelor
suntuoso sumptuous
tardar (en) to be late, to delay (in)
tarea homework
teniente lieutenant
tocadiscos *m.* record player
tonto foolish, fool
valer la pena to be worthwhile
vicio vice
volver (ue) en sí to regain one's consciousness

Lesson 10

1

Comparisons of Inequality

More . . . and *less . . .* are expressed respectively by **más** ... and **menos** ... with adjectives, adverbs and nouns.

A. Adjectives.

1. The comparative in English is usually expressed by adding *-er* to adjectives of one or two syllables *(tall—taller)* and by putting *more* in front of longer adjectives *(difficult—more difficult)*.

Spanish uses **más** with all adjectives, except for a few irregular forms discussed in Section 3 on pages 174–175.

alto	más alto	*taller*
difícil	más difícil	*more difficult*

Menos is the equivalent of the English *less* in the comparative construction.

menos interesante	*less interesting*
menos ocupado	*less busy*

¿Quién es más alto, Juan o su primo?	*Who is taller, Juan or his cousin?*
Este capítulo es más difícil que los otros.	*This chapter is more difficult than the others.*
Hoy tengo menos trabajo que ayer.	*Today I have less work than yesterday.*

2. In Spanish the superlative form is the same as the comparative when preceded by a definite article or a possessive adjective. If a noun is expressed, the article or possessive adjective will precede the noun.

Es la lección más complicada que hemos estudiado.	*It is the most complicated lesson we have studied.*
Le robaron sus más preciosas joyas.	*They stole her most precious jewels from her.*
Rosa es la más linda de la clase.	*Rosa is the prettiest in the class.*
Rosa es la muchacha más linda de la clase.	*Rosa is the prettiest girl in the class.*
Rosa es la más linda de las dos hermanas.	*Rosa is the prettier of the two sisters.*

NOTE: After a superlative **de** is used to translate *in*.

Nueva York es la ciudad más grande de los Estados Unidos.	*New York is the largest city in the United States.*

The great Spanish poet Luis de Góngora (1561–1627) wrote a charming poem in which a young bride laments the departure of her husband to fight in the wars. The opening lines are:

La más bella niña*	*The most beautiful girl*
de nuestro lugar,	*in our village,*
hoy viuda y sola	*today a widow and alone,*
y ayer por casar ...	*and yesterday about to marry . . .*

3. The following four adjectives have both regular and irregular comparative forms:

bueno	*good*	mejor	*better*
		más bueno	*better (in a moral sense)*
malo	*bad*	peor	*worse*
		más malo	*worse (in a moral sense)*

*Note that sometimes the article and the adjective precede the noun.

grande	big, large	mayor	bigger, greater, older (in reference to age or importance)
		más grande	bigger, larger, greater (size)
pequeño	small, little	menor	smaller, younger, lesser (age or importance)
		más pequeño	smaller (size)

Mejor and **peor** usually precede the noun they modify. **Mayor** and **menor** follow the noun when they refer to age.

Mi hermano menor es más grande que mi hermano mayor.	My younger (or youngest) brother is bigger than my older (or oldest) brother.
Es más bueno que el pan. (Spanish expression)	He is better than bread. (He is as good as gold.)
Son los chicos más malos de esta escuela.	They are the worst kids in this school.
Es mi mejor amigo.	He is my best friend.
No hay peor sordo que el que no quiere oír. (Proverb)	No man is more deaf (there is no worse deaf person) than he who does not want to hear.
No tengo la menor idea de lo que dijo.	I don't have the slightest idea of what he said.
El Salvador es más pequeño que Honduras, pero tiene mayor población.	El Salvador is smaller than Honduras but has a larger population.

The adjectives **mucho** and **poco** have the irregular comparative forms **más** and **menos**.

Tiene más dinero y menos amigos que nadie.	He has more money and fewer friends than anybody.

B. Adverbs.

1. Adverbs are compared in the same manner as adjectives, by placing **más** or **menos** before them.

más fácilmente	more easily	más despacio	more slowly
menos fácilmente	less easily	menos despacio	less slowly

Hable más despacio, por favor.	Speak more slowly, please.
Lo explicaron menos claramente que yo.	They explained it less clearly than I.

2. The following four adverbs have irregular comparative and superlative forms:

bien *well*	mejor *better, best*
mal *badly*	peor *worse, worst*
mucho *much*	más *more, most*
poco *little*	menos *less, least*

Quien mal dice, peor oye. *(Proverb)*	He who says bad things, hears worse.
Esa rubia me gusta más.	I like that blonde best (or better).
Donde menos se piensa, salta la liebre. *(Proverb)*	Where least expected, the hare jumps out. (Things happen when you least expect them.)

C. Nouns.

As with adjectives and adverbs, **más** (or **menos**) before the noun expresses *more* (or *less*).

Si uno tiene más suerte, es posible tener éxito con menos talento.	If one has more luck, it is possible to be a success with less talent.

D. *Than* in comparisons of inequality.

1. *More . . . than* and *less . . . than* are usually expressed by **más ... que** and **menos ... que**. To express *better than* or *worse than*, the expressions **mejor que** and **peor que** are used.

Sigue más cursos que yo.	He is taking more courses than I.
Lee más rápidamente que sus amigas y por eso ella lee más que ellas.	She reads more rapidly than her friends and therefore she reads more than they.
Es menos antipático que su hermano.	He is less obnoxious than his brother.
La biblioteca de nuestra universidad es mejor que ninguna otra.	The library of our college is better than any other.
El equipo es peor que nunca este año.	The team is worse than ever this year.

2. If there is a second clause (with a conjugated verb) and the comparison is with a noun in the first clause, **del que, de la que, de los que, de las que** must be used to express *than*.*

Tenemos más libros de los que podemos leer.	We have more books than we can read.
Anoche perdió más dinero del que gana en un año.	Last night he lost more money than he earns in a year.

If the comparison is with an adjective or an adverb **de lo que** is used.

---

*If, however, the second verb is one of mental attitude (**pensar, creer, esperar**, etc.) **de lo que** is used. Tenemos más libros de lo que tú crees. *We have more books than you think.*

Eran más fuertes de lo que sospechábamos.	*They were stronger than we suspected.*
Diviértete. Es más tarde de lo que crees.	*Enjoy yourself. It's later than you think.*

3. Before a number or a numerical expression *more than* is expressed by **más de.**

Le ofrecieron más de un millón de dólares.	*They offered him more than a million dollars.*
Faltó más de la mitad de la clase.	*More than half the class was absent.*

No ... más que before a number means *only.*

No gana más que mil pesos al mes.	*He earns only a thousand pesos a month. (exactly a thousand)*
No gana más de mil pesos.	*He earns no more than a thousand pesos. (possibly less)*

E. *The more . . . the more* is expressed in Spanish by **cuanto más ... (tanto) más;** *the less . . . the less* by **cuanto menos ... (tanto) menos;** *the more . . . the less* by **cuanto más ... (tanto) menos.**

Cuanto más come, (tanto) más engorda.	*The more he eats, the fatter he gets.*
Cuanto menos estudia, (tanto) menos aprende.	*The less he studies, the less he learns.*
Cuanto más tienen, (tanto) menos gastan.	*The more they have, the less they spend.*

EXERCISE 1

A. Complete the sentences with the comparative form of the adjective or adverb.

1. Ana baila bien pero Alicia baila _____. **2.** Esa novela es buena pero ésta es _____. **3.** Carlos es grande pero Juan y Pedro son aún _____.
4. Mi hermana mayor habla mucho pero mi hermano menor habla _____.
5. La comida de anoche fue mala pero ésta es _____. **6.** Su novio es guapo pero el mío es _____. **7.** Elena escribe mal pero Jorge escribe _____.
8. Esos documentos son de poca importancia pero éste tiene _____ importancia.

B. Insert either **de, que, de lo que,** or **del que (de la que, de los que, de las que)** in the blank.

1. Juan es más listo _____ yo. **2.** Juan es más listo _____ yo creía. **3.** México tiene más _____ cincuenta millones de habitantes. **4.** Ese equipo tiene más jugadores _____ necesita. **5.** Rosa escribe peor _____ Elena. **6.** Las crisis son más frecuentes _____ habían previsto. **7.** La foto de mi novia, para mí, vale más _____ un millón de pesos. **8.** Mi amigo gasta más dinero _____ gana.

C. Translate.

1. It is not so bad.   **2.** The more he looks at her picture, the more he falls in love with her.   **3.** (The) dog is man's best friend.   **4.** The less I see, the less it bothers *(doler)* me.

2

The Absolute Superlative

A. The adverbs **sumamente** or **extremadamente** before an adjective or adverb indicate an absolute or very high degree of the adjective or adverb without comparison to another person or thing. They are expressed in English by *most* or *extremely.*

Es sumamente lógico.	*It is most logical.*
Es extremadamente peligroso.	*It's extremely dangerous.*

B. Spanish also has a special way of expressing the absolute superlative, with the ending **-ísimo** added to the adjective. A final vowel is dropped before the **-ísimo** is added, but a change in spelling may be needed to keep the original sound of the final consonant (**co > qu, go > gu, z > c**). (See Appendix D.)

fácil	facilísimo	rico	riquísimo
mucho	muchísimo	largo	larguísimo
alto	altísimo	feliz	felicísimo

Esta sopa está riquísima.	*This soup is most delicious.*
Muchísimas gracias.	*Many, many thanks.*

The opening line of the ever popular song, *Amapola (Amapola, My pretty little poppy):*†

Amapola, lindísima amapola,	*Amapola, my most pretty Amapola,*
será siempre mi alma tuya sola	*my heart will always be yours alone . . .*

C. Some adverbs may also use the **-ísimo** to form an absolute superlative, but except for **muchísimo** (**muy** may not be used in front of **mucho**) it is rarely used because of the length of the resulting combination.

Habla muchísimo.	*He speaks very much.*
Los veo rarísimamente.	*I see them very rarely.*

Probably the longest word in the Spanish language using this construction is the Spanish equivalent of *in a most disproportionate manner:* **desproporcionadísimamente.**

EXERCISE 2

A. Substitute the **-ísimo** form for **muy**.

1. El viaje fue muy largo. **2.** Las noches de luna eran muy liñdas. **3.** José se casó con una chica muy rica. **4.** Era una muchacha muy feliz. **5.** Sus hijos eran muy inteligentes.

B. Change to the superlative in a complete sentence including the word in parentheses.

1. Ana es lindísima. (familia) **2.** Su casa es hermosísima. (barrio) **3.** Los Andes son montañas altísimas. (Sudamérica) **4.** Estos métodos son eficacísimos. (todos) **5.** Estos capítulos son dificilísimos. (libro) **6.** Buenos Aires es una ciudad grandísima. (la Argentina)

Comparisons of Equality

A. *As . . . as* is expressed in Spanish by **tan ... como** with adjectives and adverbs.

Esta lección no es tan fácil como la anterior.	*This lesson is not as easy as the previous one.*
Pronuncia tan bien como el profesor.	*He pronounces as well as the teacher.*

NOTE: **Tan** without the **como** is the equivalent of *so*.

Es tan mono.	*He's so cute.*
No seas tan modesto.	*Don't be so modest.*
—¿Qué le dijo la luna al sol?	*"What did the moon say to the sun?"*
—Tan grande y no te dejan salir de noche.	*"So big and they don't let you go out at night."*

B. *As much . . . as* is expressed by **tanto(-a) ... como;** *as many . . . as* by **tantos(-as) ... como** with nouns.

Gastó tanto dinero como tú.	*He spent as much money as you.*
Nadie tiene tanta paciencia como una buena maestra.	*Nobody has as much patience as a good teacher.*
Esta propuesta presenta tantos problemas como la otra.	*This proposal presents as many problems as the other one.*

C. *As much as* is expressed by **tanto como**.

Trabaja tanto como ella.	*He works as much as she (does).*

The last lines of the song *Muñequita linda:*[†]

Yo te quiero mucho,	*I love you a lot,*
mucho, mucho, mucho,	*very, very much,*
tanto como entonces,	*as much as at that time,*
siempre hasta morir.	*forever until I die.*

EXERCISE 3

Make the comparison one of equality.

1. Mis hermanos tienen menos amigos que mis hermanas. **2.** María es más inteligente que Carlos. **3.** Yo duermo más profundamente que una piedra. **4.** Nuestra casa es menos hermosa que la suya. **5.** Hemos escrito más cartas que ellos. **6.** Las niñas corren menos que los niños. **7.** Hace más calor en Miami que en Nueva York. **8.** Mi padre es más fuerte que el tuyo. **9.** A mí me gusta leer más que a ti. **10.** En esta universidad hay menos mujeres que hombres.

Idioms and Word Study

A. General Expressions.

al parecer	*apparently*
cada vez más más y más	*more and more*
de mal en peor	*from bad to worse*
la mayor parte	*most (the majority)*
poco a poco	*little by little*
ponerse de acuerdo	*to come to an agreement*
seguir un curso	*to take a course (academic)*
tanto mejor	*so much the better*
tanto peor	*so much the worse*
tomar el desayuno (almuerzo)	*to have breakfast (lunch)*

B. **Llevar** and **tomar**.

llevar	*to take (a person or thing from one place to another); to carry*
tomar	*to take; to drink*
Se está cansando cada vez más.	*She is getting more and more tired.*
La mayor parte de los niños chillan mucho.	*Most (of the) children shriek a great deal.*

Tomás llevó a Ana al baile.	*Tomás took Ana to the dance.*
Tomé el avión a tiempo.	*I took the plane on time.*
Tomé el libro de la mesa.	*I took the book from the table.*
Tomaron el vino.	*They drank the wine.*

C. Useful Expressions: Communication and correspondence.

¿Cuánto cuesta mandar una carta por avión a los Estados Unidos?	*How much does it cost to send an airmail letter to the United States?*
Deme diez sellos de a cincuenta pesetas.	*Give me ten 50 peseta stamps.*
Quisiera hacer una llamada a Miami.	*I would like to make a call to Miami.*
La línea está ocupada.	*The line is busy.*
No cuelgue, por favor.	*Don't hang up, please.*

EXERCISE 4

Find an ending in column B to the phrases in column A.

A	B
1. Estos niños me están molestando	**a.** al cine anoche.
2. Las relaciones entre las naciones van	**b.** se pusieron de acuerdo.
	c. en vez de quinientos. ¡Tanto mejor!
3. Tomaron el desayuno	**d.** de mal en peor.
4. Carlos me llevó	**e.** un curso de inglés.
5. Me dieron mil pesos	**f.** cada vez más.
6. Después de mucho discutir, ellos	**g.** a las nueve.
7. La mayor parte de los inquilinos	**h.** pagan un alquiler muy alto.
8. Poco a poco vamos aprendiendo	**i.** a hablar español.
9. Al parecer Rosa está	**j.** mejor que ayer.
10. El año pasado seguí	

The Conjunctions *Y* and *E*; *O* and *U*; *Pero* and *Sino*

A. Y and **e.**

Before a word beginning with **i-** or **hi-**, the conjunction **y** is replaced by **e**.

Fernando e Isabel se casaron en 1469.	*Ferdinand and Isabel were married in 1469.*
Padre e hijo fueron bárbaros e inhumanos.	*Father and son were barbarous and inhuman.*
Servicio e impuestos	*Service charges and taxes (on a bill)*

Before **hie-**, however, the **y** is retained.

Necesitan agua y hielo para preparar la limonada.	*They need water and ice to prepare the lemonade.*

B. **O** and **u**.

Before a word beginning with **o-** or **ho-**, the conjunction **o** is replaced by **u**.

¿Me puedes prestar siete u ocho dólares?	*Can you lend me seven or eight dollars?*
No se sabe si fue mujer u hombre.	*It is not known if it was a woman or a man.*

C. **Pero** and **sino**.

1. The usual word for *but* is **pero**. In literary language **mas** is sometimes used.

No aprende mucho, pero siempre viene a clase.	*He doesn't learn much, but he always comes to class.*
La comida no es muy buena aquí, pero es abundante.	*The food is not very good here, but it is plentiful.*

The final line of *Canción de otoño en primavera* by Rubén Darío (1867–1916):

¡Mas es mía el alba de oro!	*But mine is the golden dawn!*

2. If, however, *but* means *but (rather) on the contrary*, **sino** is used. The first clause must contain a negative.

En esta construcción no se usa **pero**, sino **sino**.	*In this construction one does not use **pero**, but (rather) **sino**.*
En el Brasil no hablan español, sino portugués.	*In Brazil they do not speak Spanish, but (rather) Portuguese.*

If the second part of the sentence contains a conjugated verb and if *but* means *but (rather) on the contrary*, the clause is introduced by **sino que**.

No compraron la casa sino que la alquilaron por tres meses.	*They did not buy the house, but (rather) they rented it for three months.*

NOTE: **Pero** is used if the idea of *(rather) on the contrary* is not there.

No compraron la casa pero les gustó mucho.	*They did not buy the house but they liked it a lot.*

EXERCISE 5

A. Insert **y, e, o,** or **u** in the blanks.

1. Los amoríos entre Carlos _____ Inés van de mal en peor. **2.** Se pusieron de acuerdo para empezar en septiembre _____ octubre. **3.** Poco a poco Isabel _____ Pablo van enamorándose. **4.** Usa una aguja _____ hilo para coser el botón. **5.** Los conejos comen plantas _____ hierba. **6.** La mayor parte de la novela que acabo de leer es emocionante _____ interesante.

B. Insert **pero, sino** or **sino que** in the blanks.

1. Es guapo _____ no me gusta. **2.** No es guapo _____ es simpático. **3.** No es guapo _____ feo. **4.** No encontró a Mario _____ a José. **5.** La tarea es difícil _____ poco a poco la terminaré. **6.** Ahora no vamos a tomar el desayuno _____ el almuerzo. **7.** Hace frío _____ no creo que vaya a nevar. **8.** No quiero que se lo digas tú _____ se lo diga Juan.

Basic Class Exercises

I. A. *"Rosa has many friends and cannot help but compare them."* Express the relationship of the friend in the first sentence with the one in the second.

EXAMPLE: Juan tiene diez pesos. Pablo tiene tres. *(money)*
Juan tiene más dinero que Pablo.

1. Mario tiene poca suerte. Carlos tiene mucha suerte. *(luck)* **2.** Pedro estudia mucho. José estudia poco. *(diligent)* **3.** Ana baila bien. Alicia baila mejor. *(worse)* **4.** María es lindísima. Alicia es linda. *(pretty)* **5.** Alberto es guapo. Juan es feo. *(handsome)* **6.** Mi amigo irlandés tiene veintiún años. Mi amiga inglesa tiene veintitrés. *(younger)* **7.** Dolores no puede tocar mi cabeza con la mano. Elena lo hace fácilmente. *(shorter)*

B. Complete the sentences using **que, de lo que** or **del que (de la que, de los que, de las que)**.

EXAMPLE: Yo te quiero más _____ crees.
Yo te quiero más de lo que crees.

1. La mayor parte de los estudiantes piden más dinero a sus padres _____ necesitan. **2.** En las elecciones, el candidato salió mejor _____ esperaba. **3.** Este año en la universidad se matricularon menos estudiantes _____ el año pasado. **4.** Elena siempre compra más carne _____ legumbres. **5.** El profesor era mucho más joven _____ parecía. **6.** Recibió más cartas _____ podía contestar.

C. Tell something about yourself by answering the following questions.

1. ¿Cuál es tu clase más interesante este semestre? **2.** ¿Quién es el (la) estudiante más inteligente de la clase? **3.** ¿Quién es el profesor (la profesora) que te gusta más? ¿Por qué? **4.** ¿Tienes más trabajo en tu clase de español que en otras clases? **5.** ¿Cómo se llama tu mejor amigo(-a)? ¿Es mayor o menor que tú? **6.** ¿Te gustaría casarte con la persona más famosa del mundo? ¿Por qué?

D. Here are four members of Professor Blanco's class. Tell what you can about them in Spanish, using comparisons of inequality: **más** or **menos**.

EXAMPLE: Pedro es más gordo que Rosa.

| Pedro | Carlos | Rosa | Alicia |

II. Answer the question **¿Cómo es (son) ...?** using an absolute superlative as in the example.

EXAMPLE: Juan es alto pero Ana es más alta. (¿Cómo es Ana?)
            Ana es altísima.

1. *Los Pazos de Ulloa* de Emilia Pardo Bazán es una novela larga pero *La Regenta* de Leopoldo Alas es más larga. (¿Cómo es *La Regenta?*) **2.** Mi familia es feliz pero la de él es más feliz. (¿Cómo es la de él?) **3.** Elena es pobre pero Dolores es más pobre. (¿Cómo es Dolores?) **4.** México es un país grande pero el Brasil es más grande. (¿Cómo es el Brasil?) **5.** Ana es simpática pero Alicia e Inés son más simpáticas. (¿Cómo son Alicia e Inés?) **6.** Juan es vago pero sus hermanos son más vagos. (¿Cómo son sus hermanos?)

III. Fill in the blanks with **tan, tan ... como, tanto (-a, -os, -as) ... como,** or **tanto como**.

1. En verano no me gusta nada _____ el agua fría. **2.** Rosa, ¡nunca te he visto _____ hermosa! **3.** Este curso no es _____ fácil _____ el del año pasado.
4. Nunca han llovido sobre nosotros _____ desgracias _____ las que hemos tenido este año. **5.** Me aconsejó que no fuera _____ vago _____ mi hermano.
6. Nos alegramos de que haya _____ chicos _____ chicas en este baile.

IV. A. Answer the questions using an expression from Section 4 of this lesson. (Some may have more than one possible answer.)

1. El año pasado el señor Pérez realizó sólo treinta mil pesos de sus negocios. Este año no sacó más que veinte. ¿Cómo van sus negocios? **2.** Juan se despertó a las ocho. Tenía mucha hambre. ¿Qué hizo? **3.** A Ricardo le falta un curso para graduarse. ¿Qué hará para recibir su diploma? **4.** El padre les prometió un buen regalo a sus hijos si dejaban de pelearse. ¿Qué hicieron?
5. Ana quería ir al baile. Tomás quería complacerla. ¿Qué hizo Tomás?

B. Of the five people in the following sentences three had problems which became worse. Who are they? Fill in the blanks with an idiom from Section 4, then tell which situations became worse.

1. A Elena le gusta comer y cada semana pesa medio kilo más que la semana anterior. _____ Elena está engordando. **2.** Tomás ganaba poco dinero. De repente sus amigos lo vieron gastar mucho dinero. — _____ ha ganado la lotería,—dijeron sus amigos. **3.** Rosa ganaba doscientos dólares por semana. Una semana se equivocaron y le dieron trescientos. Un amigo le dijo:—¿Se equivocaron? ¡ _____ para ti! **4.** Luisito tenía que entregar un ensayo a su maestra para el jueves. Llegó el día y Luisito no pudo terminarlo. — _____ para ti—le dijo la maestra. **5.** Al empezar el semestre, Juan estudiaba mucho pero poco a poco se interesaba más en el fútbol y estudiaba menos.—Te estás poniendo_____ vago,—le dijo la profesora.

V. A. Rewrite the sentences replacing the word in italics with the word in parentheses.

EXAMPLE: El número es setenta o *noventa.* (ochenta)
                      El número es setenta u ochenta.

1. Es una chica bonita y *hacendosa.* (inteligente) **2.** Se llama Pedro o *Pablo.* (Horacio) **3.** Me faltan setecientos o *novecientos* dólares para comprar el televisor. (ochocientos) **4.** Tengo muchos amigos griegos y *españoles.* (italianos) **5.** Esta caja está hecha de cobre y *acero.* (hierro) **6.** Pablo es un chico guapo y *simpático.* (interesante)

B. *"A Generous Friend."* Complete the following sentences using **pero, sino** or **sino que**.

1. Ricardo gasta mucho dinero obsequiando a sus amigos. No es tacaño _____ generoso. **2.** Sus asuntos van de mal en peor, _____ no pierde ánimo. **3.** La mayor parte de sus amigos no lo desaniman _____ lo animan. **4.** Poco a poco gana más dinero que antes y ya no es pobre_____ rico. **5.** No olvida a sus verdaderos amigos _____ los obsequia más que antes. **6.** No tiene problemas ahora, _____ ahorra dinero para evitarlos en el futuro.

Elective Exercises

VI. *"A Weighty Problem."* Translate.

1. Little by little Pedro and Isabel, his wife, are getting (becoming) fatter and fatter. **2.** She is not as fat as he, but apparently this is no consolation. **3.** He does not eat as much as she [does] but, nevertheless, he continues to get fatter than she. **4.** The doctor advises him not to drink beer but water. **5.** "How can I watch television without beer! **6.** It is the best way to enjoy a good football game." **7.** "Take me to the movies instead of watching television," Isabel said to him. **8.** Since they love each other very much, they came to an agreement. **9.** He watches television not more than four times a *(por)* week and they go to the movies the other nights. **10.** Pedro has stopped seeing the doctor who, incidentally, is fatter than Pedro.

VII. Fill in the blanks by translating the English words in parentheses.

Una carta a Dios

Lencho miraba el cielo esperando que cayera la lluvia que tanto necesitaba. Pronto se alegró mucho al ver caer gruesas gotas de lluvia, pero duró poco su alegría pues empezaron a caer granizos (as big as) _____ bellotas.

—Esto es (more than) _____ esperaba—dijo Lencho y vio que (little by little) _____ los granizos iban destruyendo su cosecha.

Las cosas fueron (from bad to worse) _____ y el pobre Lencho no sabía qué hacer.

—El granizo es (the worst thing in the world)_____ —pensó —pero hay alguien que nos protege; es Dios. Nadie nos quiere (as much as) ____ Dios.

Lencho decidió escribirle una carta, pidiéndole a Dios que le enviara (more than) _____ cien pesos. Al día siguiente echó la carta en la oficina de correos.

Un cartero, al ver el sobre dirigido «A Dios», (took) _____ la carta al jefe, riéndose. Éste se rió también, (but) _____ pronto, siendo un hombre compasivo, decidió contestar la carta. Al ver que se necesitaba dinero se lo pidió a los empleados, pero no pudo reunir más que setenta (or) _____ ochenta pesos.

—Esto es menos dinero (than) _____ necesita, —dijo el jefe —pero es mucho (better than) _____ nada.

Al día siguiente Lencho volvió y preguntó si había una carta para él. Se la entregaron y Lencho se alejó para leerla.

El jefe y (the majority)_____ de los empleados miraban a Lencho desde lejos. Al abrir la carta, no mostró (the slightest) _____ sorpresa al ver los billetes. (But) _____ , al contar los billetes, hizo un gesto de cólera. En seguida pidió papel y tinta y se puso a escribir. Después de terminar la carta, la echó y salió, (angrier)_____ antes.

El jefe y los empleados se apresuraron a abrir la carta. Decía la carta:

—Dios, del dinero que pedí, llegaron a mis manos (only) _____ setenta pesos. Mándame el resto, que me hace mucha falta, (but)_____ por otro camino, porque los empleados aquí son (the worst thieves in the world) _____.

ADAPTED FROM THE STORY BY THE RENOWNED MEXICAN NOVELIST, GREGORIO LÓPEZ Y FUENTES (1897 – 1966)

VIII. Review of Lesson 9.

A. Insert a preposition, if necessary, in the blank spaces.

1. Estoy pensando ahora _____ mi futura carrera. **2.** Estábamos esperando _____ nuestros amigos. **3.** Se puso a trabajar mucho _____ ser tan pobre. **4.** A todo el mundo le gusta quejarse _____ todos los otros. **5.** ¿Su hijo le pidió _____ dinero? **6.** ¿Viniste _____ el televisor? **7.** Es la tercera vez que me enamoro _____ una chica llamada Rosa. **8.** Los soldados sacrificaron la vida ____ la patria.

B. Translate the English, using an infinitive or a present participle.

1. Me gusta escuchar (the falling) de la lluvia. **2.** (While waiting for) Dolores, encontré a mi profesora. **3.** (Doing good) para el pueblo debe ser el propósito de todos los gobiernos. **4.** Oímos (the birds singing). **5.** Después de (having lunch) se puso a estudiar. **6.** (Swimming) es bueno para la salud. **7.** No conseguirás nada (by complaining). **8.** (On seeing her) por poco me desmayo.

Vocabulary

acero steel
aguja needle
alejarse to go away; to go to one side
alquiler *m.* rent
amorío love affair
animar to encourage
ánimo courage
apresurarse (a) to hurry (to)
barrio district
bellota acorn
camino road; way
carne *f.* meat

carrera race; career
cartero mailman
cobre *m.* copper
cólera anger
compasivo compassionate
complacer (zc) to please
conejo rabbit
conseguir (i, i) to succeed
correos: oficina de— post office
cosecha harvest
desafortunado unfortunate
desanimar to discourage
desgracia misfortune

desmayarse to faint
dirigido addressed; directed
echar to mail; to throw
eficaz efficient
emocionante exciting (emotional)
empeñarse (en) to insist (on)
empleado employee
entregar to deliver
equipo team
equivocarse to be mistaken
falta: me hace— I need
gesto gesture, face (grimace)
gota drop
granizar to hail (storm)
granizo hailstone
grueso thick
hábil skillful
hacendoso diligent
hierba grass

hierro iron
hilo thread
inquilino tenant
irlandés Irish
legumbre f. vegetable
matricularse to register
negocio(s) business
obsequiar to treat
pelear(se) to quarrel; to argue; to fight
prever to foresee
propósito purpose
proteger to protect
reunir to gather, collect
sobre m. envelope
tacaño miserly, stingy
tinta ink
verdadero true
virtud f. virtue

Lesson 11

1 **Relatives**

2 **Interrogatives**

3 **Exclamations**

4 **Idioms and Word Study**

5 **Indefinites**

6 **Negatives**

1 **Relatives**

Relatives connect the subordinate clause with an antecedent in the main clause.

A. Que *(that, which, who, whom).*

1. **Que,** the most commonly used of all relative pronouns, is invariable in form, and it may refer to both persons and things, regardless of gender or number, and may be a subject or object.

El hombre que dijo eso es mi ayudante.	The man who said that is my assistant.
Los objetos que cuestan mucho no se venden fácilmente.	Objects that cost a lot are not easily sold.
La casa que compramos está en malas condiciones.	The house (which, that) we bought is in poor condition.
Las señoras que ayudaste a cruzar la calle son vecinas nuestras.	The ladies (whom) you helped to cross the street are neighbors of ours.

NOTE: While English may sometimes omit the relative pronoun when it is an object in the subordinate clause (*which, that, whom* as in the last two sentences), it is never omitted in Spanish.

2. **Que** is normally used with reference to things after the prepositions **con, de, en** and **a**.* (See also section C.1 on page 191.)

Las novelas de que hablamos son bastante cortas.	The novels of which we are speaking are quite short.
El presidente presentó a los senadores las plumas con que firmó el documento.	The president presented to the senators the pens with which he signed the document.
La casa en que vivimos es grande.	The house in which we live is big.

B. Quien, quienes (*who* or *whom*) refer only to persons.

1. **Quien** is normally used after the prepositions **con, de, en** and **a**. (See also Section C.1 on page 191.)

| Los jóvenes con quienes salía eran españoles. | The young men with whom she went out were Spaniards. |
| El ingeniero de quien te hablé acaba de entrar. | The engineer I spoke to you about has just come in. |

2. **Quien** may be used instead of **que** as subject of a clause used parenthetically (set off by commas and not essential to the meaning of the sentence). In popular speech, however, **que** is used more frequently. (See also Section C.2 on page 191.)

| Mi primo José, quien (*or* que) estuvo en México el verano pasado, vive en la casa de al lado. | My cousin José, who was in Mexico last summer, lives in the house next door. |

3. **Quien** may be used instead of **que** as direct object of a verb, in which case it must be preceded by the personal **a**.

| Los ladrones que (*or* a quienes) cogieron serán encarcelados. | The thieves whom they caught will be jailed. |

*As a mnemonic device, the word **condena** (*he / she condemns*) contains the four prepostitions: con, de, en, and a.

4. **Quien** is used, especially in proverbs, in the sense of *he who,* etc. as a subject including its own antecedent. In normal speech, however, **el que,** etc. is usually used in this construction. (See Section C.3, below.)

Quien mucho habla, mucho yerra. *(Proverb)*	*He who talks a lot makes many mistakes.*
Quien busca, halla. *(Proverb)*	*He who seeks, finds. (Seek and you shall find.)*
Quien no se atreve, no pasa la mar. *(Proverb)*	*He who doesn't dare, does not cross the sea. (Nothing ventured, nothing gained.)*
Quien (El que) dice eso, miente.	*He who says that is lying.*

C. El cual (la cual, los cuales, las cuales) and el que (la que, los que, las que).

1. After prepositions (sometimes even after **con, de, en, a**) referring to persons or things, a form of **el que** or **el cual** is used. There is a popular preference for **el cual.**

Estoy buscando el edificio delante del cual (del que) dejé el coche.	*I am looking for the building in front of which I left the car.*
Finalmente realizaron las metas por las cuales (las que) habían luchado.	*They finally achieved the goals for which they had struggled.*
Leandro y sus hermanos, entre los cuales (los que) nunca hubo ninguna riña antes de la muerte de sus padres, ahora pelean siempre.	*Leandro and his brothers, among whom there never was any dispute before the death of their parents, now quarrel all the time.*
Los jóvenes con los cuales (los que) ella salía no les gustaban a sus padres.	*Her parents did not like the young men with whom she went out.*
El ingeniero del cual (del que) te hablé acaba de entrar.	*The engineer I spoke to you about has just come in.*

2. These forms are sometimes used in place of **quien** or **que** in parenthetical clauses to avoid ambiguity. (See Section B.2, page 190.)

El consejero de la reina, el cual (el que) estaba fuera del país, no supo lo que había sucedido.	*The adviser of the queen, who was out of the country, did not find out what had happened.*

3. As a compound relative including its own antecedent, **el que,** etc. (*not* **el cual**) is used.

Los que estudian aprenderán.	*Those who study will learn.*

From popular songs, quoted previously:

El que tenga un amor, que lo cuide ...	*He who may have a love, let him take care of it . . .*
Los que dicen «adiós, che», ésos no son de aquí ...	*Those who say "adiós, che," they are not from here . . .*

D. Lo que and **lo cual**.

1. When referring to a whole idea, rather than to a specific word, **lo que** and **lo cual** are used as the equivalents of *which*.

Nadie había preparado la lección, lo que (lo cual) enojó al profesor.	*No one had prepared the lesson, which annoyed the teacher.*

2. **Lo que** (*not* **lo cual**) is used to express the English relative pronoun *what (that which)*.

No comprendí lo que dijo.	*I did not understand what he said.*

From a love poem by the Peruvian poet and politician Manuel González Prada (1848–1918):

Algo me dicen tus ojos,	*Your eyes are saying something to me,*
pero lo que dicen no sé ...	*but what they are saying I do not know . . .*

E. Cuanto *(all that, as much as)* is sometimes used, especially in literary style, in place of **todo lo que**.

Les dio cuanto (todo lo que) tenía.	*He gave them all that he had.*
Trabajó cuanto pudo.	*He worked as much as he could.*

As an adjective **cuanto (-a, -os, -as)** + *a noun* is similarly used in place of **todo el (toda la, todos los, todas las)** + *a noun* + **que**.

Nos ofreció cuanto dinero (todo el dinero que) tenía.	*He offered us all the money he had.*
Ella saludó a cuantas amigas (todas las amigas que) encontró.	*She greeted all the friends she met.*

F. Cuyo (-a, -os, -as) *(whose)* is a relative possessive adjective and agrees in gender and number with the noun it modifies.

La pintora, cuyos cuadros ganaron varios premios, es mi esposa.	*The artist, whose paintings won several awards, is my wife.*

The opening words of Cervantes' *Don Quijote de la Mancha* (1605):

En un lugar de la Mancha,
   de cuyo nombre no quiero
   acordarme ...

In a town of La Mancha,
   whose name I do not wish to
   recall . . .

Whose as an interrogative (¿de quién?) is discussed in Section 2, B.3.

EXERCISE 1

A. Fill in the blanks with **que** or **quien(-es)**.

1. El hombre _____ llegó conmigo es extranjero. **2.** Los extranjeros _____
viven en este país trabajan mucho. **3.** El avión _____ acaba de llegar vino de
Buenos Aires. **4.** Esas mujeres, _____ son muy jóvenes, son profesoras.
5. El país _____ lleva el nombre del gran general Simón Bolívar se llama
Bolivia. **6.** Benito Juárez, _____ era indio, fue un gran presidente de México.

B. Fill in the blanks with **que, quien(-es), el cual (la cual, los cuales, las cuales)** or **el que (la que, los que, las que)**.

1. Son ellos de _____ hablábamos. **2.** Ésa es la puerta por _____ entramos.
3. Seguimos un curso en _____ hay que leer mucho. **4.** Llegaron a la casa
detrás de _____ encontraron el cadáver. **5.** Mañana tendrá lugar la
conferencia de_____ ya os hablé. **6.** Hablamos a nuestros amigos con _____
pensamos dar un paseo. **7.** Ésta es la mujer sin _____ no puedo vivir—mi
esposa. **8.** ¿Es María a _____ hablaste por teléfono?

C. Substitute **el que (la que, los que, las que)** for **quien(-es)**.

1. Quien dijo eso mentía. **2.** Quienes no hagan el trabajo, no recibirán su
sueldo completo. **3.** No es él quien pronunció ese magnífico discurso.
4. Rosa es quien me lo ha dicho.

2

Interrogatives

A. All interrogatives, whether in a direct or in an indirect question, bear a
written accent.

¿Quién lo rompió?
Quiero saber quién lo rompió.
Dime con quién andas y te diré
   quién eres. *(Proverb)*

Who broke it?
I want to know who broke it.
Tell me whom you go with and
   I will tell you who you are.
   (A person is judged by the
   company he keeps.)

From a popular song:

¿Qué pasó? ¿Qué sucedió?	*What happened? What occurred?*
Yo no sé qué pasó ...	*I don't know what happened . . .*

B. The most common interrogative pronouns and adjectives are:

¿qué?	*what?*
¿cuál?, ¿cuáles?	*what, which?*
¿quién?, ¿quiénes?	*who?*
¿a quién?, ¿a quiénes?	*(to) whom?*
¿cuánto?, ¿cuánta?	*how much?*
¿cuántos?, ¿cuántas?	*how many?*

1. **¿Qué?** may be a pronoun (standing alone) or an adjective (before a noun).

¿Qué quiere decir esta palabra?	*What does this word mean?*
¿Qué poemas has leído recientemente?	*What (which) poems have you read recently?*

¿Qué? is used for English *what* when asking for an explanation or definition.

¿Qué es una república?	*What is a republic?*

Two classic examples from Spanish poetry, cited earlier. From Calderón's *La vida es sueño:*

> ¿Qué es la vida? Un frenesí.
> ¿Qué es la vida? Una ilusión ...

One of Bécquer's best known *rimas:*

> —¿Qué es poesía? dices mientras clavas
> en mi pupila tu pupila azul.
> —¿Qué es poesía? —¿Y tú me lo preguntas?
> Poesía ... eres tú.

2. **¿Cuál?** (**¿cuáles?**) is a pronoun and implies a choice among several possibilities.

¿Cuál de estas dos corbatas va mejor con mi camisa?	*Which (one) of these two ties goes better with my shirt?*
¿Cuál es tu número de teléfono?	*What is your telephone number?*

¿Cuáles son tus colores favoritos?	*What (which) are your favorite colors?*
¿Cuál es la república más grande de Latinoamérica?	*Which (one) is the largest republic in Latin America?*

¿Cuál? is used instead of **¿qué?** by many people as an adjective.

¿Cuál cerveza prefieres?	*What (which) beer do you prefer?*

3. **¿Quién? ¿Quiénes?** may refer only to persons.

¿Quién sabe?	*Who knows?*
¿A quiénes vieron Uds.?	*Whom did you see?*
¿De quién recibiste una tarjeta?	*From whom did you receive a card?*

¿De quién? (**¿de quiénes?**) is used to express *whose* in the interrogative sense.

¿De quién es esta bicicleta?	*Whose bicycle is this?*

4. **¿Cuánto(-a)?** and **¿cuántos(-as)?** may be pronouns or adjectives.

¿Cuánto cuesta?	*How much does it cost?*
¿Cuánto vale?	*How much does it cost? (or is it worth?)*
¿Cuánto es?	*How much is it?*
¿Cuántos compraron?	*How many did they buy?*
¿Cuánto tiempo nos queda?	*How much time do we have left?*
¿Cuántos nietos tiene su abuela?	*How many grandchildren does his grandmother have?*

C. Four common interrogative adverbs are:

¿Por qué?	*Why?*	¿Dónde?	*Where?*
¿Cuándo?	*When?*	¿Cómo?	*How? What?*

1. The usages in both languages generally correspond.

¿Por qué no?	*Why not?*
¿Cuándo terminarán?	*When will they finish?*
¿Dónde lo hallaron?	*Where did they find it?*
¿Cómo está Ud.?	*How are you?*

The following witty *copla,* by the Spanish fabulist, Tomás de Iriarte (1750–1791), contains the four interrogative adverbs listed in Section 2.C.

—He reñido a un hostelero.	*"I scolded an innkeeper."*
—¿Por qué? ¿Cuándo? ¿Dónde? ¿Cómo?	*"Why? When? Where? How?"*
—Porque cuando donde como sirven mal, me desespero.	*"Because when where I eat they serve badly, I become exasperated."*

From the song *Quizás,* popular in English as *Perhaps:*

Siempre que te pregunto	*Whenever I ask you*
¿cuándo? ¿cómo? y ¿dónde?	*when, how and where?*
Tú siempre me respondes:	*You always answer me,*
—Quizás, quizás, quizás.	*"Perhaps, perhaps, perhaps."*

2. With verbs of motion, *Where?* is generally expressed by **¿Adónde?** rather than by **¿Dónde?**

¿Adónde vas y dónde pasarás la noche?	*Where are you going and where will you spend the night?*

3. **¿Cómo?** has the homonym (a word that is written or pronounced in the same way) **como,** which may mean *like* or *I eat* (from **comer**).

—¿Cómo como?	*"How do I eat?"*
—Como como como.	*"I eat the way I eat."*

If *how* is used in the sense of asking for an opinion, **¿qué tal?** is used. The following sentences illustrate the difference between **¿cómo?** and **¿qué tal?**

¿Cómo te gustan los huevos?	*How do you like the (your) eggs? (fried, scrambled, etc.)*
¿Qué tal te gustan los huevos?	*How do you like the eggs? (Are they good, tasty, etc.)*

4. **¿Por qué?**, *Why?*, should not be confused in spelling or pronunciation with **porque,** *because,* which is stressed on the first syllable.

The following short poem by the beloved Galician poet Rosalía de Castro (1837–1885) contains a good example of this point.

—Te amo ... ¿Por qué me odias?	*"I love you . . . Why do you hate me?"*
—Te odio ... ¿Por qué me amas?	*"I hate you . . . Why do you love me?"*
Secreto es éste el más triste	*This is the saddest and most*
y misterioso del alma.	*mysterious secret of the soul.*
Mas ello es verdad ... ¡Verdad	*But it is the truth ... A truth*
dura y atormentadora!	*hard and tormenting!*
—Me odias, porque te amo;	*"You hate me, because I love you;*
te amo, porque me odias.	*I love you, because you hate me."*

EXERCISE 2

A. Fill in the blank space with either **¿qué?** or **¿cuál? (cuáles)**.

1. ¿ _____ es la capital de Chile? **2.** ¿ _____ es la libertad? **3.** ¿ _____ casa es la tuya? **4.** ¿ _____ es su apellido? **5.** ¿ _____ significa esto? **6.** ¿ _____ chicos son tus compañeros de cuarto? **7.** ¿En _____ residencia vivía? **8.** ¿ _____ es la fecha de vuestro aniversario?

B. Write questions for which the following sentences would be the answers, using the interrogative indicated.

1. Mi número de teléfono es 367–9400. (What?) **2.** Prefiero el café con leche. (How?) **3.** Leímos quince novelas este semestre. (How many?) **4.** Mi hermana es abogada. (What?) **5.** Mis compañeras son Ana y Elena. (Who?) **6.** Este libro es de Pablo. (Whose?) **7.** Anoche conocí a dos muchachas simpatiquísimas. (Whom?) **8.** Tomaron un litro de leche. (How much?) **9.** Fui a casa de Ana para estudiar con ella. (Why? For what reason?) **10.** Necesito una cuchara para tomar la sopa. (Why? For what purpose?)

3 Exclamations

Some interrogative words are also used as exclamations.

A. ¡Qué!

1. When used before an adjective or adverb, **¡qué!** is the equivalent of *how*.

¡Qué gracioso eres!	*How witty you are!*
¡Qué macho!	*How masculine! (What a he-man!)*
¡Qué tontos son!	*How foolish they are!*
¡Qué rápidamente lo hizo!	*How quickly he did it!*

2. When used with a noun, **¡qué!** may be translated as *what* or *what a*. (Note that the indefinite article is not used in Spanish.)

¡Qué hombre!	*What a man!*
¡Qué noche!	*What a night!*
¡Qué problemas!	*What problems!*

Vaya plus the indefinite article is sometimes used in this construction instead of **¡qué!**:

¡Vaya una noche!	*What a night!*
¡Vaya unos problemas!	*What problems!*

3. If the noun is modified by an adjective the following word order is generally used: **¡qué** + *noun* + **tan** or **más** + *adjective*.

¡Qué noche tan oscura!	*What a dark night!*
¡Qué libro más pesado!	*What a dull book!*
¡Qué montañas tan altas!	*What tall mountains!*

Less frequently **¡qué!** alone is used without **tan** or **más**.

¡Qué buenos niños!	*What good children!*
¡Qué libro pesado!	*What a dull book!*

The opening lines of the beautiful *Malagueña salerosa:*†

¡Qué bonitos ojos tienes	*What beautiful eyes you have*
debajo de esas dos cejas!	*beneath those two eyebrows!*

Federico García Lorca (1898–1936), the brilliant poet and dramatist, who met a tragic death at the outbreak of the Spanish civil war, wrote the haunting *Canción de jinete* (Rider's Song). The horseman has a foreboding that disaster will overtake him before he reaches Córdoba. One stanza goes:

¡Ay, qué camino tan largo!	*Alas, what a long way!*
¡Ay, mi jaca valerosa!	*Alas, my brave pony!*
¡Ay, que la muerte me espera	*Alas, death awaits me*
antes de llegar a Córdoba!	*before I reach Córdoba!*

B. ¡Cuánto(-a)! means *how (much)!* **¡Cuántos(-as)!** means *how many!* *How* alone is frequently expressed by **¡cómo!**

¡Cuánto (cómo) te quiero!	*How I love you!*
¡Cuánto (cómo) lo siento!	*How sorry I am!*
¡Cuánto (cómo) me alegro de verte!	*How glad I am to see you!*
¡Cuántas veces se lo había dicho!	*How many times I had told it to him!*
¡Cómo engañó a todo el mundo!	*How he fooled everyone!*
¡Cómo nos mintió!	*How he lied to us!*

Gil Vicente (1470–1539), the great Portuguese poet and dramatist, wrote a number of beautiful lyrics in Spanish. One of them begins with the following two lines:

Muy graciosa es la doncella,	*Very charming is the maiden,*
¡cómo es bella y hermosa!	*how lovely and beautiful she is!*

EXERCISE 3

Make exclamations of the following sentences using the word indicated.

1. Estoy muy alegre. (qué) **2.** Es una chica muy linda. (qué) **3.** Es un jugador maravilloso. (vaya) **4.** Se espantaron. (cuánto) **5.** Tenía muchos enemigos. (cuántos) **6.** Me aburren los profesores. (cómo) **7.** Es una casa grande. (qué) **8.** Tienes bonitos ojos. (qué) **9.** Es un sinvergüenza. (vaya) **10.** Ganaron mucha plata. (cuánta)

4 Idioms and Word Study

A. General Expressions.

¡Cómo no!	*Of course! Why not?*
de buena gana	*willingly*
de mala gana	*unwillingly*
en ninguna parte ⎫ por ninguna parte ⎭	*nowhere*
es decir	*that is to say*
haber de	*to be to, to be supposed to*
¿Qué más ... ?	*What else?*
¡Qué va!	*Nonsense! Not at all! Of course not!*
valer la pena	*to be worthwhile, worth the trouble*
vale (in Spain)	*all right, O.K.*

B. Time Expressions.

hora	*hour, time of day, time (to do something)*
tiempo	*duration of time, time (abstract), weather*
vez	*time (once, twice, etc.)*
a la vez (al mismo tiempo)	*at the same time*
a tiempo	*on time*

Son las tres, es decir, es tarde.	*It's three o'clock, that is to say, it is late.*
Hemos de terminar el trabajo para mañana.	*We are (supposed) to finish the work by tomorrow.*
Estudiamos (por) dos horas.	*We studied for two hours.*
Es hora de acostarnos.	*It's time for us to go to bed.*
No tengo tiempo para eso.	*I don't have time for that.*
No lo hagas ni una vez más.	*Don't do it even once more.*
¿Cuántas veces tengo que decírtelo?	*How many times do I have to tell you (it)?*
Estudia y escucha la radio al mismo tiempo (a la vez).	*He studies and listens to the radio at the same time.*
Hay que llegar a clase a tiempo.	*It is necessary to (One must) get to class on time.*

C. Useful expressions: Medical.

No me siento bien.	*I don't feel well.*
Favor de llamar al médico.	*Please call the doctor.*
Hay que fijar cita.	*You must (It's necessary to) make an appointment.*
¿Dónde le duele?	*Where does it hurt you?*

Creo que tengo un resfriado (una fiebre).	*I think I have a cold (a fever).*
Tome dos aspirinas y llámeme por la mañana.	*Take two aspirins and call me in the morning.*

EXERCISE 4

Fill in the blanks with one of the words or expressions in this section.

1. Cuando es _____ de trabajar, siento un dolor de estómago. **2.** Ya te di cien mil pesos, ¿ _____ quieres? **3.** Lo único que quiero es que lo hagas _____.
4. El tren _____ partir a las tres pero no salió _____. **5.** Busqué a Carlota pero no la encontré _____. **6.** Hoy en día la costumbre es casarse por lo menos dos _____. **7.** —¿Te gustarían algunos bombones, Juanito?—¡ _____ !
8. —¿Te molestaría que te trajera un regalito?—¿ _____ ? **9.** Mi amigo me prestó mil dólares pero lo hizo _____ porque verdaderamente no quería prestármelos. **10.** Es difícil hablar y comer _____ aunque algunas personas lo hacen.

5 Indefinites

The most common indefinites are:

alguien	*someone*
alguno, -a, -os, -as	*some, someone (of several)*
algo	*something*

1. **Alguien** *(someone, somebody, anyone)* refers only to persons. A personal **a** precedes **alguien** when it is a direct object.

Alguien viene.	*Someone is coming.*
¿Ves a alguien?	*Do you see anybody?*

2. **Alguno** (**-a, -os, -as**) *(some, any, a few)*, used as a pronoun or an adjective, implies reference to a person or thing in a group. When it is a direct object referring to a person it is preceded by a personal **a**. Before a masculine singular noun **alguno** becomes **algún**.

Algunos de Uds. ya me conocen.	*Some of you already know me.*
Algún día me lo agradecerás.	*Some day you will thank me for it.*
Ya he saludado a algunos de los invitados.	*I have already greeted some of the guests.*

3. **Algo** *(something, anything)*.

Algo ocurre.	*Something is happening.*
Busco algo diferente.	*I am looking for something different.*
¿Tienes algo para mí?	*Do you have anything for me?*

Algo may be used adverbially in the sense of *somewhat, rather*.

Esto es algo rebuscado.   *This is rather farfetched.*

4. *Something* or *anything (at all)* may also be expressed by **cualquier cosa.**
This should not be confused with **algo.**

¿Me has traído algo?   *Have you brought me anything*
                                               (something)?

Haría cualquier cosa por ti.   *I would do anything (at all) for you.*

EXERCISE 5

Fill in the blanks with one of the following: **algo, alguno (-a, -os, -as), algún,
alguien, cualquier cosa**.

1. Esta lección es _____ difícil. **2.** Invité a varios amigos para una fiesta
y _____ dijeron que vendrían. **3.** Espero casarme _____ día. **4.** ¿Conoces
a _____ que pueda ayudarme? **5.** Por ti yo haría _____ (anything). **6.** Juana
vino ayer con _____ amigas. **7.** Este pan está _____ quemado. **8.** Para su
cumpleaños le daré _____ muy lindo.

Negatives

A. The indefinites have corresponding negatives.

alguien	nadie	*no one, nobody*
alguno (-a, -os, -as)	ninguno (-a, -os, -as)	*no one, none (of several)*
algún	ningún	*no one, none (before a* *masculine, singular noun)*
algo	nada	*nothing*

The negative word may be used before the verb, or it may follow the verb.
In the latter case, **no** precedes the verb and creates a "double negative" (wrong
in English, but required in Spanish). As a general guide, **nadie, ninguno** and
nada preferably precede the verb when they are the subject of the verb; they
follow the verb when they are the object. A personal **a** is used before **nadie** and
ninguno (referring to a person) when they are direct objects.

Nadie viene *or* No viene nadie.	*No one is coming.*
No veo a nadie *or* A nadie veo.	*I do not see anyone.*
Ninguno de Uds. me conoce *or* No me conoce ninguno de Uds.	*None of you knows me.*
No he saludado a ninguno de los invitados.	*I have not greeted any of the guests.*
No tengo ningún dinero.	*I don't have any money at all.*
Nada ocurre *or* No ocurre nada.	*Nothing is happening.*

Nada may be used adverbially in the sense of *not at all*.

Esto no es nada interesante.	*This is not at all interesting.*
—Señorita, ¿Ud. no nada nada?	*"Miss, you don't swim at all?"*
—No, señor, no traje traje.	*"No, sir, I didn't bring a suit."*
—¡Vaya, vaya!	*"My, oh my! You don't say!"*

B. Other negative words and their affirmative parallels are:

nunca, jamás	*never*	siempre	*always, ever*
tampoco	*neither*	también	*also*
ni tampoco	*not . . . either* ⎱	y también	*and also*
ni siquiera	*not even* ⎰		
ni ... ni	*neither . . . nor*	o ... o	*either . . . or*

These negatives may be used before the verb, or may follow it; in the latter case **no** precedes the verb.

1. **Nunca** and **jamás** both mean *never*, but **nunca** is more common in everyday speech.

Siempre estudia.	*He is always studying.*
Nunca estudia *or* No estudia nunca.	*He never studies.*

Jamás or **alguna vez** is used in an interrogative sentence to mean *ever*.

¿Han visto Uds. jamás (alguna vez) tanta destrucción?	*Have you ever seen so much destruction?*

Nunca jamás is a strong negation meaning *never ever* or *never again*.

Nunca jamás le prestaré dinero.	*I shall never again lend him money.*

2. **Tampoco** may be used alone, with **no** or with **ni**.

—¿Conoces a Pablo? —No.	*"Do you know Pablo?" "No."*
—¿Y a su hermano? —Tampoco.	*"And his brother?" "Not him either."*
No me ayuda tampoco *or* Tampoco me ayuda.	*He doesn't help me either.*
—¿Has estado alguna vez en Veracruz?	*"Have you ever been in Veracruz?"*
—No, señor. Ni en Tampico tampoco.	*"No, sir. Nor in Tampico either."*
—No quiero ver esa película.	*"I don't want to see that movie."*
—Ni yo tampoco.	*"Neither do I."*

3. **Ni ... ni, ni, ni siquiera** (*neither . . . nor, not even*).

No habla ni francés ni italiano.	*He doesn't speak either French or Italian.*
Ni siquiera me dio las gracias.	*He didn't even thank me.*

A sign in a neighborhood store.

Si fío, pierdo lo mío.	*If I trust, I lose what is mine.*
Si presto, al cobrar molesto.	*If I lend, I disturb when I collect.*
Si doy, a la ruina voy.	*If I give, I go to ruin.*
Para evitar todo esto,	*To avoid all this,*
ni fío, ni doy, ni presto.	*I neither trust nor give nor lend.*

When used with the subject of the sentence the **ni ... ni** construction usually has the verb in the plural.

| Ni Margarita ni su hermana vinieron | *Neither Margarita nor her sister* |
| a la fiesta. | *came to the party.* |

A single **ni** is sometimes used with the force of *not even*.

| No entiendo ni jota de lo que dijo. | *I don't understand even a little bit* |
| | *of what he said.* |

4. The various negatives are often combined in one sentence. If one of the negative words precedes the verb, **no** is not used.

—Tu nuevo novio no es ni inteligente	*"Your new boyfriend is neither*
ni guapo.	*intelligent nor handsome."*
—Ni rico tampoco. Por eso ninguna	*"Nor rich either. That's why none*
de mis amigas tratará nunca	*of my friends will ever try to take*
de quitármelo.	*him away from me."*

5. A negative is used in Spanish after comparisons when a negative is implied, and also after **sin** or **sin que**.

Mejor que nunca.	*Better than ever.*
Más que nada.	*More than anything.*
Más vale tarde que nunca.	*Better late than never.*
(Proverb)	
Más vale algo que nada. *(Proverb)*	*Something is better than nothing.*
No puedes salir sin decir nada.	*You can't leave without saying*
	anything.
Llegó sin que nadie lo supiera.	*He arrived without anyone's*
	knowing it.

A popular *copla*:

Niña de los veinte novios,	*Girl with twenty boyfriends,*
y conmigo veintiuno.	*and with me twenty-one.*
Si todos son como yo,	*If all are like me,*
te quedarás sin ninguno.	*you'll be left without any.*

EXERCISE 6

A. Change the affirmative words to the negative and make other changes if necessary.

1. Carlos es algo tacaño. **2.** También vino Ana. **3.** Dígale que algún compañero lo visitará. **4.** Siempre escribe la tarea de mala gana. **5.** O Pedro o Pablo ha prometido llevarme a la estación. **6.** Mi prima es algo perezosa. **7.** Los niños mayores, es decir, los de más de doce años, siempre se quedan en casa. **8.** He escrito a tres amigos y sé que alguno me contestará.

B. Translate the English portion of the following sentences.

1. Me gusta nadar (more than ever). **2.** (I don't know anything) del asunto. **3.** Puedes hacer (anything). **4.** ¿Ha llamado Pedro (anyone)? **5.** Elena está (prettier than ever). **6.** Me gusta la pintura (more than anything).

Basic Class Exercises

I. A. Substitute the italicized words with the words indicated and make any other changes if necessary.

1. No es *tu hermano* el que acaba de llegar.
    a. Elvira **b.** sus profesores **c.** Juan **d.** mis compañeras
2. Esta es *la casa* sin la cual sería difícil vivir.
    a. la mujer **b.** el hombre **c.** las cosas **d.** los medios
3. Vinimos con Enrique cuyo *hijo* es inteligentísimo.
    a. hija **b.** sobrinos **c.** nietas **d.** perros

B. *"Some events of interest in Spanish and Spanish-American history."* Translate the words in parentheses.

1. Los aztecas, (who) eran muy poderosos, tenían miedo de Cortés porque creían (that) era un dios. **2.** Pizarro exigió (that) Atahualpa, (who) era rey de los incas, le diera casi (all the gold that) tenía. **3.** Los franceses invadieron España en 1808, (which) dio una oportunidad a las colonias en América para levantarse contra los españoles. **4.** San Martín y Bolívar se pusieron de acuerdo, (which) facilitó el éxito de la revolución. **5.** Inglaterra, (whose) tropas ocuparon la península de Gibraltar, dijo que era suya. **6.** *Evita* es una revista musical (which) trata de la vida de Eva Perón, (whose) marido fue Juan Perón, el dictador argentino.

II. A. Give the questions which would be answered by the following sentences.
EXAMPLE: Fui a la estación.
            ¿Adónde fuiste?

1. Me llamo José López. **2.** Nos casó el cura don Fermín. **3.** Me gustó muchísimo la comedia. **4.** La etimología es el estudio del origen y desarrollo lingüístico de las palabras. **5.** Soy dentista. **6.** Costa Rica está en la América Central. **7.** Asisto a la Universidad de Puerto Rico. **8.** Domingo Faustino Sarmiento escribió la novela *Facundo*.

B. Ask a fellow student the following personal questions.

1. in what city he / she was born **2.** how old he/she is **3.** what his/her philosophy of life is **4.** which he / she prefers, wealth or happiness **5.** on whom his / her happiness depends **6.** who his / her favorite author is **7.** what novel he / she has read and what he / she thinks of it **8.** how he / she likes coffee— with sugar or without it

③

III. Write an exclamation based on the information supplied.

EXAMPLE: Ese joven es muy alto.
             ¡Qué joven más alto!

1. José está muy gordo. **2.** Come muchísimo. **3.** Le gustan mucho los bombones y los pasteles. **4.** Siempre anda muy despacio. **5.** Es un joven alegre. (Use *vaya*) **6.** Su mujer es delgada. **7.** Quiere mucho a su marido. **8.** Sabe cocinar muy bien.

④

IV. A. The following sentences do not make sense. Make them logical, substituting a word or phrase from Section 4.A on p. 199 for the words in italics.

EXAMPLE: Hay hombres de tres cabezas *en todas partes.*
             No hay hombres de tres cabezas en ninguna parte.

1. Los trenes deben llegar *tarde* siempre. **2.** Debemos hacer las tareas *de mala gana.* **3.** *Nunca merece la pena* estudiar un idioma. **4.** —Hijo, ¿quieres cinco mil dólares para comprarte un coche? —¡*Qué va*, papá! **5.** ¿Te gustaría trabajar ochenta horas por semana? *¡Cómo no!*

B. Translate the English section of the following sentences.

1. Hemos comido (four times) hoy. **2.** ¿Sabes (what time) es? **3.** (It is time) de acostarnos. **4.** (We don't have time) para eso. **5.** (At times) mis niños me vuelven loca. **6.** Ya te dije (a thousand times) que no salieras con ese vago.

⑤

V. Answer the questions using **alguien, alguno (-a, -os, -as), algún** or **algo**.

EXAMPLE: ¿Quién te besó?
             Alguien me besó.

1. ¿Quién ha llamado a la puerta? **2.** ¿Qué tiene Ud. en la mano? **3.** ¿Vendrán tus amigos a la fiesta? **4.** ¿Es difícil esta lección? **5.** ¿Cuándo piensas graduarte? **6.** ¿No hay nada en la caja? **7.** ¿Quién está en la cocina con Dina? **8.** ¿Tienes muchos(-as) novios(-as)?

⑥

VI. A. Answer the following personal questions using one of the negative words in Section 6 on pages 201–202.

EXAMPLE: ¿A quién visteis ayer?
             No vimos a nadie. (A nadie vimos.)

1. ¿Conoces un muchacho que sepa hablar bien el español? **2.** ¿Has hablado a alguien en español hoy? **3.** ¿Has visitado alguna vez las Islas Canarias? **4.** ¿Con quién piensas casarte? **5.** ¿Cuál de tus amigos ya está casado? **6.** En el verano, ¿prefieres nadar o jugar al tenis?

B. Translate the English portion of the following sentences.

1. Estoy (better than ever). **2.** Tuve la culpa (more than anyone). **3.** Lo haré (without anyone's knowing it). **4.** Te quiero (more than anything). **5.** Prefiero andar (without anyone).

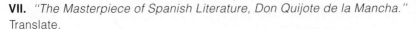

Elective Exercises

VII. *"The Masterpiece of Spanish Literature, Don Quijote de la Mancha."* Translate.

1. There has never existed any character like Don Quijote, who was created by Miguel de Cervantes. **2.** The first time I read *Don Quijote de la Mancha* I laughed and cried at the same time. **3.** What a marvelous novel it is! **4.** What is its full [complete] title? **5.** I don't know anyone who has not read it. **6.** Nonsense! I know someone who has not read it. **7.** What is life if you don't read some of the great books? **8.** They are books through which we learn what life is.

VIII. *"Moving to Another Country."* Answer the following questions.

1. ¿Conoce Ud. a alguien que haya tenido que trasladarse a otro país? **2.** Si Ud. tuviera que hacer esto, ¿a qué país iría? **3.** ¿Se da cuenta Ud. de lo difícil que es vivir en un país extranjero? **4.** ¿Cuáles son algunas cosas que hay que hacer para prepararse para vivir en otro país? **5.** ¿Preferiría Ud. ir a un país donde conoce a alguien? ¿Por qué? **6.** ¿Tiene Ud. algún amigo en un país hispano?

IX. Write the answers to the questions related to the drawings in a complete sentence. Some answers may be negative.

EXAMPLE: ¿Adónde corre el niño?
El niño corre a la escuela.

1. ¿Cuántas chicas hay en el dibujo?

2. ¿Qué animal vemos en el dibujo?

3. ¿Ve Ud. a alguien en el dibujo?

4. ¿Cuál de estos hombres lleva sombrero?

5. ¿Tiene algo en la cabeza María?   **6.** ¿ Es más alta que las otras alguna de estas chicas?

X. Review of Lesson 10.

Translate the English portion of the following sentences.

1. España produce casi (as much wine as) Italia.   **2.** No es (as expensive as that of Italy but) es muy bueno también.   **3.** (Most of) la gente del norte de España es (taller than) la del sur.   **4.** Cuando (Ferdinand and Isabella) se casaron, unieron los reinos de Aragón y Castilla.   **5.** En el siglo diez y seis España era (the most powerful country in the world).   **6.** En el siglo diez y siete el país iba (from bad to worse).   **7.** Si alguien hace algo bien sin esperar hacerlo no le decimos ("so much the worse" but "so much the better").   **8.** María e Irene no son (younger than) Jorge.   **9.** El reloj me costó (less than) quinientos pesos.
10. Vinieron a la fiesta como (seventy or eighty) invitados.

Vocabulary

aburrir to bore
acuerdo agreement
amistad *f.* friendship;
  acquaintance
apellido last name, surname
barco boat
bombón *m.* candy
cadáver *m.* corpse
cocinar to cook
conferencia lecture
cuchara spoon
desarrollo development
discurso speech; **pronunciar**
  un—to make a speech
espantar to frighten
etimología etymology
éxito success

invadir to invade
invitado guest
jugador *m.* player
lealtad *f.* loyalty
medio means
mentir (ie, i) to lie
pastel *m.* pie, pastry
plata silver; money *(colloq.)*
poderoso powerful
prestar to lend
quemar to burn
reino kingdom
sueldo salary
tiranizar to tyrannize
trasladarse to move (one's home,
  office, etc.)

Lesson 12

1. **Numerals**

2. **Time of Day**

3. **Idioms and Word Study**

4. **Dates**

5. **Diminutives and Augmentatives**

---

1 Numerals

A. Cardinal Numbers.

The cardinal numbers are invariable except **uno** and the compounds of **ciento. Uno** is shortened to **un** before a masculine noun.

1. 0–19.

0 cero	7 siete
1 un(o), una	8 ocho
2 dos	9 nueve
3 tres	10 diez
4 cuatro	11 once
5 cinco	12 doce
6 seis	13 trece

14 catorce	17 diecisiete (diez y siete)
15 quince	18 dieciocho (diez y ocho)
16 dieciséis (diez y seis)	19 diecinueve (diez y nueve

2. 20–29. The numbers 21–29 may be written as three words or as one word.

20 veinte
21 veintiuno (veinte y uno)
    veintiún libros   *21 books*
    veintiuna lecciones   *21 lessons*
22 veintidós (veinte y dos)
23 veintitrés (veinte y tres)
24 veinticuatro (veinte y cuatro)
25 veinticinco (veinte y cinco)
26 veintiséis (veinte y seis)
27 veintisiete (veinte y siete)
28 veintiocho (veinte y ocho)
29 veintinueve (veinte y nueve)

3. 30–99. Counting by tens from 30–90, the numbers end in **-nta**. The compound numbers 31 through 99 must be written as three separate words.

30 treinta
31 treinta y uno(-a)
    treinta y un niños   *thirty-one children (boys)*
    treinta y una niñas   *thirty-one children (girls)*
32 treinta y dos
40 cuarenta
50 cincuenta
60 sesenta
70 setenta
80 ochenta
90 noventa
99 noventa y nueve

4. 100–999. Ciento is followed directly by a number smaller than itself, without an intervening **y** (**ciento uno**, etc.). **Ciento** becomes **cien** before a noun or number that it modifies (**cien casas, cien mil**). Standing alone, **cien** is normally used, although **ciento** is used by many speakers.

Tengo cien *or* Tengo ciento.   *I have a hundred.*
Cien por cien, *or*
Ciento por ciento, *or*   ⎫
Cien por ciento   ⎬   *One hundred percent*
                        ⎭

Two hundred, etc, is expressed as *two hundreds,* etc., written as one word (**doscientos**) with agreement in gender with the noun it modifies.

Note the irregular forms 500, 700 and 900.

100	cien(to)	
102	ciento dos	
117	ciento diez y siete	
200	doscientos (-as)	
	doscientos lápices	*200 pencils*
	doscientas quince plumas	*215 pens*
300	trescientos (-as)	
400	cuatrocientos, (-as)	
500	quinientos (-as)	
600	seiscientos (-as)	
700	setecientos (-as)	
800	ochocientos (-as)	
900	novecientos (-as)	
	novecientos noventa y nueve dólares	*999 dollars*
	novecientas noventa y nueve pesetas	*999 pesetas*

5. **1000 (mil).** In both Spanish and English the equivalent of 2000, etc. does not use a plural form of *thousand* or **mil** (*two thousand* **dos mil**). Both English and Spanish use the plural in *thousands of dollars, thousands and thousands:* **miles de dólares, miles y miles.**

In counting above 1000, in English we may use either *a (one) thousand* or *hundred*. (1456: *one thousand four hundred fifty-six* or *fourteen hundred and fifty-six*). In Spanish we must use **mil** in this construction (1456: **mil cuatrocientos cincuenta y seis**).

1000	mil	
	Mil gracias	*A thousand thanks. Many thanks.*
1001	mil uno	
1010	mil diez	
1492	mil cuatrocientos noventa y dos	
1776	mil setecientos setenta y seis	
2001	dos mil uno	
100.000	cien mil	
200.000	doscientos mil	

NOTE: Spanish uses a period in numerals where English uses a comma.

6. **1.000.000 (un millón).** The construction is **un millón de** + *noun*.

Un millón de habitantes	*A million inhabitants*
Dos millones de pesos	*Two million pesos*

If there is an intervening number before the noun, **de** is not used.

Tres millones ochocientos cincuenta mil paquetes	*3,850,000 packages*

B. Ordinal numbers.

1. They are seldom used beyond *tenth*. They agree in gender and number with the nouns they modify.

1st	primero
2nd	segundo
3rd	tercero
4th	cuarto
5th	quinto
6th	sexto
7th	séptimo (*usually pronounced* sétimo)
8th	octavo
9th	noveno (nono *is used in titles*)
10th	décimo

2. Ordinal numbers generally precede the noun. As was pointed out in Lesson 3, Section 1.D, **primero** and **tercero** drop the -o before a masculine singular noun.

el primer día	*the first day*
la primera vez	*the first time*
el tercer hombre	*the third man*
la segunda fila	*the second row*
la Quinta Avenida	*Fifth Avenue*

C. Special uses of cardinal and ordinal numbers.

1. With days of the month, except for **primero,** the cardinal numbers are used.

el primero de enero	*January 1st*
el dos de mayo	*May 2nd*

2. With volumes, chapters, streets, etc., either an ordinal or cardinal numeral may be used up to *ten (tenth)*. Above *eleven*, usually a cardinal numeral is used.

el segundo capítulo	*the second chapter*
capítulo dos	*chapter two*
el quinto párrafo	*the fifth paragraph*
párrafo cinco	*paragraph five*
el siglo veinte	*the 20th century*
la Calle cuarenta y dos	*42nd Street*

3. In expressions containing both a cardinal and an ordinal, in English the ordinal usually comes first. In Spanish the cardinal precedes.

las diez primeras páginas	*the first ten pages*

4. In titles the ordinal numbers are used only through *tenth;* above that the cardinals are used. The definite article of this construction in English *(Philip the Second)* is omitted in Spanish.

Carlos V (quinto) fue el padre de Felipe II (segundo).	*Charles V was the father of Philip II.*
Alfonso XIII (trece) abdicó en 1931.	*Alfonso XIII abdicated in 1931.*
Isabel II (segunda) reinó durante la época de las guerras carlistas.	*Isabel II reigned during the period of the Carlist Wars.*

D. Fractions.

1. *One half, a half,* or *half a* is **medio. Medio** is used as an adjective and agrees with the noun it modifies. **La mitad (de)** is a noun and means *half of.*

Cómprame un kilo y medio de cebollas.	*Buy me one and a half kilos of onions.*
Necesitamos también media docena de huevos.	*We also need half a dozen eggs.*
Usamos solamente la mitad de las zanahorias.	*We used only half of the carrots.*
La mitad de los obreros participaron en la huelga.	*Half of the workers took part in the strike.*

Medio may also be used adverbially.

Está todavía medio dormida.	*She is still half asleep.*

2. *One third* is **un tercio.** Other fractions are formed as in English, with a cardinal number on top and an ordinal number underneath.

¼ un cuarto	⅖ dos quintos	⅛ un octavo
¾ tres cuartos	⅙ un sexto	⅑ un noveno
⅕ un quinto	⅐ un séptimo	⅒ un décimo

3. In popular usage the word **parte** *(part)* is often used.

⅓ la tercera parte   ⅕ la quinta parte
⅔ dos terceras partes

E. Collective numbers.

un par (de)	*a pair (of), a couple (of)*
una docena	*a dozen*
una decena	*ten, about ten*
una centena *or* un centenar	*a hundred, about a hundred*
un millar	*a thousand*
un par de zapatos	*a pair of shoes*
una docena de huevos	*a dozen eggs*

A stirring stanza from the *Canción del pirata* by one of Spain's greatest romantic poets, José de Espronceda (1808–1842):

Veinte presas	*Twenty ships*
hemos hecho	*we have seized*
a despecho	*despite*
del inglés,	*the English,*
y han rendido	*and a hundred nations*
sus pendones	*have surrendered*
cien naciones	*their banners*
a mis pies.	*at my feet.*

From a dramatic recitation about a would-be Don Juan:

Rubias, morenas, tengo centenas,	*Blondes, brunettes, I have hundreds,*
tengo un surtido de todo color.	*I have a supply of every color.*
Tengo mil novias, tengo mil novias,	*I have a thousand girlfriends, I have a thousand girlfriends,*
de los amores yo soy el campeón ...	*in love affairs I am the champion . . .*

EXERCISE 1

Write out the following completely in Spanish.

1. 906 casas **2.** 531 inglesas **3.** Enrique IV **4.** Luis XIV **5.** 100.000 pesos **6.** 5 más 16 son 21 **7.** ¾ **8.** *one dozen* naranjas **9.** 104 páginas **10.** 2.781 ciudades **11.** 3.000.000 de soldados **12.** el año 1469 **13.** el 15 de abril **14.** el 1° de julio **15.** *half* muerta **16.** ½ kilo **17.** *half* de mi dinero **18.** el *17th* siglo

2

Time of Day

A. The verb **ser** is used to express *to be* in telling time.

1. With the exception of **es** for one o'clock, the plural **son** is used to indicate the hour. In the past tense, the imperfect is used.

¿Qué hora es?	*What time is it?*
Es la una.	*It is one o'clock.*
Son las dos.	*It is two o'clock.*

¿Qué hora era?	*What time was it?*
Era la una.	*It was one o'clock.*
Eran las dos.	*It was two o'clock.*
¿Qué hora será?	*What time can it be?*
Serán las seis y media.	*It must be 6:30.*
¿Qué hora sería?	*What time could it have been?*
	(I wonder what time it was.)
Serían las nueve.	*It must have been nine o'clock.*

2. Minutes after the hour are indicated by **y** plus the number. *Half past* is expressed by **y media** or **y treinta**. *A quarter after* is **y cuarto** or **y quince**.

Es la una y veinte.	*It is 1:20.*
Son las tres y cinco.	*It is 3:05.*
Eran las ocho y veinte.	*It was 8:20.*
Son las seis y media (treinta).	*It is 6:30.*
Eran las cuatro y cuarto (quince).	*It was 4:15.*

3. Time after the half hour is usually expressed by giving the next hour and using **menos** plus the number of minutes.

Son las dos menos veinte y cinco.	*It is twenty-five to two. (It is 1:35)*
Eran las diez menos cuarto (quince).	*It was a quarter to ten. (It was 9:45)*

We may also add the minutes to the hour even beyond the half hour, as in English. The last example above may be expressed as: **Eran las nueve y cuarenta y cinco.**

A popular alternate way of expressing time before the hour is to use the verb **faltar**.

Faltan diez minutos para las siete.	*It is ten minutes to seven. (It is 6:50)*

B. *At* is expressed by **a**.

¿A qué hora?	*At what time?*
a la una y cuarto	*at 1:15*
a las once menos cinco	*at five to eleven (at 10:55)*

At about is **a eso de** or **como a**.

Llegaron a eso de las cinco (como a las cinco).	*They arrived at about five o'clock.*

C. A.M. is **de la mañana**, P.M. is **de la tarde** (until about 7 P.M.) and **de la noche** (generally after 8 P.M.)

Los bancos abren a las nueve de la mañana y cierran a las tres de la tarde.	*Banks open at 9 A.M. and close at 3 P.M.*
Son las diez de la noche.	*It is 10 P.M.*

De la madrugada is used to refer to the very early hours between 1 and 4 A.M.

Se durmió a las dos de la madrugada.   *He fell asleep at 2 A.M.*

If the hour is not specified, *in the morning, in the afternoon, in the evening* are rendered by **por la mañana, por la tarde, por la noche.** In Mexico and some other countries of Spanish America **en la mañana,** etc. is preferred.

Por la mañana voy a la escuela,   *In the morning I go to school, in*
  por la tarde trabajo y por la noche   *the afternoon I work and in the*
  estudio.   *evening I study.*

De noche means *at* (or *by*) *night*; **de día,** *by day.*

Es peligroso caminar en el parque   *It's dangerous to walk in the park*
  de noche.   *at night.*

The lascivious Corregidor (mayor), attempting to seduce Frasquita, the miller's beautiful wife, in Pedro Antonio de Alarcón's (1833–1891) delightful novelette, *El sombrero de tres picos,* says:

¡De día, de noche, a todas horas,   *By day, by night, at all hours,*
  en todas partes, sólo pienso en ti!   *everywhere, I think only of you!*

D. In railroad, airline, theater, movie and other official schedules, the 24-hour timetable is usually used.

El tren sale a las 14:20. (catorce   *The train leaves at 2:20 P.M.*
  y veinte)
La última función es a las 21   *The last performance is at 9 P.M.*
  (veintiuna) horas.

The great Spanish playwright and poet Federico García Lorca (1898–1936) wrote a gripping elegy on the death of his friend, the bullfighter Ignacio Sánchez Mejías. The opening line, *a las cinco de la tarde,* is repeated in every other line of the entire first part of the poem.

A las cinco de la tarde.   *At five o'clock in the afternoon.*
Eran las cinco en punto de la   *It was exactly five o'clock in the*
  tarde.   *afternoon.*

The *copla* about the number of days in the months of the year:

Treinta días trae noviembre,   *November has thirty days,*
con abril, junio y septiembre;   *along with April, June and*
                                          September;
de veinte y ocho sólo hay uno;   *there is only one of twenty-eight;*
los demás de treinta y uno.   *the rest (have) thirty-one.*

EXERCISE 2

A. Write out the following.

1. 1:30 P.M. **2.** 9:40 A.M. **3.** 2:15 P.M. **4.** 10:20 P.M. **5.** 3:10 A.M.

B. Translate the English section of the following sentences.

1. Prefiero quedarme en casa (in the morning). **2.** (At night) me gusta bailar. **3.** Cuando llegué a casa (it was 2 A.M.). **4.** Me encontraré con Silvia (about ten-thirty). **5.** El tren sale para Barcelona (at 11 P.M.). **6.** Mañana te quiero aquí (at 1 o'clock). **7.** Nos veremos (about four-twenty). **8.** (It was five-forty) cuando llegamos al aeropuerto.

Idioms and Word Study

A. More Time Expressions.

a estas horas	*at this time (hour), at such an hour*
a fines de (marzo)	*toward the end of (March)*
a mediados de (abril)	*toward the middle of (April)*
a principios de (mayo)	*toward the beginning of (May)*
a tiempo	*on time*
amanecer	*to get light, to dawn*
anochecer	*to grow dark, to be nightfall*
anteayer	*the day before yesterday*
da la una, dan las dos	*the clock strikes one, the clock strikes two*
de hoy en ocho (quince) días	*a week (two weeks) from today*
madrugar	*to rise early*
a (la) medianoche	*at midnight*
a (*or* al) mediodía	*at noon*
pasado mañana	*the day after tomorrow*
el reloj se adelanta (se atrasa)	*the watch is fast (is slow)*
en adelante	*henceforth, from now on, from then on*
en punto	*sharp (on the dot)*
hacerse tarde	*to be (get) late*
llegar tarde	*to be (arrive) late*
(las siete) y pico	*a little after (seven)*

B. **Volver** and **devolver**.

devolver	*to return (give back)*
volver	*to return (to a place)*
volver loco	*to drive crazy*

C. *To miss.*

echar de menos	*to miss (a person or something*
extrañar (Span. Am.)	*mentally)*
perder	*to miss a thing (train, etc.)*

¿Qué haces aquí a estas horas?   *What are you doing here at this hour?*

Lo haré a mediados de junio.   *I'll do it around the middle of June.*

Vámonos; se está haciendo tarde.   *Let's go; it's getting late.*

Volveré a casa para el jueves.   *I'll return home by Thursday.*

Nunca me devuelven los libros que les presto.   *They never return the books I lend them.*

Cuando te cases, te echaré de menos.   *When you get married, I will miss you.*

Si no te das prisa, perderás el tren.   *If you don't hurry, you'll miss the train.*

EXERCISE 3

A. Complete the sentences in column *A* with a phrase from column *B*.

A	B
1. Cuando me gradúe	**a.** pero María siempre llega a las once y pico.
2. La clase empieza a las once	**b.** o se lo diré a papá.
3. Con sus preguntas estos niños	**c.** echaré de menos la vida universitaria.
4. Me levanté tarde	**d.** me vuelven loca.
5. Hoy es miércoles;	**e.** y por eso perdí el tren.
6. Devuélveme mi bicicleta	**f.** anteayer fue lunes.
7. En adelante piénsalo bien	**g.** antes de decir que sí.
8. Es preciso	**h.** no llegar tarde a la clase.

B. Fill in the blanks with one of the words or idioms in this section.

1. Siempre debemos llegar a clase _____. **2.** Casi todo el mundo paga el alquiler _____ mes. **3.** Cuando _____ doce, sabemos que es medianoche. **4.** Si son realmente las seis, y mi reloj dice las seis y diez, _____. **5.** Si son realmente las seis, y mi reloj dice las seis menos diez, _____ . **6.** Salen los espectros _____ en punto.

4 Dates

Spanish does not use capitals for months of the year or days of the week.

A. The months.

enero	agosto
febrero	septiembre (pronounced and often
marzo	written *setiembre*)
abril	octubre
mayo	noviembre
junio	diciembre
julio	

B. Day of the month.

¿Cuál es la fecha?	
¿Qué fecha es?	*What is today's date?*
¿A cuántos estamos?	
Hoy es el 15 (quince) de enero.	*Today is January 15.*
Estamos a 15 de enero de 1994	*It is January 15, 1994.*
(mil novecientos noventa y cuatro).	

Note that **de** is used before the month and before the year. In giving the day of the month, Spanish uses the ordinal number only for the *first* (**primero**). The cardinal numbers are used in all other cases.

El primero de enero.	*January 1st.*
El dos de mayo.	*May 2nd.*
Es el catorce de marzo (*or*	*It is March 14th.*
Estamos a catorce de marzo).	

English *on* (a certain date) is not expressed with a preposition in Spanish.

Las clases empiezan el primero de febrero y terminan el veinticuatro de mayo.	*Classes begin on February 1st and end on May 24th.*
¿Cuándo es tu cumpleaños? Es el treinta de abril.	*When is your birthday? It is April 30th.*

The **el** is omitted before a date when following a day of the week.

Llegó el martes, doce de julio.	*He arrived on Tuesday, July 12th.*

C. Days of the week.

lunes *Monday*	viernes *Friday*
martes *Tuesday*	sábado *Saturday*
miércoles *Wednesday*	domingo *Sunday*
jueves *Thursday*	

D. Day of the week.

The definite article is used before the days of the week except after the verb **ser.** The **on** is not translated. Note that the plural is used for habitual action.

¿Qué día es (hoy)?	*What day is it (today)?*
Hoy es lunes.	*Today is Monday.*
Ayer fue domingo.	*Yesterday was Sunday.*
Tuvimos un examen el jueves.	*We had an exam on Thursday.*
Los domingos van a la iglesia.	*They go to church on Sundays.*

EXERCISE 4

"Some important dates in Spanish history." Write out the dates in Spanish.

1. Cortés llegó a México en (February, 1519) y terminó la conquista de los aztecas en (August, 1521). **2.** (In January, 1531) Francisco Pizarro partió para conquistar el imperio incaico con menos de doscientos soldados. **3.** La Guerra de la Independencia Española empezó (May 2, 1808). **4.** La victoria de los rebeldes en la batalla de Ayacucho dio fin a la Guerra de la Independencia de Hispanoamérica (on October 9, 1824). **5.** El reinado de Isabel II de España empezó (on November 8, 1843) y duró hasta (September 30, 1868) cuando la revolución la obligó a salir de España. **6.** La Guerra Civil empezó en España (on July 17, 1936) y terminó (on April 1, 1939).

Diminutives and Augmentatives

A. There are a number of endings which may be added to nouns and adjectives to give a feeling of smallness and/or affection. They are especially common in "babytalk" and when one is trying to be "cute" or affectionate.

1. The most common diminutive ending is **-ito, -ita** which replaces the final vowel. A final **c** or **g** changes to **qu** or **gu.** Some of the more usual words are:

abuela	abuelita	*granny*
libro	librito	*little book*
hija	hijita	*little (dear) daughter, child*
casa	casita	*(cute) little house*
chico	chiquito	*little boy*
barco	barquito	*little boat*
amigo	amiguito	*(little) friend*
delgado	delgadito	*nice and thin*
trago	traguito	*little drink, "shot"*
pájaro	pajarito	*little (cute) bird*
hembra	hembrita	*baby girl*

Juan	Juanito	*Johnny*
estrella	estrellita	*little star*
Isabel	Isabelita	*little (dear) Isabel*
querida	queridita	*darling, dearest*
Paco	Paquito	*Frankie*
viejo	viejito	*nice old man*

Certain adverbs may take the **-ito** (**-ita**) ending.

Ahorita vengo. (Mex.)	*I'm coming right away.*
Tempranito	*Bright and early*

2. Another common ending is **-cito**.

mamá	mamacita	*mommy, dear mother*
papá	papacito	*papa, daddy*
joven	jovencito	*young man, young fellow*
mujer	mujercita	*little woman*
bote	botecito	*little boat*
madre	madrecita	*dear mother*
viaje	viajecito	*little trip*
varón	varoncito	*baby boy*
amor	amorcito	*dear love*

3. Other endings include **-ecito, -illo, -ecillo, -uelo**.

ventana	ventanilla	*little window, car window*
chico	chiquillo	*little boy, kid*
pan	panecillo	*roll*
flor	florecita	*little flower*
plaza	plazuela	*little square*
voz	vocecita	*little voice*
pueblo	pueblecito	*little town, village*

Diminutives appear quite frequently in songs as in the popular favorite, *Muñequita linda.*[†]

Muñequita linda,	*Pretty little doll,*
de cabellos de oro,	*with golden hair,*
de dientes de perla,	*with teeth of pearl,*
y labios de rubí ...	*and ruby lips . . .*

4. Paradoxically, some diminutive endings sometimes have a sarcastic or pejorative connotation.

autor	autorcillo	*second-rate author, so-called author*
rey	reyezuelo	*petty king*

Since it is sometimes difficult for a non-native speaker to know which diminutive ending is to be added, the student is advised not to use diminutives unless he / she has seen or heard them used correctly.

B. There are also augmentative endings, which denote largeness and / or ugliness. The most common augmentative ending is **-ón, -ona;** **-ona** is associated with female persons while **-ón** is used with male persons or things of either gender.

hombre	hombrón	*big man*
mujer	mujerona	*big woman*
silla	sillón *(m.)*	*armchair*

In two fairly common words, however, the **-ón** ending expresses a reverse meaning:

| rata | *rat* | ratón *(m.)* | *mouse* |
| calle | *street* | callejón *(m.)* | *alley* |

EXERCISE 5

Replace the diminutives and augmentatives with the base word.

1. Ven acá, Miguelito. **2.** Espérame un ratito. **3.** Su hermano es un abogadillo que no vale nada. **4.** Comí un pedacito de pan con queso. **5.** ¿Me quieres hacer un favorcito? **6.** Pablo es un muchachón de catorce años.

Basic Class Exercises

I. A. *"More Historical Information."* Write out the numerals in Spanish.

1. Granada fue conquistada por los Reyes Católicos en 1492. **2.** Según varios historiadores, Hernán Cortés empezó la conquista de México en 1519 con unos 509 soldados, 200 indios, 32 caballos y 4 piezas de artillería. **3.** Más tarde, 1000s de indios, enemigos de los aztecas, lo ayudaron. **4.** Durante la conquista murieron más de la ½ de sus soldados. **5.** Felipe V fue el 1er rey borbón de España. **6.** Alfonso XIII tuvo que abdicar en 1931. **7.** En España hay unos 40.000.000 habitantes. **8.** Hay aproximadamente 21 países de habla española.

B. Answer in Spanish.

1. ¿Aproximadamente cuántos habitantes hay en los Estados Unidos? **2.** ¿Cuál fue su primera clase hoy? **3.** ¿Cómo se llama el papa actual de los católicos? **4.** ¿En qué año nació Ud.? **5.** ¿Cuántos días hay en un año? **6.** Si yo le ofreciera compartir un millón de dólares conmigo, ¿preferiría la mitad o cinco octavos? **7.** ¿Cuántos centímetros hay en un metro? **8.** ¿En qué siglo vivimos?

2

II. Answer in Spanish.

1. ¿Qué hora es? **2.** ¿A qué hora empieza esta clase? **3.** ¿A qué hora almuerza Ud.? **4.** ¿Qué hace Ud. los domingos por la mañana? **5.** ¿A qué hora de la mañana suele Ud. levantarse? **6.** ¿Prefiere Ud. trabajar de día o de noche? **7.** ¿A qué hora se acuesta Ud.?

3

III. A. Complete the sentences by selecting one of the items indicated.

1. Cuando se rompió el compromiso, Ana no quiso _____ la sortija.
   a. volver **b.** tomar **c.** devolver
2. _____ no comas los guisantes con el cuchillo.
   a. Al otro día **b.** En adelante **c.** Si tienes sed
3. Cuando mi novio mira la televisión, _____ .
   a. se hace daño **b.** tiene frío **c.** me vuelve loca
4. Cuando me case, _____ a mis amigos.
   a. ahorcaré **b.** echaré de menos **c.** volveré locos
5. ¿Qué dirá su novia si_____ ?
   a. se vuelve Ud. loco **b.** llega Ud. tarde **c.** ella desaparece

B. Translate the English portion of the following sentences.

1. (If I don't arrive on time), perderé la apuesta. **2.** (The clock was striking eleven) cuando entraron los ladrones. **3.** Siempre (toward the end of the month) me encuentro sin dinero. **4.** (Two weeks from today) ya no seré soltera. **5.** Dame el último besito pues (it is getting late). **6.** (At this time) estarán ya cerca de su casa. **7.** Te devolveré el libro (around the middle of the month). **8.** (The day after tomorrow) será viernes.

4

IV. A. Match the date with the important event in Spanish and Spanish-American history; then write out the date in Spanish.

1. la fiesta nacional de España
2. la fiesta nacional de México
3. el descubrimiento de las Américas
4. la muerte del general Franco en España
5. la derrota de Fulgencio Batista por Fidel Castro en Cuba

a. October 12, 1492
b. May 2, 1808
c. September 16, 1821
d. January 1, 1959
e. November 20, 1975

Answers: 1 b, 2 c, 3 a, 4 e, 5 d

B. Answer the following personal questions.

1. ¿Cuándo nació Ud.? **2.** ¿En qué mes y año piensa Ud. graduarse de esta universidad? **3.** ¿En qué día del mes pagan sus padres el alquiler? **4.** ¿Qué días de la semana tiene Ud. la clase de español? **5.** ¿Qué día de la semana prefiere Ud.? **6.** ¿En qué meses tiene Ud. vacaciones? **7.** ¿En qué mes del año le gustaría casarse? ¿Por qué? **8.** ¿Qué mes del año prefiere Ud.? ¿Por qué?

V. A. Translate.

1. ¡Mira a Luisito! ¡Ya es un hombrecito! **2.** Los chiquillos estaban jugando en la calle. **3.** Se cree gran cosa pero es un autorcillo de mala muerte. **4.** No me beses; tu boca tiene un olorcillo a ajo. **5.** El niño se puso el traje nuevecito. **6.** A las diez suena la campanilla. **7.** Mi hermano es ya un solterón de cuarenta años. **8.** Su casa tenía dos salas y un salón para las fiestas.

B. Make one sentence from each of the following groups of words.

EXAMPLE: Tomasito / varoncito / mono.
              Tomasito es un varoncito muy mono.

1. Teresa / besito / novio   **2.** Ana / vocecita / fina   **3.** Mario / paseo / plazuela
4. fiesta / tener lugar / salón   **5.** ahorita / Pedro / venir / verme
6. amiguitos / andar / despacito

Elective Exercises

VI. *"A Birthday Party."* Translate.

1. Paquita was born on April 1, 1971. **2.** She invited twenty-one friends to a birthday party on Saturday, April 3rd. **3.** To animate the party some came dressed like Henry the Eighth, Louis the Fourteenth and Charles the Fifth.
4. Everyone made fun of Henry the Eighth, calling him the petty king of England. **5.** The guests almost drove him crazy, taking away his crown for having murdered so many wives. **6.** At midnight sharp they stopped dancing to allow Paquita to open the packages with the gifts. **7.** One gift was a little gold watch (use diminutive) that must have cost five hundred dollars. **8.** At one–twenty in the morning everyone went home, somewhat tipsy, but happy.

VII. Review of Lesson 11.

A. Fill in the blanks with an exclamation, an interrogative, a relative adjective or pronoun.

1. ¿ _____ vendrás a verme? **2.** Allí viene el profesor _____ hijos son amigos míos. **3.** No comprendo _____ estás diciendo. **4.** Tráeme la cajita dentro de _____ metí mi sortija. **5.** ¡ _____ comida tan rica! **6.** _____ llegue primero recibirá un premio. **7.** Perdió sus guantes sin _____ tendrá las manos muy frías. **8.** ¡ _____ una chica inteligente! **9.** El novio de María, _____ es director de su compañía, es muy guapo. **10.** ¡ _____ me quería mi abuelita!

B. Translate the English section of the following sentences.

1. No lo encuentro (anywhere). **2.** ¿Conoces (anyone) que hable italiano?
3. (They are to) darme la respuesta mañana. **4.** Tú no te puedes imaginar (how high they are). **5.** No tengo (any time at all) para esas cosas. **6.** ¿(How

many times) tengo que decirte que no lo hagas? **7.** ¿Quieres que te ayude? (Of course!) **8.** Tiene mucho dinero, (that is), es riquísimo. **9.** Se lo pregunté a varios estudiantes pero (no one) supo contestar. **10.** Esperamos que (it has been worth while) estudiar este libro.

Vocabulary

acción share (of stock)
actual present (now)
ahorcar to hang
apuesta bet
atreverse (a) to dare
borbón Bourbon
campana bell
colgar(se) (ue) to hang (oneself)
compartir to share
compromiso engagement (to marry)
espectro ghost
fin *m.* end; **dar—** to end
guisante *m.* pea
historiador *m.* historian
incaico Incan *(adj.)*
kilo(gramo) kilogram (2.2 lbs.)

mojarse to get wet
mono cute
monstruo monster
muerte; de mala— of little importance
nacimiento birth
olor *m.* odor
partido game (match)
premio prize
rayo ray (of lightning)
rebelde *m., f.* rebel
reinado reign
soler (ue) to be accustomed to, usually
soltero bachelor
varón *m.* male child; man

Review of Lessons 7–12

I. Write the appropriate form of the verb in parentheses.

1. Prefieren que lo (coger) tú. **2.** Querían que (cantar) nosotros. **3.** Sabíamos que ellos no se lo (decir) ayer. **4.** Aunque tú (volver) al poco rato, no te esperaré. **5.** Si nosotros no (ponerse) de acuerdo, no podremos hacer nada. **6.** Siento que tú no (venir) ayer. **7.** No hay nadie que (tener) la culpa. **8.** Me miran como si yo (ser) un tonto. **9.** En cuanto ellos nos (ver), se pusieron a gritar. **10.** No te habrías hecho daño si tú (tener) cuidado. **11.** Su padre le dio diez mil dólares para que él se (comprar) un coche nuevo. **12.** ¿Conoces a alguien que (tocar) la guitarra? **13.** Se cayó en la calle, de modo que (llamar) la atención de todos. **14.** La eché de menos aun antes de que ella (salir) para el Perú. **15.** Aunque (llover) ayer, jugaron al fútbol. **16.** Lo haré sin que vosotros me lo (mandar).

II. Complete the suspended sentence by making the first sentence subordinate.

1. Has llevado una vida tranquila. Nos alegramos de que _____. **2.** Me estaba tomando el pelo. Era posible que _____. **3.** Juan tiene celos. Parece mentira que _____. **4.** La mayor parte de los estudiantes estudian mucho. No dudo que _____. **5.** Volvió ayer. Me sorprende que _____. **6.** Me habéis tomado por español. Es imposible que _____.

III. Fill in the blanks with either **por** or **para**.

1. _____ médico, sabe pintar muy bien. **2.** Se sacrificó _____ su hermano. **3.** Fueron a la fuente _____ agua. **4.** El trabajo estará listo _____ la semana que viene. **5.** Compré un regalo _____ el jefe de mi hermana porque ella estaba enferma. **6.** Salieron _____ España.

IV. Express the relationship of the first sentence to the second.

1. David es guapo. Roberto es más guapo. **2.** Ana tiene muchas flores. Carmen también tiene muchas flores. **3.** Su hermano tiene veinte y tres años. El mío tiene veinte. **4.** Elena canta bien. Rosa canta mejor. **5.** Eduardo y Pedro son vagos. Tomás también es vago. **6.** María es gorda. Carlos es menos gordo.

V. Fill in the blanks with **de, que, de lo que,** or **del que (de la que, de los que, de las que)**.

1. Esta taza de café tiene menos azúcar _____ la otra. **2.** Su hijo es más guapo _____ él. **3.** Tu profesor es más amable _____ decías. **4.** Compró su coche por más _____ diez mil dólares. **5.** Tenía más corbatas _____ necesitaba. **6.** Juega mejor _____ creíamos.

VI. Fill in the blanks with the correct form of one of the following: **que, qué, quien, quién, cual, cuál, el cual, lo que, cuyo, como, cómo, cuanto, cuánto, el que, qué tal, lo cual**.

1. ¿De _____ es este ensayo? **2.** ¿ _____ es su dirección? **3.** ¡ _____ nariz tan larga! **4.** Salí con Roberto, _____ hermanas son hermosísimas. **5.** Ahí vienen varios chicos entre _____ veo a Pablo. **6.** ¡ _____ me alegro de verte, chico! **7.** Esa es la ventana por_____ entraron los ladrones. **8.** Los héroes _____ más hicieron por la independencia fueron Bolívar y San Martín. **9.** ____ estudia mucho, sabe mucho. **10.** Su novio llegó tarde a la cita, _____ la enojó mucho. **11.** ¿ _____ valen estas corbatas? **12.** ¿ _____ te gusta el baile?

VII. Change the negative words to the affirmative and vice versa, making any other necessary changes.

1. Tengo algo en la mano izquierda. **2.** Esta lección no es nada difícil. **3.** ¿No has visto a ningún compañero hoy? **4.** Nosotros también fuimos a la conferencia. **5.** No conozco a nadie que sepa bailar el tango. **6.** O Dolores o Carmen me ayudará.

VIII. Translate.

1. I was born on the twenty-fifth of July, nineteen hundred sixty-five. **2.** It was ten-thirty in the morning when we got home. **3.** I was *(quedar)* astonished at *(de)* how tall she was. **4.** She didn't even look at me. **5.** Have you ever gone to a bullfight? **6.** By getting up at six o'clock you can be there in time. **7.** After eating, I like to rest. **8.** By reading a great deal you will improve your vocabulary.

Appendix A

Answers to Section Exercises

Lesson 1

EXERCISE 1

1. la juventud **2.** el tema **3.** la educación **4.** la cabeza **5.** la artista
6. la inmortalidad **7.** la mano **8.** el día **9.** la cumbre **10.** el Misisipí
11. la sobrina **12.** el tren **13.** el artista **14.** la flor **15.** el martes
16. la be **17.** la libertad **18.** el agente **19.** el mapa **20.** el cura

EXERCISE 2

1. las crisis **2.** las mujeres **3.** los comedores **4.** las luces **5.** los jueves
6. los idiomas **7.** los cafés **8.** las lumbres **9.** los corazones **10.** los
portugueses **11.** las paredes **12.** los paraguas **13.** los poetas **14.** los
reyes **15.** los exámenes **16.** las ciudades **17.** las camareras **18.** las noticias

EXERCISE 3

A. 1. no **2.** sí **3.** no **4.** sí **5.** sí **6.** sí **7.** sí **8.** no **9.** sí **10.** sí
11. sí **12.** sí

B. 1. ¿Quién sabe? **2.** no sabe nada **3.** Conozco ... no sé **4.** no saben
bailar. **5.** No conozco ... conocerla.

C. 1. a. Nos gusta b. Nos gusta c. Nos gustan d. Nos gustan e. Nos
gusta **2.** a. Me gusta b. Me gusta c. Me gusta d. Me gustan e. Me gusta

D. 1. No nos gusta **2.** Le gustan **3.** Me gustan **4.** Les gusta **5.** No nos
importa **6.** Te, le, os *or* les faltan

EXERCISE 4

A. 1. a. nosotros vendemos b. ellos venden c. vosotros vendéis d. tú vendes e. yo vendo **2.** a. Pedro espera b. tú esperas c. yo espero d. María y Elena esperan e. vosotros esperáis **3.** a. nosotros volvemos b. yo vuelvo c. ellos vuelven d. vosotros volvéis e. tú vuelves **4.** a. vosotros no cerráis b. tú no cierras c. Uds. no cierran d. yo no cierro e. ella no cierra **5.** a. yo sirvo b. Ud. sirve c. vosotros servís d. mi hermano y yo servimos e. tú sirves **6.** a. tú prefieres b. vosotros preferís c. Juan y Ana prefieren d. la gente prefiere e. nosotros preferimos

B. 1. ellos traducen, están, piensan, van, tienen, salen **2.** yo traigo, sé, cojo, conozco, sigo, vengo **3.** nosotros merecemos, decimos, somos, caemos, conseguimos, vencemos **4.** él quiere, puede, oye, dice, se lava, sigue **5.** yo salgo, doy, soy, venzo, pongo, hago **6.** tú oyes, eres, estás, duermes, dices, vienes **7.** Uds. envían, se acuestan, continúan, construyen, cogen **8.** vosotros tomáis, sabéis, vivís, volvéis, pensáis

C. 1. I have been hoping to marry you for two years. **2.** We have been eating for three hours and now my stomach hurts me. **3.** They have been living in Buenos Aires since last month. **4.** I have been in love with you since the first day I met you. **5.** They have not smoked for one year. **6.** I have been reading this novel for three hours. **7.** He has not received a letter from his girlfriend for two weeks.

Lesson 2

EXERCISE 1

1. — **2.** El **3.** el **4.** — **5.** el **6.** El **7.** La **8.** El **9.** — **10.** — **11.** el **12.** la **13.** la **14.** el

EXERCISE 2

1. lo alta que era, qué alta era. **2.** lo mejor. **3.** lo misterioso. **4.** lo bien que toca, qué bien toca. **5.** lo más pronto posible, cuanto antes. **6.** lo bello, lo hermoso.

EXERCISE 3

1. — **2.** — **3.** — **4.** un **5.** — **6.** una, una **7.** —

EXERCISE 4

1. hace frío, hace mal tiempo **2.** hace calor **3.** hay luna **4.** hay (hace) viento **5.** hay (hace) sol **6.** nieva **7.** llueve **8.** sale **9.** salgo **10.** dejas

EXERCISE 5

A. 1. Nosotros tomábamos, comíamos, vivíamos, hacíamos, queríamos **2.** yo sacaba, cogía, comenzaba, hacía, era **3.** Ud. encontraba, volvía, sentía, pedía, ponía **4.** tú decías, pagabas, leías, empezabas, te vestías **5.** vosotros sabíais, robabais, preferíais, hablabais, podíais **6.** ellas reñían, se divertían, empezaban, tenían, iban

B. 1. I hadn't seen my friend Consuelo for many years. **2.** We had been eating for three hours when I got sick. **3.** We had been living in Buenos Aires for a year when we had to return to the United States. **4.** How long had you been waiting for the train? **5.** We had been travelling through the country for two months when we met the President.

EXERCISE 6

A. 1. Nosotros tomamos, comimos, vivimos, hicimos, quisimos **2.** Ud. encontró, volvió, sintió, pidió, puso **3.** yo saqué, cogí, comencé, hice, pude **4.** tu dijiste, pagaste, leíste, empezaste, te vestiste **5.** vosotros supisteis, robasteis, preferisteis, hablasteis, pudisteis **6.** ellas riñeron, se divirtieron, empezaron, tuvieron, fueron

B. 1. Eran **2.** tenía **3.** conocimos **4.** sabías, tenía **5.** era, tenía **6.** fuiste, vi **7.** compró, era **8.** Hacía, eran **9.** dejó **10.** almorcé, tenía

Lesson 3

EXERCISE 1

1. la chica inglesa **2.** una niña encantadora **3.** los temas fáciles **4.** los lápices azules **5.** el famoso dramaturgo Calderón **6.** una muchacha cortés **7.** los parientes alemanes **8.** los verdes pinos **9.** mi viejo profesor **10.** mi tía vieja **11.** el primer capítulo **12.** el pobre millonario **13.** las casas populares **14.** la mujer burlona **15.** los animales feroces **16.** una actriz grande *or* una gran actriz **17.** un buen orador *or* un orador bueno **18.** la tercera lección **19.** Santo Domingo **20.** las lecciones difíciles

EXERCISE 2

A. **1.** felizmente **2.** difícilmente **3.** alegremente **4.** ruidosamente
5. inteligentemente **6.** lentamente

B. **1.** rápidos **2.** apresurada **3.** lentos **4.** felices **5.** tranquilos

EXERCISE 3

1. está ... está **2.** es **3.** es **4.** es **5.** es **6.** es **7.** está **8.** está **9.** es
10. es ... están **11.** es **12.** es ... es **13.** está **14.** está **15.** estás
16. estás **17.** son **18.** Es **19.** Estáis **20.** eres ... eres

EXERCISE 4

1. c. **2.** b **3.** b **4.** b **5.** c **6.** a **7.** b **8.** c

EXERCISE 5

1. volverá, dudará, sabrá, escribirá, vendrá **2.** empezaremos, sentiremos,
diremos, entenderemos, tendremos **3.** saldrás, comprenderás, llegarás,
pondrás, vivirás **4.** devolveréis, podréis, insistiréis, pediréis, seréis
5. dormirán, cabrán, dirán, valdrán, cogerán **6.** estaré, vendré, haré,
perderé, saldré

EXERCISE 6

1. a. comprendería b. comprenderíamos c. comprenderían
d. comprenderías e. comprenderíais **2.** a. preferiría b. preferirías
c. preferiríais d. preferiría e. preferiría **3.** a. haríamos b. haría c. haría
d. harían e. harías **4.** a. tendrías b. tendría c. tendrían d. tendrían
e. tendríamos

Lesson 4

EXERCISE 1

1. su **2.** mis **3.** nuestros **4.** mío **5.** suyo **6.** su **7.** su **8.** sus
9. tu **10.** vuestro

EXERCISE 2

A. 1. ... en el mío   **2.** La mía y la tuya ...   **3.** ... en el suyo   **4.** ... es (la) mía   **5.** ... a la suya   **6.** El tuyo y el nuestro ...   **7.** ... (los) míos ... los tuyos   **8.** ... el suyo   **9.** el mío ... el vuestro   **10.** ... las suyas y la mía

B. 3. el de él   **5.** la de ellos (ellas)   **8.** el de ella   **10.** las de él

EXERCISE 3

1. esta   **2.** ese   **3.** este   **4.** estos   **5.** esas   **6.** estos   **7.** aquella   **8.** aquel

EXERCISE 4

A. 1. ésos   **2.** éste   **3.** éstos   **4.** éstas   **5.** ésas   **6.** aquél   **7.** la de Juan   **8.** la

B. 1. eso   **2.** esto   **3.** esta   **4.** éstos   **5.** ese   **6.** eso   **7.** esto   **8.** las

EXERCISE 5

A. 2   **B.** 1   **C.** 3   **D.** 2   **E.** 3   **F.** 2   **G.** 3   **H.** 2

EXERCISE 6

1. hemos dicho   **2.** habías escrito   **3.** habremos terminado   **4.** había visto   **5.** habían aprendido   **6.** había abierto   **7.** he traído   **8.** habéis hecho   **9.** has llegado   **10.** habrá pasado

Lesson 5

EXERCISE 1

A. 1. Ellos   **2.** ella   **3.** ella   **4.** él   **5.** él   **6.** él, ella

B. 1. conmigo   **2.** tú y yo   **3.** sí (misma)   **4.** él   **5.** ellos (ellas)   **6.** ti, contigo   **7.** ellas   **8.** mí (mismo)

EXERCISE 2

1. Queremos hacerla.   **2.** ¿Lo (le) habéis visto?   **3.** Díganle que su mujer está buscándolo.   **4.** Ya se lo dije.   **5.** No lo coja Ud.   **6.** Guillermo Tell no dio en la manzana y su hijo se la comió.   **7.** La aceptó pero al día siguiente se la devolvió. **8.** ¿Os las escribió el Presidente? **9.** Los ladrones le robaron mucho dinero. **10.** Quítasela.

EXERCISE 3

1. se **2.** se **3.** te **4.** Se **5.** — **6.** se

EXERCISE 4

1. llegó a ser **2.** dar un paseo **3.** Se da (dio, *etc*.) cuenta de **4.** a propósito **5.** se puso **6.** hacerse **7.** cuanto antes **8.** A lo lejos **9.** me vuelvo

EXERCISE 5

A. 1. Se abrió la ventana. **2.** Se encenderán las luces más tarde. **3.** Se ha terminado la lección. **4.** Se cerraron las puertas. **5.** Se limpia el cuarto a menudo. **6.** Ya se ha lavado el coche.

B. 1. Abrieron la ventana. **2.** Encenderán las luces más tarde. **3.** Han terminado la lección. **4.** Cerraron las puertas. **5.** Limpian el cuarto a menudo. **6.** Ya han lavado el coche.

C. 1. está **2.** es **3.** fue **4.** serán **5.** están **6.** fue

EXERCISE 6

A. 1. tomando **2.** escribiendo **3.** diciendo **4.** teniendo **5.** durmiendo **6.** pidiendo **7.** volviendo **8.** acostándose **9.** saliendo **10.** vistiéndose

B. 1. se está poniendo (está poniéndose) **2.** Estábamos dando **3.** Está lloviendo **4.** Estábamos vistiéndonos (nos estábamos vistiendo) **5.** estáis haciendo **6.** estoy llamándolo (lo estoy llamando) **7.** estás diciendo **8.** Estoy levantándome (me estoy levantando)

Lesson 6

EXERCISE 1

yo:	rompa, escriba, piense, haga, diga
ellos:	se acuesten, cojan, aprendan, pidan, discutan
tú:	charles, saques, sigas, vuelvas, pierdas
nosotros:	sintamos, nos durmamos, entendamos, devolvamos, empecemos
Ud.:	goce, pague, ponga, conozca, caiga

vosotros: traigáis, busquéis, lleguéis, traduzcáis, os quedéis

yo: sea, vaya, haya, sepa, esté

EXERCISE 2

A. 1. No volváis temprano. **2.** No se acuesten Uds. **3.** No me des un beso. **4.** No se lo digan Uds. **5.** No comas ahora. **6.** Que no se acuesten los niños. **7.** No nos levantemos a las seis. **8.** No se vayan Uds. **9.** No le pida Ud. dinero a su padre. **10.** No os acostéis. **11.** No te levantes. **12.** No lo hagas.

B. 1. Contesta esas preguntas. **2.** Vuelve temprano. **3.** Escribe la lección. **4.** Decid eso. **5.** Ponte el abrigo. **6.** Sigue hablando. **7.** Dale tu rubí. **8.** Levantaos temprano. **9.** Véndele tu casa. **10.** Acuéstate ahora. **11.** Sacadlo. **12.** Sal de tu cuarto.

C. 1. Demos un paseo. **2.** Acostémonos. **3.** Digámoselo. **4.** Saquemos el dinero.

EXERCISE 3

1. c **2.** a **3.** b **4.** c **5.** b **6.** b **7.** a **8.** c

EXERCISE 4

A. 1. Será necesario que nosotros estudiemos (estudiemos nosotros). (Subject may go before or after the verb.) **2.** Tengo miedo de que mi hija no se case. **3.** Creo que tú la has visto. **4.** Conviene que Uds. vayan de compras ahora. **5.** Se alegran de que yo pueda venir mañana. **6.** No creo que se equivoquen ellos.

B. 1. devuelva **2.** tengo **3.** piense **4.** es **5.** pasen **6.** sabe **7.** expliques

Lesson 7

EXERCISE 1

1. hayan tenido mucho éxito **2.** se haya hecho daño **3.** hayas vuelto a verla **4.** me haya enfermado **5.** lo hayan dicho Uds. **6.** hayáis querido hacerlo

EXERCISE 2

1. saliéramos (saliésemos), tradujéramos (tradujésemos), volviéramos (volviésemos) **2.** te dieras (dieses) cuenta, vencieras (vencieses), siguieras (siguieses) **3.** supieran (supiesen), pudieran (pudiesen), se alegraran (se alegrasen) de **4.** dijera (dijese), enviara (enviase), vendiera (vendiese) **5.** me levantara (me levantase), me fuera (me fuese), empezara (empezase) **6.** os divirtierais (os divirtieseis), vinierais (vinieseis), os acostarais (os acostaseis)

EXERCISE 3

1. hubieras (hubieses) vuelto **2.** hubiera (hubiese) sucedido **3.** hubieras (hubieses) dado **4.** hubieran (hubiesen) dicho **5.** hubieran (hubiesen) estado

EXERCISE 4

1. encendiera (encendiese) **2.** realizó (or any indicative tense) **3.** dé **4.** volviéramos (volviésemos) **5.** escojamos **6.** estuvieran (estuviesen) [hubieran (hubiesen) estado] **7.** era (fue, había sido) **8.** podáis

EXERCISE 5

1. hubiéramos (hubiésemos) tenido **2.** hace **3.** diera (diese) **4.** íbamos **5.** fuera (fuese) **6.** habría (hubiera) dicho

EXERCISE 6

A. 1. Quisiera ... **2.** Pudieras ... **3.** Quisiéramos ... **4.** Debiéramos ... **5.** Pudieran ...

B. 1. vengan mañana **2.** lo harán **3.** lo hagan **4.** llueva mañana **5.** (que) me dé una *A* **6.** lo hizo ella

C. 1. ¡Ojalá (que) fuera (fuese, sea) posible! **2.** ¡Ojalá (que) hubiera (hubiese) sido así! **3.** Tal vez [Quizá(s)] lo haga. **4.** Tal vez [Quizá(s)] lo dijo. **5.** ¡Ojalá (que) no llueva! **6.** ¿Dijo eso? ¡Ojalá que sí! (¡Ojalá!)

EXERCISE 7

1. realizó **2.** lleva una vida **3.** nos dimos (dábamos, habíamos dado) cuenta **4.** ¿Qué le parece ... ? **5.** no tengo nada que ver con **6.** dio las gracias **7.** están de acuerdo

Lesson 8

EXERCISE 1

A. 1. ¿Conoces una secretaria que hable español? **2.** ¿Buscáis un chico que toque la guitarra? **3.** Espero casarme con un hombre que se enamore perdidamente de mí. **4.** ¿Dónde tienes un televisor que funcione bien? **5.** Llame un abogado que se especialice en divorcios.

B. 1. The one who arrives first will dance with the queen. *El que* is an indefinite (unknown) person. **2.** Those who did the work well passed the exams. *Los que* refers to specific persons. **3.** He doesn't understand what you told him yesterday. *Lo que* is a known quantity (what you said). **4.** He will not understand what you will (may) tell him. *Lo que* refers to an unknown quantity; you haven't told him yet. **5.** Wherever you (may) go, you will not be well received. *Dondequiera* refers to an indefinite (unknown) place. **6.** However much he strove, he got nothing out of it. The clause makes a statement of fact. **7.** Whoever you are (may be), I will not open the door. *Quienquiera* refers to an indefinite (unknown) person.

EXERCISE 2

1. Aunque tuviera (tuviese) tiempo, no iría contigo. **2.** Te di ocho mil dólares para que te compraras (comprases) un coche. **3.** Te di ocho mil dólares de modo que podías (pudiste) comprarte un coche. **4.** Dijo (decía) que volvería cuando tuviera (tuviese) más dinero. **5.** Siempre cuando venía, le ofrecía una taza de café. **6.** Lo haría con tal (de) que estuviéramos (estuviésemos) de acuerdo. **7.** A veces salía (salí) de casa sin que se dieran (diesen) cuenta mis padres. **8.** Aunque no tenía (tuvo) la culpa, la castigaban (castigaron). **9.** Me lo dijo antes (de) que yo se lo pidiera (pidiese). **10.** No te lo diría a menos que prometieras (prometieses) callarlo.

EXERCISE 3

1. A veces (Algunas veces) **2.** dejar de **3.** llama la atención **4.** a la derecha ... a la izquierda **5.** Al principio *or* A veces **6.** pensáis ... de **7.** de nuevo **8.** pienso en **9.** piensas

Lesson 9

EXERCISE 1

A. 1. con 2. — 3. en 4. De 5. — 6. de 7. a 8. de 9. a 10. —
11. de 12. de 13. — 14. de 15. en

B. 1. — 2. a 3. a 4. a 5. a

EXERCISE 2

A. 1. on behalf of *or* for the sake of 2. implied comparison (considering the fact that) 3. intended for 4. through 5. in exchange for 6. for a period of time 7. by a certain time 8. destination 9. object of an errand 10. for the sake of 11. because of 12. on behalf of ... intended for

B. 1. por la mañana *or* por lo general 2. por favor *or* ¡por Dios! 3. por lo menos 4. por casualidad 5. por primera vez 6. por fin 7. por lo visto
8. Por todas partes *or* Por aquí 9. por todas partes *or* por aquí 10. por Dios *or* por favor

EXERCISE 3

1. Le (Lo) tomé por 2. la conoció 3. por poco se rompe 4. se puso a
5. Estábamos para salir 6. no es para tanto 7. al otro día (al día siguiente)
8. a las dos horas 9. Encontré 10. Estábamos por 11. De ningún modo.
(De ninguna manera.) 12. Al poco rato

EXERCISE 4

A. 1. Comiendo 2. (El) comer 3. ver 4. No fumar 5. siguió trabajando
6. cantar 7. Al ver 8. Repitiendo 9. (El) estudiar 10. Andaban diciendo

B. 1. Yendo. 2. Esperándola 3. Siendo así 4. Hablando contigo

Lesson 10

EXERCISE 1

A. 1. mejor 2. mejor 3. más grandes 4. más 5. peor 6. más guapo
7. peor 8. menor

B. 1. que 2. de lo que 3. de 4. de los que 5. que 6. de lo que 7. de
8. del que

C. 1. No es tan malo. **2.** Cuanto más mira su foto, (tanto) más se enamora de ella. **3.** El perro es el mejor amigo del hombre. **4.** Cuanto menos veo, (tanto) menos me duele.

EXERCISE 2

A. 1. larguísimo **2.** lindísimas **3.** riquísima **4.** felicísima **5.** inteligentísimos

B. 1. Ana es la más linda de la familia. **2.** Su casa es la más hermosa del barrio. **3.** Los Andes son las montañas más altas de Sudamérica. **4.** Estos métodos son los más eficaces de todos. **5.** Estos capítulos son los más difíciles del libro. **6.** Buenos Aires es la ciudad más grande de la Argentina.

EXERCISE 3

1. Mis hermanos tienen tantos amigos como mis hermanas. **2.** María es tan inteligente como Carlos. **3.** Yo duermo tan profundamente como una piedra. **4.** Nuestra casa es tan hermosa como la suya. **5.** Hemos escrito tantas cartas como ellos. **6.** Las niñas corren tanto como los niños. **7.** Hace tanto calor en Miami como en Nueva York. **8.** Mi padre es tan fuerte como el tuyo. **9.** A mí me gusta leer tanto como a ti. **10.** En esta universidad hay tantas mujeres como hombres.

EXERCISE 4

1. f **2.** d **3.** g **4.** a **5.** c **6.** b **7.** h **8.** i **9.** j **10.** e

EXERCISE 5

A. 1. e **2.** u **3.** y **4.** e **5.** y **6.** e

B. 1. pero **2.** pero **3.** sino **4.** sino **5.** pero **6.** sino **7.** pero **8.** sino que

Lesson 11

EXERCISE 1

A. 1. que **2.** que **3.** que **4.** quienes (que) **5.** que **6.** quien (que)

B. 1. quienes (los cuales) **2.** la cual (la que) **3.** que (el cual) **4.** la cual (la que) **5.** que (la cual) **6.** quienes (los cuales) **7.** la cual (la que) **8.** quien (la cual, la que)

C. 1. El que **2.** Los que **3.** el que **4.** la que

EXERCISE 2

A. 1. Cuál **2.** Qué **3.** Qué (Cuál) **4.** Cuál **5.** Qué **6.** Qué (Cuáles)
7. qué (cuál) **8.** Cuál

B. 1. ¿Cuál es tu (su) número de teléfono? **2.** ¿Cómo prefieres (prefiere) el
café? **3.** ¿Cuántas novelas leyeron Uds. (leísteis) este semestre? **4.** ¿Qué es
tu (su) hermana? or ¿Cuál es la profesión de tu (su) hermana? **5.** ¿Quiénes son
tus (sus) compañeras? **6.** ¿De quién es este (ese) libro? **7.** ¿A quiénes
conociste (conoció Ud.) anoche? **8.** ¿Cuánta leche tomaron? **9.** ¿Por qué
fuiste (fue Ud.) a casa de Ana? **10.** ¿Para qué necesitas (necesita Ud.) una
cuchara?

EXERCISE 3

1. ¡Qué alegre estoy! **2.** ¡Qué chica tan (más) linda! **3.** ¡Vaya un jugador
maravilloso! **4.** ¡Cuánto se espantaron! **5.** ¡Cuántos enemigos tenía!
6. ¡Cómo me aburren los profesores! **7.** ¡Qué casa tan (más) grande!
8. ¡Qué bonitos ojos tienes! **9.** ¡Vaya un sinvergüenza! **10.** ¡Cuánta plata
ganaron!

EXERCISE 4

1. hora **2.** ¿qué más? **3.** de buena gana **4.** había de ... a tiempo. **5.** en
ninguna parte **6.** veces **7.** ¡Cómo no! **8.** ¡Qué va! **9.** de mala gana
10. a la vez

EXERCISE 5

1. algo **2.** algunos **3.** algún **4.** alguien **5.** cualquier cosa **6.** algunas
7. algo **8.** algo

EXERCISE 6

A. 1. Carlos no es nada tacaño. **2.** Tampoco vino Ana or Ana no vino
tampoco. **3.** Dígale que ningún compañero lo visitará. **4.** Nunca escribe la
tarea de mala gana. **5.** Ni Pedro ni Pablo ha(n) prometido llevarme a la
estación. **6.** Mi prima no es nada perezosa. **7.** Los niños mayores, es decir,
los de más de doce años, nunca se quedan en casa. **8.** He escrito a tres
amigos y sé que ninguno me contestará.

B. 1. más que nunca **2.** No sé nada (Nada sé) **3.** cualquier cosa
4. a alguien **5.** más bonita que nunca **6.** más que nada

Lesson 12

EXERCISE 1

1. novecientas seis **2.** quinientas treinta y una **3.** Cuarto **4.** Catorce
5. cien mil **6.** cinco más dieciséis (diez y seis) son veintiuno (veinte y uno)
7. tres cuartos **8.** una docena de **9.** ciento cuatro **10.** dos mil setecientas
ochenta y una **11.** tres millones **12.** mil cuatrocientos sesenta y nueve
13. quince **14.** primero **15.** medio **16.** medio **17.** la mitad **18.** el siglo
diecisiete (diez y siete)

EXERCISE 2

A. 1. la una y media (y treinta) de la tarde. **2.** las diez menos veinte de la
mañana **3.** las dos y cuarto (y quince) de la tarde **4.** las diez y media (y
treinta) de la noche **5.** las tres y diez de la madrugada

B. 1. por la mañana **2.** De noche (Por la noche) **3.** eran las dos de la
madrugada **4.** a eso de las diez y media **5.** a las veintitrés (veinte y tres)
6. a la una **7.** a eso de las cuatro y veinte **8.** Eran las seis menos veinte

EXERCISE 3

A. 1. c **2.** a **3.** d **4.** e **5.** f **6.** b **7.** g **8.** h

B. 1. a tiempo **2.** a principios del **3.** dan las doce **4.** el reloj se adelanta
5. mi reloj se atrasa **6.** a (la) medianoche

EXERCISE 4

1. febrero de mil quinientos diez y nueve ... agosto de mil quinientos veinte y
uno **2.** en enero de mil quinientos treinta y uno **3.** el dos de mayo de mil
ochocientos ocho **4.** el nueve de octubre de mil ochocientos veinte y cuatro
5. el ocho de noviembre de mil ochocientos cuarenta y tres ... el treinta de
septiembre de mil ochocientos sesenta y ocho **6.** el diez y siete de julio de mil
novecientos treinta y seis ... el primero de abril de mil novecientos treinta y nueve

EXERCISE 5

1. Miguel **2.** rato **3.** abogado **4.** pedazo **5.** favor **6.** muchacho

Appendix B

Deceptive Cognates

There are literally thousands of words that are the same or similar in appearance in English and Spanish and have the same meaning in both languages. There are also, however, many instances where appearances are deceiving and words that look alike are quite different in meaning. The following list includes some of the most common words in this category:

acción In addition to meaning *action*, it is also used in business to mean *share, stock*. **Las acciones de la compañía:** *The company's stock* (or *shares*).

actual Means *present, current* and not *actual* which is **real, verdadero. El presidente actual no ejerce el verdadero poder:** *The present president does not exercise the actual power.* **Actualmente:** *at the present time. Actually:* **en realidad, de veras, realmente.**

asistir Means *to attend* and requires **a** before a noun. **Casi nunca asiste a sus clases:** *He almost never attends class. To assist* is **ayudar.**

colegio General term for *school* rather than *college*, which is **universidad.**

conferencia *Lecture* as well as *conference.*

decepción *Disappointment, deception. Deception* is usually **engaño.**

desgracia *Misfortune.* **¡Qué desgracia!:** *What a misfortune!* **Desgraciadamente:** *unfortunately. Disgrace:* **deshonra.**

disgusto *Unpleasantness, annoyance* rather than *disgust* (**asco**). **Me da asco:** *It disgusts me.* **Tuve un disgusto con mi cuñado:** *I had an unpleasant incident with my brother-in-law.*

embarazada Does not mean *embarrassed*, which is **avergonzado, desconcertado,** or **turbado. Está embarazada** is one way of saying *She is pregnant.*

éxito *Success.* **Su nueva comedia tuvo un gran éxito:** *His new play was a great success. Exit:* **salida.**

fastidioso *Annoying, bothersome.* **Fastidiar** is a commonly used verb. **No me fastidies:** *Don't bother (annoy) me.* Likewise, the noun **fastidio. Es un fastidio:** *It's a bother (nuisance, inconvenience).* It is difficult to find an equivalent for *fastidious*. Several possibilities are **melindroso, quisquilloso, exigente, difícil de complacer.**

242

firma *Signature.* A business firm is **compañía** or **casa** (**comercial**).

grosería The adjective **grosero** means *rude* or *coarse* and **grosería** is *rudeness* or *coarseness.* The English word *grocery* is known by a variety of terms in the various parts of the Hispanic world. Usually **tienda de ultramarinos** in Spain; **tienda de abarrotes** in Mexico; **bodega** in Cuba and Venezuela; **almacén** in Argentina, Uruguay and Chile; **colmado** in Puerto Rico.

idioma *Language. Idiom* is **modismo**. **Hay muchos modismos en cada idioma.** *There are many idioms in every language.*

indiano This is a special term used to refer to a Spaniard who went to the Spanish colonies in the new world and returned to Spain with great wealth. *Indian* is **indio**.

introducir Means *introduce* in the sense of bringing up a topic in conversation or to insert physically. *To introduce a person* is **presentar**.

largo *Long. Large* is **grande**.

lectura *Reading. Lecture* is **conferencia**.

librería *Bookstore. Library* is **biblioteca**.

molestar May mean *molest* but usually is the equivalent of *to bother, disturb, annoy.* **Siento molestarlo:** *I'm sorry to bother you.* **No es ninguna molestia:** *It's no trouble* (or *bother*).

oficio *Trade, occupation. Office* is **despacho** or **oficina**.

pariente This is the general word for a *relative. Parent* is **padre** or **madre**; *parents:* **padres**.

pretender *To attempt, try to. To pretend:* **fingir**.

propaganda Not only *propaganda* but also *advertising, publicity.*

regular In addition to *regular* may mean *average, so-so, O.K.* **¿Cómo estás? Regular:** *How are you? So-so; O.K.*

sano *Healthy* rather than *sane,* which is **cuerdo**. Note the expression **sano y salvo:** *safe and sound.*

sensible *Sensitive. Sensible* may be **sensato, cuerdo, razonable, de buen sentido. Es una persona muy sensible:** *He is a very sensitive person.*

sentencia Means *sentence* only in a judicial sense. May also mean a *saying* or *proverb.* The Spanish word for *sentence* in grammar is **frase** or **oración**.

simpático This is one of the finest compliments that can be given to a person. It is roughly the equivalent of *pleasant, charming, congenial, nice. Sympathetic:* **compasivo**.

suceso *Event, occurrence, happening.* The verb **suceder** means *to happen, occur. Success:* **éxito**.

sujeto Means *subject* only in the grammatical sense. It may also mean, colloquially, *fellow, guy,* in a derogatory sense. A subject in school is **asignatura, materia, curso.** When it is the equivalent of *topic, subject is* rendered by **tema.** When it refers to a citizen of a country, *subject* is **súbdito, ciudadano.**

tipo Not only *type* but also colloquially used in a derogatory sense for *guy, character.* **No me gusta ese tipo:** *I don't like that guy.* Note the expression **tipo de cambio:** *rate of exchange.*

Appendix C

Songs

Adiós, muchachos

Adiós, muchachos, compañeros de mi vida,
barra querida de aquellos tiempos.
Me toca a mí hoy emprender la retirada,
debo alejarme de mi buena muchachada.
Adiós, muchachos, ya me voy y me resigno,
contra el destino nadie la talla;
se terminaron para mí todas las farras,
mi cuerpo enfermo no resiste más.

Allá en el rancho grande

Allá en el rancho grande,
allá donde vivía,
había una rancherita
que alegre me decía, que alegre me decía:

Te voy a hacer tus calzones,
como los usa el ranchero;
te los comienzo de lana,
te los acabo de cuero.

Amapola

Amapola, lindísima Amapola,
será siempre mi alma tuya sola.
Yo te quiero, amada niña mía,
igual que ama la flor la luz del día.
Amapola, lindísima Amapola,
no seas tan ingrata y ámame.
Amapola, Amapola,
¿cómo puedes tú vivir tan sola?

Amor

Amor, amor, amor,
nació de ti, nació de mí,
de la esperanza.

Amor, amor, amor,
nació de Dios, para los dos,
nació del alma.

Sentir que tus besos anidaron en mí,
igual que palomas mensajeras de luz,
saber que mis besos se quedaron en ti,
haciendo en tus labios la señal de la cruz.

Bésame

Bésame, bésame mucho,
como si fuera esta noche la última vez.
Bésame mucho, que tengo miedo perderte,
perderte después.

Quiero tenerte muy cerca,
mirarme en tus ojos,
estar junto a ti.
Piensa que tal vez mañana
ya estaré lejos, muy lejos de aquí.

Canción mixteca

¡Qué lejos estoy del suelo donde he nacido!
Intensa nostalgia invade mi pensamiento.
Y al verme tan solo y triste cual hoja al viento,
quisiera llorar, quisiera morir, de sentimiento.

¡Oh, tierra del sol, suspiro por verte!
Ahora que lejos yo vivo sin luz, sin amor.
Y al verme tan solo y triste cual hoja al viento,
quisiera llorar, quisiera morir, de sentimiento.

Cielito lindo

De la Sierra Morena, cielito lindo, viene bajando
un par de ojitos negros, cielito lindo, de contrabando.

¡Ay, ay, ay, ay!, canta y no llores,
porque cantando se alegran
Cielito lindo, los corazones.

Ese lunar que tienes, cielito lindo, junto a la boca,
no se lo des a nadie, cielito lindo, que a mí me toca.

La cucaracha

La cucaracha, la cucaracha,
ya no puede caminar
porque no tiene, porque le falta
marijuana que fumar.

Las de quince son de oro,
las de veinte son de plata,
las de treinta son de cobre,
y las otras son de lata.

Para sarapes, Saltillo,
Chihuahua para soldados;
para mujeres, Jalisco,
y para amar, toditos lados.

Isabelita

A las cinco por Florida
muy bien vestida pasa Isabel;
su silueta distinguida
es perseguida como la miel:
pues no hay hombre que al mirarla
no se empeñe en conquistarla,
pero nadie ha conseguido
ser preferido por Isabel.

Isabelita, porteña bonita,
figura exquisita de gracia sin par,
Isabelita, la calle palpita,
la gente se agita al verla pasar,
y nadie sabe su gran dolor,—
Isabelita busca un amor.

Cuando fina y elegante,
rosa fragante pasa Isabel,
va arrastrando tras su gracia
y aristocracia todo un tropel;
pues no hay hombre que en seguida
no le ofrezca su alma y vida,
mas el príncipe soñado
aún no ha llegado, ... ¡Pobre Isabel!

Malagueña salerosa

¡Qué bonitos ojos tienes, debajo de esas dos cejas,
debajo de esas dos cejas, qué bonitos ojos tienes!
Ellos me quieren mirar, pero si tú no los dejas,
pero si tú no los dejas, ni siquiera parpadear.

Malagueña salerosa, besar tus labios quisiera,
besar tus labios quisiera, malagueña salerosa,
y decirte, niña hermosa, que eres linda y hechicera,
que eres linda y hechicera, como el candor de una rosa.

Si por pobre me desprecias, yo te concedo razón,
yo te concedo razón, si por pobre me desprecias.
Yo no te ofrezco riqueza, te ofrezco mi corazón,
te ofrezco mi corazón a cambio de mi pobreza.

Las mañanitas

Estas son las mañanitas
que cantaba el Rey David,
a las muchachas bonitas
se las cantamos aquí.

Despierta, mi bien, despierta,
mira que ya amaneció;
ya los pajarillos cantan,
la luna ya se metió.

Muñequita linda

Muñequita linda, de cabellos de oro,
de dientes de perla y labios de rubí.
Dime si me quieres, como yo te adoro,
si de mí te acuerdas, como yo de ti.

A veces escucho un eco divino,
que envuelto en la brisa parece decir:
yo te quiero mucho, mucho, mucho, mucho,
tanto como entonces, siempre hasta morir.

Vals del estudiante

Yo tengo un amor que me tiene penando,
por el que dejé de seguir estudiando.
Dejando los libros y en vez de estudiar,
con ansias me pongo a cantar.

Yo por ti no voy a la escuela,
yo por ti no voy a estudiar,
yo por ti no voy al colegio,
y es por ti que no soy colegial.

Yo tengo un amor que me causa tormento,
su ardiente mirar no lo olvido un momento.
Cogiendo los libros y en vez de cantar,
con ansias me pongo a estudiar.

Yo por ti he vuelto a la escuela,
yo por ti he vuelto a estudiar,
yo por ti he vuelto al colegio,
y es por ti que tendré que triunfar.

Appendix D

Syllabication, Stress and Orthography

Syllabication

A single consonant between single vowels goes with the following vowel:
a-me-ri-ca-no, a-mi-go, Pa-na-má. Two consonants together are usually divided:
has-ta, don-de, Ar-gen-ti-na. If, however, the second consonant is **l** or **r**, both
consonants generally go with the following vowel: **ha-blar, fe-bre-ro, Ma-drid.**
Note: **ch, ll** and **rr** are considered single letters of the alphabet and must not be
divided: **mu-cha-cho, ca-lle, ja-rro.**

A diphthong is a combination of two weak vowels (**i** and **u**) or a strong (**a, e, o**) and
a weak vowel. Strong vowels are separated: **ve-o, le-er, ma-es-tro.** A combination
of a strong and weak vowel or two weak vowels is treated as a single vowel for
syllabication purposes: **pia-no, ciu-dad, Bue-nos Ai-res,** unless a written accent
mark on a weak vowel breaks up the diphthong: **rí-o, pa-ís, ba-úl, Ma-rí-a.**

Stress

1. Words that end in a vowel or **n** or **s** are normally stressed on the next to the last
   syllable: **hom-bre, es-cri-ben, sa-lu-dos.**
2. Words that end in a consonant, except **n** or **s**, are stressed on the last syllable:
   se-ñor, pa-red, a-ni-mal.
3. All exceptions to the above rules are indicated by a written accent on the
   stressed vowel: **a-quí, es-ta-ción, Mé-xi-co.**

Orthography

Note the following spelling patterns for the letters **c, z, qu, g** and **j.**

	hard *c* (k)	hard *g*	Castilian *th* Spanish-American *s*	aspirate *h*	*gu* (gw)
a	**ca**sa	**ga**nar	**za**pato	**ja**rro	a**gua**
o	**co**mo	**go**ma	**zo**na	**jo**ven	anti**guo**
u	**cu**ra	**gu**sto	a**zul**	**ju**rar	
e	**que**so	pa**gué**	empe**cé**	**ge**nte, mu**je**r	ver**güe**nza
i	a**quí**	se**guir**	**ci**nco	**gi**gante, tra**ji**ste	ar**güi**r

Appendix E

REGULAR VERBS

	1 (-ar)	2 (-er)	3 (-ir)
Infinitive	tomar *to take*	comer *to eat*	vivir *to live*
Present Participle	tomando *taking*	comiendo *eating*	viviendo *living*
Past Participle	tomado *taken*	comido *eaten*	vivido *lived*

Present Indicative	*I take, do take,*
	   am taking, etc.
	tomo
	tomas
	toma
	tomamos
	tomáis
	toman
		I eat, do eat,
		   am eating, etc.
		como
		comes
		come
		comemos
		coméis
		comen
			I live, do live,
			   am living, etc.
			vivo
			vives
			vive
			vivimos
			vivís
			viven

Imperfect Indicative	*I was taking,*
	   used to take,
	   took, etc.
	tomaba
	tomabas
	tomaba
	tomábamos
	tomabais
	tomaban
		I was eating,
		   used to eat,
		   ate, etc.
		comía
		comías
		comía
		comíamos
		comíais
		comían
			I was living,
			   used to live,
			   lived, etc.
			vivía
			vivías
			vivía
			vivíamos
			vivíais
			vivían

Preterite	*I took, did take,*
	   etc.
	tomé
	tomaste
	tomó
	tomamos
	tomasteis
	tomaron
		I ate, did eat,
		   etc.
		comí
		comiste
		comió
		comimos
		comisteis
		comieron
			I lived, did live,
			   etc.
			viví
			viviste
			vivió
			vivimos
			vivisteis
			vivieron

Future	I shall (will) take, etc.	I shall (will) eat, etc.	I shall (will) live, etc.
	tomaré	comeré	viviré
	tomarás	comerás	vivirás
	tomará	comerá	vivirá
	tomaremos	comeremos	viviremos
	tomaréis	comeréis	viviréis
	tomarán	comerán	vivirán
Conditional	I should (would) take, etc.	I should (would) eat, etc.	I should (would) live, etc.
	tomaría	comería	viviría
	tomarías	comerías	vivirías
	tomaría	comería	viviría
	tomaríamos	comeríamos	viviríamos
	tomaríais	comeríais	viviríais
	tomarían	comerían	vivirían
Present Subjunctive	(that) I (may) take, etc.	(that) I (may) eat, etc.	(that) I (may) live, etc.
	(que) tome	(que) coma	(que) viva
	(que) tomes	(que) comas	(que) vivas
	(que) tome	(que) coma	(que) viva
	(que) tomemos	(que) comamos	(que) vivamos
	(que) toméis	(que) comáis	(que) viváis
	(que) tomen	(que) coman	(que) vivan
Imperfect Subjunctive (-ra form)	(that) I took, might take, etc.	(that) I ate, might eat, etc.	(that) I lived, might live, etc.
	(que) tomara	(que) comiera	(que) viviera
	(que) tomaras	(que) comieras	(que) vivieras
	(que) tomara	(que) comiera	(que) viviera
	(que) tomáramos	(que) comiéramos	(que) viviéramos
	(que) tomarais	(que) comierais	(que) vivierais
	(que) tomaran	(que) comieran	(que) vivieran
Imperfect Subjunctive (-se form)	(que) tomase	(que) comiese	(que) viviese
	(que) tomases	(que) comieses	(que) vivieses
	(que) tomase	(que) comiese	(que) viviese
	(que) tomásemos	(que) comiésemos	(que) viviésemos
	(que) tomaseis	(que) comieseis	(que) vivieseis
	(que) tomasen	(que) comiesen	(que) viviesen

COMPOUND TENSES OF REGULAR VERBS

Perfect Infinitive	haber tomado *to have taken*	haber comido *to have eaten*	haber vivido *to have lived*
Perfect Participle	habiendo tomado *having taken*	habiendo comido *having eaten*	habiendo vivido *having lived*

Present Perfect Indicative *I have taken, eaten, lived, etc.*	he has ha hemos habéis han	tomado	comido	vivido
Past Perfect Indicative *I had taken, eaten, lived, etc.*	había habías había habíamos habíais habían	tomado	comido	vivido
Preterite Perfect *I had taken, eaten, lived, etc.*	hube hubiste hubo hubimos hubisteis hubieron	tomado	comido	vivido
Future Perfect *I will have taken, eaten, lived, etc.*	habré habrás habrá habremos habréis habrán	tomado	comido	vivido
Conditional Perfect *I would have taken, eaten, lived, etc.*	habría habrías habría habríamos habríais habrían	tomado	comido	vivido
Present Perfect Subjunctive *(that) I (may) have taken, eaten, lived, etc.*	(que) haya (que) hayas (que) haya (que) hayamos (que) hayáis (que) hayan	tomado	comido	vivido

Past Perfect Subjunctive (-ra form) *(that) I had taken, eaten, lived, etc.*	(que) hubiera (que) hubieras (que) hubiera (que) hubiéramos (que) hubierais (que) hubieran	tomado	comido	vivido
Past Perfect Subjunctive (-se form)	(que) hubiese (que) hubieses (que) hubiese (que) hubiésemos (que) hubieseis (que) hubiesen	tomado	comido	vivido

STEM-CHANGING VERBS

(Note: only tenses with stem-changing forms are included.)

1st or 2nd Conjugation, e > ie
pensar (ie) *to think*
Present: pienso, piensas, piensa; pensamos, pensáis, piensan
Present Subjunctive: (que) piense, pienses, piense; pensemos, penséis, piensen
Formal Commands: piense Ud., piensen Uds.

1st or 2nd Conjugation, o > ue
volver (ue) *to return*
Present: vuelvo, vuelves, vuelve; volvemos, volvéis, vuelven
Present Subjunctive: (que) vuelva, vuelvas, vuelva; volvamos, volváis, vuelvan
Formal Commands: vuelva Ud., vuelvan Uds.

3rd Conjugation, e > ie, e > i
mentir (ie, i) *to tell a lie*
Present Participle: mintiendo
Present: miento, mientes, miente; mentimos, mentís, mienten
Preterite: mentí, mentiste, mintió; mentimos, mentisteis, mintieron
Present Subjunctive: (que) mienta, mientas, mienta; mintamos, mintáis, mientan
Imperfect Subjunctive: (que) mintiera (—se), mintieras, mintiera; mintiéramos, mintierais, mintieran
Formal Commands: mienta Ud., mientan Uds.

3rd Conjugation, e > i
pedir (i, i) *to ask for*
Present Participle: pidiendo
Present: pido, pides, pide; pedimos, pedís, piden
Preterite: pedí, pediste, pidió; pedimos, pedisteis, pidieron
Present Subjunctive: (que) pida, pidas, pida; pidamos, pidáis, pidan

Imperfect Subjunctive: (que) pidiera (—se), pidieras, pidiera; pidiéramos, pidierais, pidieran
Formal Commands: pida Ud., pidan Uds.

3rd Conjugation, o > ue, o > u
dormir (ue, u) *to sleep*
Present Participle: durmiendo
Present: duermo, duermes, duerme; dormimos, dormís, duermen
Preterite: dormí, dormiste, durmió; dormimos, dormisteis, durmieron
Present Subjunctive: (que) duerma, duermas, duerma; durmamos, durmáis, duerman
Imperfect Subjunctive: (que) durmiera (—se), durmieras, durmiera; durmiéramos, durmierais, durmieran
Formal Commands: duerma Ud., duerman Uds.

IRREGULAR VERBS

(**Note:** only tenses with irregular forms are included.)

andar *to go; to walk*
Preterite: anduve, anduviste, etc.
Imperfect Subjunctive: (que) anduviera (—se), anduvieras, etc.

caer *to fall*
Present Indicative: caigo, caes, etc.
Present Subjunctive: (que) caiga, caigas, etc.
Preterite: caí, caíste, cayó; caímos, caísteis, cayeron
Imperfect Subjunctive: (que) cayera (—se), cayeras, etc.
Present Participle: cayendo
Past Participle: caído

dar *to give*
Present Indicative: doy, das, etc.
Present Subjunctive: dé, des, etc.
Preterite: di, diste, etc.
Imperfect Subjunctive: (que) diera (—se), dieras, etc.

decir *to say*
Present Indicative: digo, dices, dice; decimos, decís, dicen
Present Subjunctive: (que) diga, digas, etc.
Preterite: dije, dijiste, dijo; dijimos, dijisteis, dijeron
Imperfect Subjunctive: (que) dijera (—se), dijeras, etc.
Future: diré, dirás, etc.
Conditional: diría, dirías, etc.
Command: di (tú)
Present Participle: diciendo
Past Participle: dicho

estar *to be*
Present Indicative: estoy, estás, está; estamos, estáis, están
Present Subjunctive: (que) esté, estés, esté; estemos, estéis, estén
Preterite: estuve, estuviste, etc.
Imperfect Subjunctive: (que) estuviera (—se), estuvieras, etc.

haber *to have*
Present Indicative: he, has, ha; hemos, habéis, han
Present Subjunctive: (que) haya, hayas, etc.
Preterite: hube, hubiste, etc.
Imperfect Subjunctive: (que) hubiera (—se), hubieras, etc.
Future: habré, habrás, etc.
Conditional: habría, habrías, etc.

hacer *to make; to do*
Present Indicative: hago, haces, etc.
Present Subjunctive: (que) haga, hagas, etc.
Preterite: hice, hiciste, hizo; hicimos, hicisteis, hicieron
Imperfect Subjunctive: (que) hiciera (—se), hicieras, etc.
Future: haré, harás, etc.
Conditional: haría, harías, etc.
Command: haz (tú)
Past Participle: hecho

ir *to go*
Present Indicative: voy, vas, va; vamos, vais, van
Present Subjunctive: (que) vaya, vayas, etc.
Imperfect Indicative: iba, ibas, iba; íbamos, ibais, iban
Preterite: fui, fuiste, fue; fuimos, fuisteis, fueron
Imperfect Subjunctive: (que) fuera (—se), fueras, etc.
Command: ve (tú)
Present Participle: yendo

oír *to hear*
Present Indicative: oigo, oyes, oye; oímos, oís, oyen
Present Subjunctive: (que) oiga, oigas, etc.
Preterite: oí, oíste, oyó; oímos, oísteis, oyeron
Imperfect Subjunctive: (que) oyera (—se), oyeras, etc.
Future: oiré, oirás, etc.
Conditional: oiría, oirías, etc.
Present Participle: oyendo
Past Participle: oído

poder *to be able*
Present Indicative: puedo, puedes, puede; podemos, podéis, pueden
Present Subjunctive: (que) pueda, puedas, pueda; podamos, podáis, puedan
Preterite: pude, pudiste, etc.
Imperfect Subjunctive: (que) pudiera (—se), pudieras, etc.

Future: podré, podrás, etc.
Conditional: podría, podrías, etc.
Present Participle: pudiendo

poner *to put*
Present Indicative: pongo, pones, etc.
Present Subjunctive: (que) ponga, pongas, etc.
Preterite: puse, pusiste, etc.
Imperfect Subjunctive: (que) pusiera (—se), pusieras, etc.
Future: pondré, pondrás, etc.
Conditional: pondría, pondrías, etc.
Command: pon (tú)
Past Participle: puesto

querer *to want; to love*
Present Indicative: quiero, quieres, quiere; queremos, queréis, quieren
Present Subjunctive: (que) quiera, quieras, quiera; queramos, queráis,
  quieran
Preterite: quise, quisiste, etc.
Imperfect Subjunctive: (que) quisiera (—se), quisieras, etc.
Future: querré, querrás, etc.
Conditional: querría, querrías, etc.

saber *to know*
Present Indicative: sé, sabes, etc.
Present Subjunctive: (que) sepa, sepas, etc.
Preterite: supe, supiste, etc.
Imperfect Subjunctive: (que) supiera (—se), supieras, etc.
Future: sabré, sabrás, etc.
Conditional: sabría, sabrías, etc.

salir *to go out, leave*
Present Indicative: salgo, sales, etc.
Present Subjunctive: (que) salga, salgas, etc.
Future: saldré, saldrás, etc.
Conditional: saldría, saldrías, etc.
Command: sal (tú)

ser *to be*
Present Indicative: soy, eres, es; somos, sois, son
Present Subjunctive: (que) sea, seas, etc.
Imperfect Indicative: era, eras, era; éramos, erais, eran
Preterite: fui, fuiste, fue; fuimos, fuisteis, fueron
Imperfect Subjunctive: (que) fuera (—se), fueras, etc.
Command: sé (tú)

tener *to have*
Present Indicative: tengo, tienes, tiene; tenemos, tenéis, tienen
Present Subjunctive: (que) tenga, tengas, etc.

Preterite: tuve, tuviste, etc.
Imperfect Subjunctive: (que) tuviera (—se), tuvieras, etc.
Future: tendré, tendrás, etc.
Conditional: tendría, tendrías, etc.
Command: ten (tú)

traer *to bring*
Present Indicative: traigo, traes, etc.
Present Subjunctive: (que) traiga, traigas, etc.
Preterite: traje, trajiste, trajo; trajimos, trajisteis, trajeron
Imperfect Subjunctive: (que) trajera (—se), trajeras, etc.
Present Participle: trayendo
Past Participle: traído

valer *to be worth*
Present Indicative: valgo, vales, etc.
Present Subjunctive: (que) valga, valgas, etc.
Future: valdré, valdrás, etc.
Conditional: valdría, valdrías, etc.

venir *to come*
Present Indicative: vengo, vienes, viene; venimos, venís, vienen
Present Subjunctive: (que) venga, vengas, etc.
Preterite: vine, viniste, etc.
Imperfect Subjunctive: (que) viniera (—se), vinieras, etc.
Future: vendré, vendrás, etc.
Conditional: vendría, vendrías, etc.
Command: ven (tú)
Present Participle: viniendo

ver *to see*
Present Indicative: veo, ves, ve; vemos, veis, ven
Present Subjunctive: (que) vea, veas, etc.
Imperfect Indicative: veía, veías, veía; veíamos, veíais, veían
Preterite: vi, viste, etc.
Imperfect Subjunctive: (que) viera (—se), vieras, etc.
Past Participle: visto

Vocabulary

SPANISH—ENGLISH

(**Note:** the Spanish-English vocabulary does not include easily recognizable cognates. Gender has not been indicated for masculine nouns ending in **-o**, and for feminine nouns ending in **-a, -ción, -dad, -tad, -tud,** or **-umbre.**)

A

a at; to; for; from; on; ___ (**los tres días**) after (three days)
abajo down
abierto open, opened
abogado lawyer
abono fertilizer; payment; installment; guarantee; endorsement; subscription
abrigo overcoat; shelter
abuela grandmother
abuelo grandfather; ___ -s grandfathers, grandparents
aburrido bored; boring
aburrir to bore
acabar to end, finish; ___ **de** to have just
acaloradamente heatedly
acción action; share of stock
acerca de about, concerning
acero steel
aconsejar to advise
acordarse (ue) (de) to remember
acostar (ue) to put to bed; ___ -se to go to bed
actriz *f.* actress
actual present (time)

acudir to rush, hasten, come (to the aid of)
acuerdo agreement; **estar de** ___ to be in agreement, agree
adelante forward, onward; **en** ___ henceforth, from now on
además (de) beside, besides; moreover, in addition (to)
adonde where (with verbs of motion)
aeropuerto airport
afortunado lucky, fortunate
afuera outside
agente *m.* policeman; agent
(el) **agua** *f.* water
aguantar to tolerate, stand, put up with
aguja needle
ahí there (near person addressed)
ahogarse to drown; to choke
ahora now
ahorcar to hang
ajo garlic
albañil *m.* mason, bricklayer
alegrarse (de) to be glad, happy (to)
alegre happy, cheerful, joyous
alejarse to go away, move off; to withdraw, be aloof

alemán German

algo something, anything; *(adv.)* somewhat

alguien someone, somebody; anyone, anybody

algún, alguno some, any; algunos a few, some

(el) alma *f.* soul

alquiler *m.* rent

alto tall

alumno pupil

allá there (over there)

allí there

(el) ama *f.* housewife

amable pleasant, nice, kind

amapola poppy

amar to love

amarillo yellow

amenazar to threaten

amigo (-a) friend

amistad acquaintance; friend (*m.* or *f.*); friendship

amor *m.* love

amorío love affair

ancho wide

andante: caballero ____ knight errant

andar *(irreg.)* to walk; to go

anidar to come to rest; to make a nest

animar to encourage

ánimo courage

anoche last night

ansia anxiety

antaño formerly, in the old days

antes before; *(prep.)* ____ de before; *(conj.)* ____ (de) que before; cuanto ____ as soon as possible

antiguo ancient, old; former

año year; tener (tres) ____ -s to be (three) years old; ¿Cuántos años tiene Ud.? How old are you?

aparecer (zc) to appear

apellido surname

aplastar to crush

aplazar to postpone

apoyar to support

aprender to learn

apresuradamente hurriedly, hastily

apresurarse (a) to hurry (to)

apuesta bet

apuntar to point, aim; to note (in writing); to mend, stitch; to sharpen

aquel (aquella) *(adj.)* that (over there); aquellos (aquellas) those; aquél etc. *(pron.)* that one, etc.

aquello *(neuter)* that

aquí here; por ____ this way, through here

árbol *m.* tree

archiduque *m.* archduke

arrastrar to drag (along)

arrepentirse (ie, i) to repent

arriba up

arrugado wrinkled

artista *m.* or *f.* artist; actor; actress

ascender (ie) to go up, rise

así thus, in this manner, that way

asistir (a) to attend

asombrar to amaze; ____ -se (de) to wonder; to be surprised

(el) aspa *f.* wing (of windmill)

asunto matter, subject

ataque *m.* attack

atreverse (a) to dare (to)

aumenter to increase

aun even

aún still, yet

aunque although, even though, even if

avión *m.* airplane

ayer yesterday

ayudar to help, assist

azúcar *m.* sugar

azul blue

B

bailar to dance

bailarín *m.* dancer (male); bailarina *f.* dancer (female)

baile *m.* dance

bajar to descend, go down

bajo under; *(adj.)* short

bandeja tray

baño bath; cuarto de ____ bathroom; traje de ____ bathing suit

barato cheap, inexpensive

barca boat

barco boat; ship; ____ de vela sailboat

barra (Argentina) "gang" of friends

barrio district

bastante enough; quite

bastar to be enough, suffice

bastón *m.* cane

beber   to drink
Bélgica   Belgium
belleza   beauty
bellota   acorn
bendito   blessed
besar   to kiss
beso   kiss
bien   well; very; good, fine; *m.*   good, benefit
billete *m.*   bill (money); ticket
blanco   white
bobo   fool, "dummy"
boca   mouth
boda   wedding
bola   ball
bolsa   bag (paper); handbag; stock exchange
bombón *m.*   candy, sweet
bonito   pretty
borbón *(noun, adj.)*   Bourbon
borracho   drunk; *(noun)* drunkard
borrador *m.*   eraser
borrar   to erase
bosque *m.*   woods, forest
bostezar   to yawn
bote *m.*   (row) boat
brazo   arm
bromear   to joke
buen(o)   good
burlón   scoffing, mocking; *(noun)* scoffer
busca   search; en ___ de   in search of
buscar   to look for

C

caballero   gentleman; knight
caballo   horse
cabello   hair
caber *(irreg.)*   to fit
cabeza   head
cada   each, every
cadáver *m.*   body (corpse)
caer *(irreg.)*   to fall; ___ -se   to fall; dejar ___   to drop
café *m.*   café; coffee
cafetera   coffee pot
caja   box; cash register
cajera   cashier
cajón *m.*   drawer (of a chest or desk)
calabacero   pumpkin farmer
calabaza   pumpkin

calentar (ie)   to heat
caliente   warm, hot
calor *m.*   warmth, heat; hace ___   it is warm (weather); tener ___   to be warm (person)
calzones *m. pl.*   trousers, breeches
callar(se)   to keep quiet
calle *f.*   street
camarero   waiter
cambiar   to change; to exchange
cambio   exchange; change; a ___ de   in place of; en ___ on the other hand
caminar   to walk
camino   road; way; seguir el ___   to continue on one's way
camisa   shirt
campana   bell
canción   song
cansado   tired; tiresome
cansar   to tire; to bore; ___ -se   to become tired
cantar   to sing
cantante *m.* or *f.*   singer
capaz   capable
capítulo   chapter
cara   face
cárcel *f.*   jail
caro   dear, expensive
carrera   race; career
carta   letter
cartero   mailman
casa   house, home; a ___   home (with verb of motion); en ___   at home; salir de ___   to leave the house
casado   married
casar   to marry, match; ___ -se (con)   to get married (to)
casi   almost
caso   case; hacer ___ (a or de)   to pay attention (to), heed
castigar   to punish
ceder   to yield, give in
ceja   eyebrow
celos *m.*   jealousy; tener ___   to be jealous
centena   hundred
centro   center; downtown
cereza   cherry
cerrar (ie)   to close
cerveza   beer

cielo sky; heaven

cine *m.* cinema, movies

cirujano surgeon

ciudad city

claro clear; clearly; certainly, of course

clavel *m.* carnation

cobre *m.* copper

cocinar to cook

coche *m.* car, automobile; carriage

coger to seize, catch; to take; to pick up

colegial *m.* schoolboy

colegio school

cólera anger

colgar(se) (ue) to hang (oneself)

colina hill

comedia play, comedy

comenzar (ie) to begin, commence

comer to eat; ___ -se to eat up

comida meal; food

como *(adv.)* as, as though, like, such as; how; *(conj.)* since, as long as; ¿Cómo? What? How?; ¡Cómo no! Of course!

cómoda chest of drawers

cómodo comfortable

compañero companion; ___ de cuarto roommate

compartir to share

compasivo compassionate, sympathetic

complacer (zc) to please

comportarse to behave

compra purchase; ir de ___ -s to go shopping

comprar to buy

comprender to understand, comprehend

compromiso engagement (to marry); appointment, date

conducir (zc) to lead; to drive (a car)

conejo rabbit

conferencia lecture; conference

conmigo with me

conmoverse (ue) to be moved, affected

conocer (zc) to know, be acquainted with; to meet, make one's acquaintance

conocido known, well-known

conseguir (i, i) to obtain; to succeed in

consistir en to consist of (be based upon)

contestar to answer

contigo with you

contra against

contrario contrary; al ___ on the contrary

convenir *(irreg.)* to be suitable, necessary, a good idea

convertir (ie, i) to be suitable, to change

copa goblet

corazón *m.* heart; corazoncito darling

corbata necktie

correo mail; oficina de ___ -s post office

correr to run

cortar to cut

corte *f.* court (of justice); *(m.)* cut

cosa thing

cosecha harvest

coser to sew

crear to create

creer to think, believe

criada servant, maid

cruz *f.* cross

cruzar to cross

cuaderno notebook

cual like, as; cada ___ each one; el (la) ___ , los (las) ___ -es who, the one(s) who, whom, which; lo ___ which; ¿cuál? which? which one? what (which)?

cualquier(a) any; anyone (at all)

cuando when, whenever; de vez en ___ from time to time

cuanto as much as, as many as; all that; ___ antes as soon as possible; en ___ as soon as; ¿cuánto? how much?; ¿cuántos? how many?

cuarto quarter; room

cubierto (de) covered (with)

cucaracha cockroach

cuchara spoon

cuchillo knife

cuenta bill (in a restaurant); account; tener en ___ to bear in mind, take into account

cuero leather

cuerpo body
cuidado care; **tener** ___ to be careful
cuidadoso careful
cuidar (de) to take care (of)
culpa blame; fault; **tener la** ___ to be to blame
culpable guilty
cumbre summit
cumpleaños *m.* birthday
cura *m.* priest
cuyo whose

Ch

chaqueta jacket
charla talk, chat
charlar to chat, talk
chico (-a) boy, girl; **chiquillo (-a)** little boy, little girl
chocar to collide
chófer (chofer) *m.* chauffeur; driver
choque *m.* collision

D

daño damage, harm; **hacer(se)** ___ to hurt (oneself)
dar *(irreg.)* to give; **dar en** to strike, hit; ___ **-se cuenta de** to realize, take into account
de of; from; about; in; by; made of; as, with
debajo (de) beneath, underneath
deber to be obliged to; should, ought to; to owe
decano dean
decir *(irreg.)* to say, tell; **es** ___ that is (to say)
dedo finger
dejar to leave (behind), abandon; to let, allow; ___ **de+**inf. to stop; **no** ___ **de** not to fail to
delgado slim, thin
demasiado too, too much
deporte *m.* sport
derecho right; straight ahead; *(noun)* law; (customs) duty; **a la derecha** to (on) the right
derrota defeat
desagradable unpleasant
desarrollo development
desatar to untie
desayuno breakfast

descuidar to neglect
desde from, since
desdeñar to scorn, disdain
desear to want, wish, desire
desgracia misfortune
desgraciadamente unfortunately
desmayarse to faint
despacio slow(ly)
despedir (i, i) to dismiss, fire, send away; ___ **-se (de)** to take leave (of), say goodbye (to)
despertar (ie) to awaken; to wake up; ___ **-se** to wake up
despreciar to scorn
después afterwards; then, later; ___ **(de)** after
desvanecerse (zc) to faint
detrás (de) behind, in back of
devolver (ue) to return, give back
día *m.* day; **de** ___ by day, in the daytime; **hoy (en)** ___ nowadays
dibujo drawing, sketch
difícil difficult
dinero money
dios, diosa god, goddess; **Dios** God; **¡Dios mío!** For Heaven's sake!
dirección address
dirigir to address; to direct; ___ **-se a** to address; to go to
discurso speech; **pronunciar un** ___ to make a speech
discutir to discuss; to argue
disfrutar (de) to enjoy, have the benefit of
disparar to shoot, fire; to go off (gun)
disparate *m.* nonsense
distinto different
distraído absent-minded
divertirse (ie, i) to enjoy oneself, have a good time
doblar to fold; to turn (a corner)
doler (ue) to ache, hurt; **me duele la cabeza** my head aches
dolor *m.* pain, grief, sorrow
domingo Sunday
donde where, in which; ___ **-quiera** wherever
dormir (ue, u) to sleep; ___ **-se** to fall asleep, go to sleep
dos two; **los** ___ both
dramaturgo dramatist, playwright

dudar to doubt
dulce sweet
durante during
duro hard

E

e and (before words beginning with **i** or **hi**, except **hie**)
ebrio drunk
echar to throw; to mail; ____ **de menos** to miss
edad age; **¿Qué edad tiene?** How old is he / she?
eficaz efficient
ejercicio exercise
ejército army
el the; ____ **que** he who, the one who; **los que** those who, the ones who
elegir (i, i) to elect; to select
embargo; sin ____ however, nevertheless
embestir (i, i) to attack, assail
emocionante exciting, emotional
empeñarse (en) to insist (upon)
empezar (ie) (a) to begin (to)
empleado employee
en in; into; at; on; ____ **casa** at home; ____ **cuanto** as soon as; ____ **punto** on the dot; ____ **vez de** instead of
enamorado (de) in love (with)
enamorarse (de) to fall in love (with)
encantador charming
encantar to delight, charm, enchant; **le encanta bailar** she loves to dance
encanto charm
encender (ie) to light; to turn on (a light)
encontrar (ue) to find, meet; ____ **-se (con)** to meet (with), run into
enfermarse to become (get) sick
enfermo sick, ill
engordar(se) to get fat
enojar to anger, annoy; ____ **-se** to become (get) angry
ensayo essay
enseñar to teach; to show
entender (ie) to understand
enterarse (de) to find out (about), become informed (about)
enterrar (ie) to bury

entonces then, at that time
entrada entrance; ticket (to a movie, theater, etc.)
entre among, between
entregar to deliver, hand over
entretanto meanwhile, in the meantime
enviar to send
envuelto enveloped, wrapped
equipaje *m.* baggage, bags
equipo team
equivocarse to make a mistake, be mistaken
escándalo uproar, row, scandal
escaparate *m.* shop window
escoger to choose
esconder(se) to hide (oneself)
escribir to write
escritor *m.* writer
escuchar to listen (to)
escudero squire (of a knight)
escuela school
ese (-a, -os, -as) *(adj.)* that, those; **ése**, etc. *(pron.)* that one, those
esforzarse (ue) (por) to strive (to)
esmeralda emerald
eso *(pron.)* that; ____ **es** that's it; **por** ____ for that reason, therefore
espantar to frighten
español Spanish; *(m.)* Spaniard
especializarse to specialize; to major
espectro ghost
esperanza hope
esperar to hope; to wait (for); to expect
esposo (-a) husband, wife
esquiar to ski
estado state
estar *(irreg.)* to be; **está bien** all right
este (-a, -os, -as) *(adj.)* this, these; *(pron.)* **éste**, etc. this one, these
estimado esteemed, highly regarded
esto *(pron.)* this
estómago stomach
estropear to damage
estudiantil *(adj.)* student; scholastic
estudiar to study
exigir to demand, require
éxito success
explicación explanation
explicar to explain

exterior: política ____ foreign policy
extranjero foreign, foreigner

F

fácil easy

falta lack; hacer ____ to need, be lacking; me hace mucha falta I need it very badly

faltar to need, be lacking; ____ (a) to be absent (from)

farra wild time, spree

fe *f.* faith

fecha date

felicidad happiness

feliz happy

feo ugly

feroz ferocious

fiesta fiesta; holiday; party

fin *m.* end; a fines de at the end of; dar ____ (a) to put an end (to); por ____ finally

final: al ____ at the end

fingir to pretend

flaqueza weakness

flor *f.* flower

fósforo match

francés French; *(m.)* Frenchman

frase *f.* phrase, sentence

frente *m.* front; *(f.)* forehead

fresco fresh

frío cold; hace ____ it is cold (weather); tener ____ to be cold (person)

frontera border, boundary

fuente *f.* fountain; source; serving bowl, platter

fuera (de) out, outside (of)

fulano so and so

fumar to smoke

función function; performance (theater, film, etc.)

funcionar to work, function

fusilar to shoot, execute

fútbol *m.* soccer; ____ americano football

G

gana desire; de buena ____ willingly; de mala ____ unwillingly; tener ____ -s (de) to feel like (doing something)

ganar to earn; to win; to gain

garbanzo chick pea

gastar to spend (money)

gaviota sea gull

general: por lo ____ in general

gente *f.* people

gesto gesture, face (expression)

gigante *m.* giant

gobierno government

golosina sweet, candy

golpe *m.* blow

gordo fat

gota drop

gozar (de) to enjoy; to possess

gracia grace, beauty; ____ -s thanks, thank you

gran(de) big, large; great

granizar to hail (storm)

granizo hail (stone)

griego Greek

gris gray

gritar to shout

grueso thick; stout

guante *m.* glove

guapo handsome

guardar to keep, preserve

guerra war

guisante *m.* pea

guisar to cook

gustar to be pleasing; to like; ____ más to like better (best), prefer

gusto pleasure; taste

H

haber to have *(as auxiliary verb);* ____ de to be (supposed) to; hay there is, there are; había there was, there were

hábil skillful

hablador talkative

hablar to speak

hacendoso diligent

hacer *(irreg.)* to make, do; hace buen (mal) tiempo the weather is good (bad); hace calor it is warm; hace frío it is cold; hace viento it is windy; ¿Qué tiempo hace? What is the weather like?; hace (un año) + *pret.* or *imp.* (one year) ago; hace (un año) que + *pres.* for (one year) . . . ;

¿Cuánto tiempo hace ... ? How long has it been . . . ?; ____ **caso a** (or **de**) to pay attention to, heed; ____ **un papel** to play a role; ____ **un viaje** to take a trip; ____ **-se** to become; ____ **(-se) daño** to hurt (oneself); ____ **-se tarde** to be (get) late

(el) **hacha** *f.* axe

hallar to find

(el) **hambre** *f.* hunger; **tener** ____ to be hungry

hasta even; until

hay there is, there are; ____ **que** it is necessary, one must

hechicero bewitching, enchanting

helado ice cream

herido wounded

hermano(-a) brother, sister; ____ **-s** brothers; brother(s) and sister(s)

hermoso beautiful

hermosura beauty

hielo ice

hierba grass

hierro iron

hijo son; ____ **-s** sons; children

hilo thread

historiador *m.* historian

hoja leaf

hojalata tin plate

hola hello

hombre *m.* man

honrado honest

hora hour; time; **¿A qué** ____ **?** At what time?; **es** ____ **de** it is time to; **¿Qué** ____ **es?** What time is it?

hortelano vegetable farmer

hospedar to give lodging

hoy today; ____ **(en) día** nowadays

huerta orchard; vegetable garden

hueso bone

huevo egg

huir to flee, run away

húmedo humid

hundir to submerge, drown; ____ **-se** to sink, drown

I

idioma *m.* language

idolatrar to idolize

igual equal; **al** ____ **que** the same as

impedir *(i, i)* to impede, prevent

impermeable *m.* raincoat

importar to matter, be important; **no me importa** it doesn't matter to me

incaico Incan

indio Indian

influir to influence

ingeniero engineer

Inglaterra England

ingrato ungrateful

inolvidable unforgettable

inquilino tenant

invadir to invade

invierno winter

invitado guest

ir *(irreg.)* to go; ____ **-se** to go (away), leave; **¡qué va!** go on! nonsense!

irlandés Irish; *m.* Irishman

izquierdo left; **a la izquierda** to (on) the left

J

jardín *m.* garden

jefe *m.* chief, head, boss

joven *m.* or *f.* young man; young woman; *(adj.)* young

jueves *m.* Thursday

juez *m.* or *f.* judge

jugador *m.* player

jugar (ue) to play (a game); ____ **al tenis** to play tennis

junto(s) together; **junto a** near, next to

jurar to swear

juventud *f.* youth

K

kilo(gramo) kilogram (2.2 lbs.)

kilómetro kilometer ($\frac{5}{8}$ of a mile)

L

la the; her; it; you; ____ **que** she who, the one who; **las que** the ones *(f.)* who

labrador *m.* farmer

ladrón *m.* thief, crook

lana wool

lápiz *m.* pencil

lástima pity

lavar(se) to wash (oneself)

leal loyal

lección lesson
leer to read
legumbre *f.* vegetable
lejos far; a lo ____ in the distance
lengua language
lento slow
letrero sign
levantar to raise, lift; ____ -se to get up
ley *f.* law
libre free
libro book
líder *m.* leader
limpiar to clean
lindo pretty, beautiful
lío difficulty, mess
listo ready; smart, clever; estar ____ to be ready; ser ____ to be smart, clever
litro liter (slightly more than a quart)
loco crazy, insane
lograr to succeed in, achieve
luchar to fight, struggle
luego then, afterwards
lugar *m.* place, town; tener ____ to take place
lumbre light
luna moon; hay ____ the moon is out
lunar *m.* mole, beauty mark
lunes *m.* Monday
luz *f.* light

Ll

llamar to call; ____ la atención to attract attention; ____ por teléfono to phone; ____ -se to be named, called
llanto crying, weeping
llegar to arrive; ____ tarde to arrive late, to be late; ____ a ser to become (get to be)
lleno full; ____ de filled with, full of
llevar to carry, bring; to wear; ____ una vida to lead a life; ____ -se to take (along), to carry off; ____ -se bien to get along well
llover (ue) to rain
lluvia rain

M

madrugada (early) morning
maestro (-a) teacher

mago magician
maíz *m.* corn
mal *m.* bad, evil
mal(o) bad; badly; hace mal tiempo the weather is bad
malagueña woman from Málaga
maleta suitcase, valise; hacer la(s) ____ (s) to pack one's bag(s)
mandar to send; to command, order
manejar to drive (a car)
mano *f.* hand
manzana apple
mañana morning; tomorrow; de la ____ A.M. (with time of day); por la ____ in the morning
mañanitas morning songs
máquina machine
marco frame
marido husband
marinero sailor
martes *m.* Tuesday
más more; most; ____ de more than (before a number); ____ que more than; ¿qué ____ ? what else?
matar to kill
matricularse to register (for a course)
matrimonio matrimony; married couple
mayor greater, greatest; older, oldest; big, major; serious
medianoche *f.* midnight
médico doctor
medio means; por ____ de by means of
mejor better, best
menor less, least; younger, youngest; smaller, smallest
menos less; least; except; minus; a ____ que unless; por lo ____ at least
mensajero messenger
mente *f.* mind
mentir (ie, i) to lie, tell a lie
mentiroso liar
menudo: a ____ often
mercado market
merecer (zc) to merit, deserve
mes *m.* month
mesa table, desk
meter to put (in); to insert; la luna se metió the moon set

miedo fear; **tener** ____ to be afraid
miel *f.* honey
mientras (que) while
miércoles *m.* Wednesday
mil one thousand
mirar to look (at), watch
mismo same; very; **ahora** ____ right now; **aquí** ____ right here; **hoy** ____ this very day
mitad *f.* half
mixteca Mixtecan (Mexican Indian tribe)
modista dressmaker
mojar to wet; ____ **-se** to get wet
molestar to bother, annoy
molino mill; ____ **de viento** windmill
mono cute; *(m.)* monkey
montar to mount; to assemble (machinery); ____ **a caballo** to ride horseback
morder (ue) to bite
moreno dark, brunet(te)
morir (ue, u) (-se) to die
motocicleta motorcycle
mozo young man; porter; waiter
muchacha girl
muchachada group of friends
muchacho boy
muchedumbre crowd
mucho much, a great deal; ____ **-s, (-as)** many
mudarse to move (one's home)
muerte *f.* death; **de mala** ____ of little importance (insignificant)
muerto dead
mujer *f.* woman; wife
mundial *(adj.)* world
mundo world; **todo el** ____ everybody
muñequita little doll (*dim.* of **muñeca**)
muy very

N

nacer (zc) to be born
nacimiento birth
nada nothing; (not) anything
nadar to swim
nadie no one, nobody; (not) anyone, (not) anybody
naranja orange
nariz *f.* nose
necesitar to need

negar (ie) to deny
negocio(s) business
negro black
nevar (ie) to snow
nevera refrigerator
ni nor; not even; ____ ... ____ neither . . . nor
nieve *f.* snow
ningún, ninguno no; no one or none (of a group); not any; neither (of them); **de ningún modo, de ninguna manera** not at all
niño (-a) little boy, little girl
noche *f.* night; **de** ____ at night; **de la** ____ P.M. (with time of day); **esta** ____ tonight; **por la** ____ at night
nombrar to name; to appoint
nombre *m.* name
nota note; grade
noticia(s) news
novio (-a) boyfriend, girlfriend; fiancé(e)
nube *f.* cloud
nuevo new; **de** ____ again
nunca never, (not) ever

O

o or; ____ ... ____ either . . . or
obedecer (zc) to obey
obsequiar to treat, make a gift to; to flatter with attention; to court
odiar to hate
ojalá I hope that . . ., I wish that . . ., if only
ojo eye; ¡ ____ ! look out!
olvidar to forget; ____ **-se de** to forget; **olvidársele** to forget, **se me olvidó hacerlo** I forgot to do it
orden *f.* order, command; *m.* order (chronological, physical, etc.)
oreja ear
orilla shore
oro gold
otro other, another; **otra vez** again

P

padre *m.* father; ____ **-s** father(s) and mother(s), parents
pagar to pay (for)
página page

país *m.* country, nation
palabra word
pálido pale
paloma dove
papa *m.* pope
papel *m.* paper; **hacer un** ____ to play a role
paquete *m.* package
par *m.* pair; **sin** ____ without peer
para for, for the purpose of; in order to; by (a certain time); toward; ____ **que** so that; ¿ ____ **qué?** why?; **estar** ____ to be about to
paraguas *m.* umbrella
paraíso paradise
parar(se) to stop
parecer **(zc)** to seem, appear; ____ **-se (a)** to resemble
pared *f.* wall
pareja couple
pariente *m.* or *f.* relative
parpadear to wink, blink
parte *f.* part; **en (por) todas** ____ **-s** everywhere
partido game (match); ____ **de fútbol** soccer game
pasado past, last; **el mes** ____ last month
pasar to happen; to pass; to spend (time); ¿**qué le pasa?** what is the matter with you (her, him)?; ¿**qué pasa?** what is the matter?
paseo walk, ride; **dar un** ____ to take a walk, ride
pastel *m.* pie, pastry
patria fatherland
paz *f.* peace
pedazo piece
pedir **(i, i)** to ask (for), request
pegar to stick, attach; to hit, strike
pelear to fight; to quarrel, argue
película film, movie
peligro danger
pelo hair; **tomar el** ____ to "kid," tease
pena grief; distress; **valer la** ____ to be worthwhile
penar to grieve, worry
pensar **(ie)** to think; to intend; ____ **en** to think about (turn one's thoughts to); ____ **de** to think about (opinion)

peor worse; worst; **de mal en** ____ from bad to worse
pequeño small, little
perder **(ie)** to lose
perdidamente wildly, hopelessly
perezoso lazy
perla pearl
pero but
perro dog
perseguir **(i, i)** to pursue, follow closely; to persecute
personaje *m.* person (of importance); character
pesado heavy; boring
pescar to fish
picaflor *m.* hummingbird
pico beak; point; bit; **El sombrero de tres picos** The Three-Cornered Hat; **las siete y** ____ a little after seven
piedra rock, stone
pierna leg
pino pine tree
pintar to paint
pintoresco picturesque
pintura painting
piscina swimming pool
pizarra chalkboard, blackboard
plata silver; money *(colloquial)*
platino platinum
playa beach, shore
plaza plaza, square; bull ring
población population
pobre poor; unfortunate; (*m.* or *f.*) poor man, poor woman
pobreza poverty
poco little; **por** ____ almost; ____ **-s** few, a few, some
poder **(ue)** *(irreg.)* to be able
poderoso powerful
política policy; politics
político political *(adj.);* politician
pollo chicken
poner *(irreg.)* to put, place; ____ **un telegrama** to send a telegram; ____ **-se** to put on (clothing); ____ **-se a + *inf.*** to begin; ____ **-se + *adj.*** to become (get); ____ **-se de acuerdo** to come to an agreement
por for, because of; on account of; for the sake of; by; per; through,

throughout; along; around; in place of; in exchange for; during; ____ **favor** please

porteño resident of Buenos Aires

preferir (ie, i) to prefer

pregunta question; **hacer una** ____ to ask a question

preguntar to ask; ____ **por** to ask for, inquire about; ____ **-se** to ask oneself, wonder

premio prize

prender to arrest

prestar to lend; ____ **atención** to pay attention

prever to foresee

primer(o) first

primo (-a) cousin

príncipe *m.* prince

prisa hurry; **tener** ____ to be in a hurry

probar (ue) to prove; to taste (food); to try

prometer to promise

pronto soon; **de** ____ suddenly

propio one's own

propósito purpose; **a** ____ by the way

proteger to protect

próximo next

prueba proof; test

publicar to publish

pueblo town, village; people

puerta door

pues well, then; since (because)

puesto vendor's stand; post, job

Q

que that; which; who; whom; **el mismo** ____ the same as; **lo** ____ what (that which); **más (menos)** ____ more (less) than; **¿qué ... ?** what (which) . . . ?; **¡qué ... !** what (a) . . . !; **¡qué va!** go on! nonsense!

quedar(se) to remain, stay; to be (result of an action)

quejarse (de) to complain (about)

querer (ie) *(irreg.)* to wish, want; to love; ____ **decir** to mean

querido dear, darling, beloved

quien (-es) who, whom; he (she, they) who, the one(s) who; **¿de quién(-es)?** whose?

quienquiera whoever

quinientos five hundred

quitar to take away, remove; to take off, take from; ____ **-se** to take (clothing) off (oneself)

quizá(s) perhaps, maybe

R

rancherita girl who lives or works on a ranch

rango rank

raro strange; rare

rascacielos *m.* skyscraper

rato little while; short time; **al poco** ____ after a while

ratoncito mouse

rayo ray, lightning

razón *f.* reason; **tener** ____ to be right; **no tener** ____ to be wrong

realizar to realize, fulfill, accomplish

rebelde *m.* or *f.* rebel

recibir to receive

recibo receipt

recoger to pick (up), gather

recordar (ue) to remember

recto straight

recuerdo remembrance, souvenir

refresco soft drink, refreshment

regalar to give (a gift) (of)

regalo gift, present

reglamento rule, regulation

regresar to return, go (come) back

reina queen

reinado reign

reino kingdom

reír(se) (i, i) (de) to laugh (at)

reloj *m.* watch, clock

reñir (i, i) to scold; to quarrel; to fight; ____ **-se** to quarrel; to fight

repartir to distribute

repente; de ____ suddenly

repetir (i, i) to repeat

repicar to tap

resbalar(se) to slip, slide; to skid

respuesta answer

resultar to turn out, result

retrato photograph, portrait

reunir to gather, collect; ____ **-se** to meet

revista magazine; review; ____ **musical** musical comedy

rey *m.* king; ___ -es kings, king(s) and queen(s)

rico rich; delicious; *(m.)* rich man

riña quarrel; fight

riqueza wealth

robar to steal

rodar (ue) to roll

rodilla knee; **de** ___ -s on one's knees

rogar (ue) to beg, beseech

rojo red

romance Romance (derived from Latin); **lenguas** ___ -s Romance languages

romper to break, tear

ropa clothing

ruido noise

ruta route

S

sábado Saturday

saber *(irreg.)* to know, find out; ___ + *inf.* to know how to; ___ **a** to taste of

sacar to take out, pull out; to get, obtain (grades)

sacerdote *m.* priest

sal *f.* salt

sala living room

saleroso witty, lively, charming

salir *(irreg.)* to go out, leave; ___ **bien (mejor)** to do well (better); ___ **bien (mal) en un examen** to pass (fail) an exam; ___ **de casa** to leave the house

salón *m.* large room; classroom

salud *f.* health

saludar to greet

salvar to save

sed *f.* thirst; **tener** ___ to be thirsty

seguida: en ___ at once, immediately

seguir (i, i) to follow; to continue, keep on; to take (a course)

según according to

segundo second

seguro sure, certain; safe

semáforo traffic light

semana week; **la** ___ **que viene** next week

sentado seated, sitting down

sentarse (ie) to sit down

sentir (ie, i) to feel (something); to feel sorry, regret; ___ **-se** to feel

señal *f.* sign

señalar to point out, indicate

señor *m.* Mr., sir; gentleman

señora Mrs., lady; madam

señorita Miss; young lady

ser *(irreg.)* to be; ___ **de** to become of, to happen to; to be made of; to come (be) from

servir (i, i) to serve; ___ **de** to serve as

si if; whether; **como** ___ as if

sí yes; **para** ___ to himself, herself, etc.

siempre always; **para** ___ always, forever

siglo century

siguiente following, next; **al día** ___ (on) the following day

silueta silhouette

silla chair

simpático nice, likable, congenial

sin without

sino (que) but, but rather

sinvergüenza *m.* or *f.* scoundrel

siquiera: ni ___ not even

sitio place

sobre about; over; on top of; on; *(m.)* envelope

sobrino (-a) nephew, niece

socio member; partner

sol *m.* sun; **hace (hay)** ___ it is sunny

soldado soldier

soler (ue) to be accustomed to, be in the habit of

solo alone, lone; simple

sólo only

soltar (ue) to let go; to loosen

soltero (-a) bachelor; unmarried woman

sombrero hat

sonar (ue) to sound; to ring (a bell)

sonreír(se) (i, i) to smile

sonrisa smile

soñar (ue) (con) to dream (about)

sorprender to surprise

sortija ring

suceder to happen

sucio dirty

suegro (-a) father-in-law; mother-in-law

sueldo salary

suelo land, soil, ground

sueño dream; sleep; tener ____ to be sleepy

suerte *f.* luck; fate, destiny; tener ____ to be lucky, fortunate

suéter *m.* sweater

sugerir (ie, i) to suggest

sumamente very, extremely

suntuoso sumptuous, lavish

suponer *(irreg.)* to suppose

supuesto: por ____ of course

sur *m.* south

surtido supply, assortment

suspirar to sigh

T

tacaño miserly, stingy

tachuela tack

tal such (a); con ____ (de) que provided that; ____ vez perhaps; ¿qué ____ ? how goes it?; ¿qué tal ... ? how . . . ?

talonario: libro ____ stub book

tallar to cut, carve; to deal (cards)

tallo stalk, stem

también also, too

tampoco neither, (not) either

tan as; so; ____ ... como as . . . as

tanto so much, as much; ____ peor so much the worse; ____ -s as many, so many; ____ (-s) como as much (many) as; ____ (-s) ... como as much (many) . . . as

taquilla box office

tardar (en) to be late, delay; to take (a certain amount of time) to

tarde late; *f.* afternoon

tarea homework

taza cup

té *m.* tea

televisor *m.* television set

tema *m.* subject, theme

temer to fear, be afraid (of)

temprano early

tener *(irreg.)* to have, possess; ____ (tres) años to be (three) years old; ____ calor to be warm; ____ celos to be jealous; ____ cuidado to be careful; ____ en cuenta to bear in mind, take into account; ____ éxito to be successful; ____ frío to be cold; ____ ganas (de) to feel like doing something; ____ hambre to be hungry; ____ la culpa to be guilty, be to blame; ____ lugar to take place; ____ miedo to be afraid; ____ prisa to be in a hurry; ____ que + *inf.* to have to, must; _ razón to be right; no ____ razón to be wrong; ____ sueño to be sleepy; ____ suerte to be lucky; ____ vergüenza to be ashamed; ¿qué tiene Ud.? (él, ella) what is the matter with you? (him, her); ¿qué edad tiene (Ana)? how old is (Ana)?

teniente *m.* lieutenant

tercer(o) third

tiempo time; weather; a ____ in time, on time; ¿cuánto ____ hace ... ? how long . . . ?

tienda store

tinta ink

tío (-a) uncle, aunt; ____ -s uncles; aunt(s) and uncle(s)

tiranizar to tyrannize

tiza chalk, piece of chalk

tocadiscos *m.* record player

tocar to touch; to play (a musical instrument); me toca a mí it belongs to me; it's my turn

todavía yet, still; ____ no not yet

todo all; every; whole; ____ el día all day; todos los días every day

tomar to take; to drink; ____ el pelo to tease; to "kid"

tonto foolish; *(m.)* fool

torear to fight bulls

torero bull fighter

trabajador hardworking

trabajar to work

trabajo work

traducir (zc) to translate

traer *(irreg.)* to bring, carry

traje *m.* suit; dress; ____ de baño bathing suit

trama plot

trasladarse to move (one's home, office, etc.)

tratar to treat; ____ (**de**) to try (to), to deal (with)

tren *m.* train

tribu *f.* tribe

triste sad

tristeza sadness

tropa troop

tropel *m.* crowd, mob; jumble, confusion

U

u or (before word beginning with **o** or **ho**)

último last

único unique; only

unir to unite, join

uña fingernail, toenail

uva grape

V

vacaciones *f. pl.:* **estar de** ____ to be on vacation

vago lazy; vague

valer (*irreg.*) to be worth, cost; ____ **la pena** to be worth while;

vale O.K.

vals *m.* waltz

varios several

varón *m.* male child; man

vaso glass

vecino neighbor; resident

vela sail; **barco de** ____ sailboat

vencer to win, overcome, conquer

vendedor *m.* seller, vendor

vender to sell

venir (*irreg.*) to come; (**el año**) **que viene** next (year); **viene haciéndose** is (gradually) becoming

ventana window

ver (*irreg.*) to see; **tener que** ____ **con** to have to do with

verano summer

verdad *f.* truth; ¿**verdad?** right? isn't that so?

verdadero true

verde green

verduras vegetables, greens

vergüenza shame; **tener** ____ to be ashamed

vestido dress

vestir(se) (**i, i**) to dress (oneself)

vez *f.* time; **de** ____ **en cuando** from time to time; **otra** ____ again; **por primera** ____ for the first time; **tal** ____ perhaps; **una** ____ once; **dos veces,** twice, etc.

viajar to travel

viaje *m.* trip; **¡buen** ____ **!** have a good trip!; **hacer un** ____ to take a trip

vicio vice, bad habit

vida life

viejo old; old man

viento wind; **hacer** ____ to be windy

viernes *m.* Friday

vino wine

virtud virtue

vivir to live

vivo lively, vivacious, alive

volar (**ue**) to fly

volver (**ue**) to return; to turn; ____ **a** + *inf.* (to do something) again; ____ **en sí** to regain consciousness; ____ **loco** to drive crazy; ____ **-se** to become, turn into; ____ **-se loco** to go (become) crazy

voz *f.* voice

Y

y and

ya already; now; ____ **no** no longer

Z

zanahoria carrot

zapato shoe

zarzuela *zarzuela* (musical comedy or operetta)

English—Spanish

A

able: to be ____ poder (ue) *(irreg.)*
about de, acerca de; **to be ____ to**
  estar para, estar a punto de
accident accidente *m.*
acquainted: to be ____ with conocer (zc)
actor actor *m.*
actress actriz *f.*
advise aconsejar
afraid: to be ____ (of) tener miedo
  (de), temer
afterwards después, luego,
  más tarde
again otra vez, de nuevo; volver (ue)
  a + *inf.*
ago: (four months) ____ hace (cuatro
  meses)
agreement acuerdo; **to come to**
  an ____ ponerse de acuerdo
alcohol alcohol *m.*
allow dejar, permitir
almost casi
although aunque
always siempre
among entre
angry enfadado, enojado
animate animar
another otro
answer respuesta, contestación; *(v.)*
  responder, contestar
any algún, alguno

anyone alguien; **____ at all**
  cualquier(a)
anything algo; **____ at all** cualquier
  cosa; nada *(neg.)*
anywhere en cualquier parte; en
  ninguna parte *(neg.)*
apparently por lo visto, al parecer
arrive llegar (a)
ashamed avergonzado; **to be ____**
  estar avergonzado, avergonzarse,
  tener vergüenza
ask preguntar (question); **____ a**
  question hacer una pregunta;
  ____ for preguntar por; **____ (for)**
  (request) pedir (i, i)
astonished atónito, asombrado
attention atención; **to pay ____**
  prestar atención; hacer caso a (de)
  (heed)
attractive bello, hermoso, guapo
author autor(-a)

B

bad mal *m.; (adj.)* mal(o); **from ____**
  to worse de mal en peor
badly mal
bag maleta (**baggage**)
bank banco
baseball béisbol *m.*
be ser; estar; **to ____ from** ser de;
  they are to . . . han de ...
beach playa

bear: to ____ in mind tener en cuenta
beautiful hermoso, bello, lindo, bonito
beauty belleza
because porque; **____ of** a causa de; por
bed cama; **to go to ____** acostarse (ue)
beer cerveza
before antes (de); delante (de)
beg rogar (ue); suplicar
begin empezar (ie) (a), comenzar (ie) (a), ponerse a + *inf.*
believe creer
best mejor; **the ____ part** lo mejor; **best-looking** (el) más guapo
better mejor; **it is ____** es mejor, más vale; **____ than ever** mejor que nunca
big grande
bird pájaro
birthday cumpleaños *m.;* **____ party** fiesta de cumpleaños
bite morder (ue)
black negro
blackboard pizarra
blame culpa; **to be to ____** tener la culpa
blind ciego
blue azul
boat barco, bote *m.*
book libro
bored aburrido; **boring** aburrido
born: to be ____ nacer (zc)
bother *(v.)* molestar
boyfriend novio
Brazil el Brasil
break *(v.)* romper
bright inteligente, listo (**smart**)
broom escoba
brother hermano
building edificio
bullfight corrida (de toros)
busy ocupado
but pero; sino, sino que
buy comprar

C

candy bombón *m.,* caramelo
car coche *m.,* carro
career carrera
careful cuidadoso; **to be ____** tener cuidado

cat gato
chair silla
change *(v.)* cambiar
chapter capítulo
character personaje *m.*
Charles V Carlos Quinto
charming encantador
chemistry química
children niños; hijos
China la China
choose escoger
city ciudad
class clase *f.*
classroom sala (de clase), salón *m.,* aula
clean limpio; *(v.)* limpiar
close *(v.)* cerrar (ie)
coffee café *m.;* **____ pot** cafetera
cold frío; **it is ____** hace frío; **to be ____** tener frío (person)
college universidad
come venir *(irreg.)*
company compañía
compassionate compasivo
complain quejarse (de)
complete completo
consent consentir (ie, i) (en)
consolation consuelo
contemporary contemporáneo
continue seguir (i, i), continuar
cook *(v.)* cocinar, cocer (ue), guisar
copper cobre *m.*
correct *(v.)* corregir (i, i)
cost *(v.)* costar (ue)
count *(v.)* contar (ue)
country país *m.* (**nation**); campo (**opp. of city**)
courage valor *m.*
court corte *f.,* tribunal *m.*
crazy loco; **to drive ____** volver loco; **to go ____** volverse loco
create crear
crime crimen *m.*
crown corona
cry llorar
cup taza

D

dance baile *m.; (v.)* bailar
danger peligro
dangerous peligroso

dark oscuro; **to get ____** anochecer (zc)
day día; **the ____ after tomorrow**
    pasado mañana
deal: a great ____ mucho
dear querido (**beloved**); caro (**expensive**)
declare declarar
depend (on) depender (de)
desk mesa
diamond diamante *m.*
die morir (ue, u)
difficult difícil
difficulty dificultad
diligent aplicado, hacendoso
divorce divorcio; **to get a ____**
    divorciarse
do hacer *(irreg.)*
doctor médico(-a); doctor(-a)
dog perro
dollar dólar *m.*
door puerta
down abajo; **____ the street** calle
    abajo
dozen docena
dress vestido; *(v.)* vestir(se) (i, i)
drink *(v.)* beber; tomar
drive *(v.)* conducir (zc), manejar

E

eagle (el) águila *f.*
ear oreja
early temprano
earn ganar
easy fácil
eat comer
either o; **____ . . .or** o ... o
eldest mayor
end fin *m.;* final *m.*
engagement compromiso
England Inglaterra
English inglés, inglesa; **____ man**
    inglés *m.*
enjoy gozar (de); **____ oneself**
    divertise (ie, i)
enough bastante
establish establecer (zc), fundar
even though aunque
everyone todo el mundo
everything todo; todo lo que
evidently evidentemente
exam examen *m.*
exist existir

expensive caro
extremely sumamente,
    extremadamente
eye ojo

F

fall caer(se); **to ____ in love (with)**
    enamorarse (de)
falling *(n.)* caída; el caer
fast rápido, ligero
fat gordo
father padre
father-in-law suegro; **____ and**
    mother-in-law suegros
fattening: is less ____ engorda menos
favor favor *m.;* **to be in ____ of** estar
    por
favorite favorito, preferido; predilecto
feed dar de comer
feel sentir (ie, i); sentirse
female hembra
fiancé(e) novio (-a)
figuratively en sentido figurado
film película
finally al fin, por fin, finalmente
finger dedo
first primer(o); **at ____** al principio;
    for the ____ time por primera vez
fish pez *m. (in water)*; pescado
fit caber *(irreg.)*
flower flor *f.*
follow seguir (i, i)
food comida
fool tonto
football fútbol (americano)
for por; para
forbid prohibir
foreign extranjero
forget olvidar, olvidarse (de)
fork tenedor *m.*
former aquél, etc.
France Francia
French francés, francesa; **____ man**
    francés *m.*
Friday viernes *m.*
friend amigo, (-a); **boy ____** novio;
    girl ____ novia
frog rana
fruit fruta; **____ tree** árbol frutal
fun: to make ____ (of) burlarse (de)
future futuro

G

game juego, partido (**match**)
garden jardín *m.*
generous generoso
German alemán, alemana; *m.* alemán
get recibir; conseguir (i, i); obtener; coger; **to ___ good grades** sacar buenas notas; **to ___ up** levantarse; **to ___ married** casarse
gift regalo
give dar *(irreg.)*
girl muchacha, chica
glad contento, alegre
go ir *(irreg.);* **to ___ away** irse; **to ___ out** salir *(irreg.);* **to ___ to bed** acostarse (ue)
gold oro
grade nota
great gran(de)
green verde
guest huésped *m.;* invitado

H

habit costumbre; **bad ___** vicio
half *(adj.)* medio; *(n.)* mitad
hand mano *f.;* **on the other ___** en cambio
handsome guapo
happily felizmente
happiness felicidad
happy feliz, alegre
hard duro; difícil; fuerte
hasten (to) apresurarse (a)
hat sombrero
have tener *(irreg.);* **to ___ a good time** divertirse (ie, i)
hello hola
help *(v.)* ayudar
henceforth en adelante
Henry VIII Enrique Octavo
here aquí; acá; **right ___** aquí mismo
high alto
history historia
hit *(v.)* pegar, golpear; chocar (con) **(collide)**
home casa; **at ___** en casa
hope *(v.)* esperar
hot caliente; **it is ___** hace (mucho) calor; **to be ___** tener (mucho) calor

hour hora
house casa
how como; cómo; qué tal; lo ... que; **___ much?** ¿cuánto?; **___many?** ¿cuántos (-as)?
hunger (el) hambre *f.;* **to be (very) hungry** tener (mucha) hambre
hurry prisa; **to be in a ___** tener prisa
hurt hacer daño; doler (ue); **to get ___** hacerse daño
husband marido, esposo

I

ice cream helado
idea idea
ideal ideal
impede impedir (i, i)
important importante
impossible imposible
improve mejorar
incidentally a propósito
incredible increíble
independence independencia
insist (on) insistir (en)
instead: ___ of en vez de
insurance seguro; **___ policy** póliza de seguro
intelligent inteligente
interest *(v.)* interesar
invisible invisible
Italian italiano

J

jokester bromista; burlón, burlona
judge juez *m.* or *f.*
just: to have ___ acabar de + *inf.*

K

keep guardar; **___ on** seguir (i, i) + *pres. part.*
kids chicos
kilometer kilómetro
kind amable
king rey; **petty ___** reyezuelo
kiss beso; *(v.)* besar; **little ___** besito
knife cuchillo
know saber *(irreg.);* conocer (zc)

L

language lengua; idioma *m.*
last último; pasado; ___ **night** anoche; ___ **week** la semana pasada
late tarde; **it is getting** ___ se hace tarde; **to be (arrive)** ___ llegar tarde
later más tarde, despúes
latter éste, etc.
laugh (at) reír(se) (de)
lead conducir (zc); ___ **a life** llevar una vida
learn aprender; ___ **(find out)** saber
leave salir *(irreg.)* (de), irse; **to** ___ **(behind)** dejar, abandonar
left izquierdo; **to the** ___ a la izquierda
lend prestar
less menos; **the** ___ ... **the** ___ cuanto menos ... (tanto) menos
lesson lección
letter carta
liar mentiroso (-a)
life vida
like como; *(v.)* querer; gustar; **I would** ___ quisiera, me gustaría
listen escuchar
little poco; pequeño; ___ **by** ___ poco a poco
long largo; ___ **time** largo tiempo; **how** ___ ? ¿cuánto tiempo?
look mirar; parecer (zc); **to** ___ **for** buscar
lot: a ___ **of** mucho
Louis XIV Luis Catorce
love amor *m.;* amar, querer *(irreg.);* **to fall in** ___ **(with)** enamorarse (de)
lunch almuerzo; **to have** ___ almorzar (ue), tomar el almuerzo

M

maid criada
majority la mayor parte, mayoría
make hacer *(irreg.)*
male varón
man hombre
many muchos; **how** ___ ? ¿cuántos (-as)?
map mapa *m.*

market mercado; **super** ___ supermercado
marry casar(se) (con)
marvelous maravilloso
mathematics matemáticas
matter asunto; cosa; **no** ___ **how little (he studies)** por poco que (estudia, estudie); **what's the** ___ ? ¿qué pasa? ¿qué tiene?
meal comida
mean *(v.)* querer decir, significar
medicine medicina
meet encontrar (ue) **(run into);** conocer (zc) **(make the acquaintance of)**
Mexico México
middle medio; **around the** ___ **of the (month)** a mediados del (mes)
midnight medianoche *f.*
milk leche *f.*
mind mente *f.*
miss echar de menos, extrañar
mom mamá
Monday lunes
money dinero
month mes *m.*
moon luna; **the** ___ **is out** hay luna
more más; **the** ___ ... **the** ___ cuanto más ... (tanto) más
morning mañana; **in the** ___ por la mañana; **(with hour)** de la mañana
mother madre, mamá; ___ **-in-law** suegra
mouse ratón *m.*, ratoncito
movies cine *m.*
much mucho; **too** ___ desmasiado; **very** ___ muchísimo
murder matar; asesinar
must deber; **(obligation)** tener que + *inf.;* **(probability)** *future or conditional or* deber (de)
mysterious misterioso

N

napkin servilleta
necessary necesario; **it is** ___ es necesario, es preciso, hay que
need necesitar; hacer falta
neither ni; ___ ... **nor** ni ... ni
nevertheless sin embargo
next próximo, siguiente

nice simpático
night noche *f.;* at ____ de noche; por
   la noche; last ____ anoche
nonsense tontería; ____ ! ¡qué va!
nor ni
not no; ____ at all de ninguna
   manera, de ningún modo; ¡qué va!
nothing nada; to have ____ to do
   with no tener nada que ver con
novel novela
novelist novelista *m.* or *f.*
now ahora
nowadays hoy (en) día
nurse enfermera (for the sick)

O

o'clock: it is one ____ es la una; it is
   two ____ son las dos
of course ¡por supuesto!, ¡claro!
often a menudo, muchas veces
old viejo; ____ -er más viejo; mayor;
   how ____ is he? ¿cuántos años
   tiene? ¿qué edad tiene?; to be
   (eight) years ____ tener (ocho) años
only solamente, sólo
open *(v.)* abrir; *(adj.)* abierto
order *(v.)* mandar, ordenar; pedir;
   in ____ to para
other otro
owe deber

P

pack: ____ one's bag(s) hacer la(s)
   maleta(s)
package paquete *m.*
pale pálido
paper papel *m.*
parents padres *m.*
part parte *f.;* the bad ____ lo malo
party fiesta
pass *(v.)* pasar; ____ an exam salir
   bien en un examen
pay pagar; ____ attention prestar
   atención; (heed) hacer caso
peace paz *f.;* to keep ____ mantener
   la paz
peaceful tranquilo
pencil lápiz *m.*
perhaps acaso, quizá(s), tal vez
person persona
petty king reyezuelo

philosophy filosofía
piano piano
pick *(v.)* escoger; ____ up recoger,
   coger
picture foto *(f.),* retrato; (film)
   película
plate plato
play tocar (an instrument);
   jugar (ue) a (a game)
pleasure gusto; placer *m.;* with ____
   con mucho gusto
policy póliza (insurance); política
   (governmental); insurance ____
   póliza de seguro
poor pobre
popcorn rosetas de maíz
popular popular
Portuguese portugués *m.; (adj.)*
   portugués, portuguesa
possible posible
powerful poderoso
prefer preferir (ie, i)
president presidente *m.*
pretty lindo, bonito, hermoso
prevent impedir (i, i)
price precio
problem problema *m.*
promise *(v.)* prometer
provided that con tal (de) que
put poner *(irreg.)*

Q

quality cualidad (personal); calidad
   (material)
question pregunta; to ask a ____
   hacer una pregunta
quiet callado (silent); tranquilo; to
   keep ____ callar(se)

R

rabbit conejo
rain lluvia; *(v.)* llover (ue)
read leer
reality realidad
realize darse cuenta (de);
   (accomplish) realizar
really realmente, verdaderamente, de
   veras
reason razón *f.* recommend
   recomendar (ie)
record player tocadiscos *m.*

red rojo
reflect reflejar
refuse *(v.)* no querer, negarse (ie) (a), rehusar
regret *(v.)* sentir (ie, i)
remain quedar(se)
repeat repetir (i, i)
reply *(v.)* contestar, responder
rest *(v.)* descansar
restaurant restaurante *m.*, restorán *m.*
return volver (ue), regresar; **(give back)** devolver (ue)
rich rico
right derecho; **to be** ____ tener razón; ____ **now** ahora mismo
ring sortija, anillo
rise *(v.)* subir, levantarse; ____ **up (rebel)** levantarse, rebelarse
run correr

S

sake: for (her) ____ por (ella)
Saturday sábado
saucer platillo
say decir *(irreg.); that* is to ____ es decir
school escuela; **to have** ____ **(classes)** tener clase(s)
scoundrel sinvergüenza *m.* or *f.*
seat asiento
see ver *(irreg.)*
seem parecer (zc)
select escoger
sell vender
send enviar, mandar
sentence frase *f.*, oración
September se(p)tiembre
sharp agudo; afilado; **(with the hour)** en punto
shopping: to go ____ ir de compras
short corto; bajo; **after a** ____ **while** al poco rato
should deber
sick enfermo, malo
sign letrero, cartel *m.*
silver plata
since ya que, puesto que, como; **(time)** desde
sincerely sinceramente
sing cantar
sister hermana

sit **(down)** sentarse (ie)
sleep sueño; *(v.)* dormir (ue, u); **to be** ____ **-y** tener sueño
slightest menor
slow despacio, lento; ____ **-ly** despacio, lentamente
smart inteligente, listo
smile *(v.)* sonreír(se)
smoke *(v.)* fumar
snow nieve *f.; (v.)* nevar (ie)
snowball bola de nieve
so así; tan; ____ **much the better (worse)** tanto mejor (peor)
sociology sociología
something algo
sometimes algunas veces, a veces
son hijo
soon pronto; **as** ____ **as possible** cuanto antes, lo más pronto posible
sorry: to be ____ sentir (ie, i)
soul (el) alma *f.*
soup sopa
Spaniard español *m.;* española *f.*
Spanish español, española
speak hablar
spoon cuchara
stadium estadio
stand **(up)** levantarse
state estado
stay quedar(se)
still todavía; aún
stone piedra
stop *(v.)* **(pause)** detener(se), parar(se); **(cease)** dejar de
story cuento, historia
street calle *f.*
strict severo, estricto
strike *(v.)* ____ **the hour** dar la hora
strong fuerte
student estudiante *m.* or *f.*
study estudiar
stupid estúpido, bruto
succeed lograr; conseguir (i, i); tener éxito
successful: to be ____ tener éxito
suddenly de repente, de pronto
sugar azúcar *m.*
summer verano
Sunday domingo

support (provide for) mantener
   (*irreg.*)
surprised sorprendido; to be ____
   sorprenderse, estar sorprendido
sweep (*v.*) barrer
sweetheart novio (-a)
swim (*v.*) nadar

T

tablecloth mantel *m.*
take tomar; llevar; ____ for tomar
   por; ____ away quitar;
   ____ out sacar
talk hablar
tall alto
tea té *m.*
teacher maestro (-a); profesor(a)
teaspoon cucharita
television televisión
tell decir (*irreg.*)
tennis tenis *m.*
terrible terrible
than que; del que, etc.
thanks gracias
that que; ese, etc.; eso; aquel, etc;
   aquello
then entonces; luego, después
there ahí, allí, allá; ____ is (are) hay;
   ____ was (were) había, hubo;
   ____ will be habrá
thief ladrón *m.*
thin delgado
thing cosa
think creer, pensar (ie)
this este, esta; esto
throw tirar, arrojar
Thursday jueves *m.*
time tiempo; hora; vez; at the same
   ____ al mismo tiempo, a la vez; at
   this ____ a estas horas; for the
   first ____ por primera vez; from
   _ to ____ de vez en cuando;
   it is ____ to es hora de; on ____
   a tiempo; to have a good ____
   divertirse (ie, i); what ____ is it?
   ¿qué hora es?
tipsy borrachito
tired cansado
title título
today hoy
tomorrow mañana

too también; demasiado; ____ much
   demasiado
touch (*v.*) tocar
traffic tráfico
translate traducir (zc)
tree árbol *m.*
trip viaje *m.*; to take a ____ hacer un
   viaje
true verdadero; it is ____ es verdad
try tratar (de)
Tuesday martes *m.*
turn (*v.*) (corner, page) doblar

U

ugly feo
umbrella paraguas *m.*
uncle tío
understand entender (ie), comprender
unfortunate desafortunado
United States Estados Unidos
universal universal
university universidad
unless a menos que
until hasta; hasta que

V

vacation vacaciones *f. pl.*
visit (*v.*) visitar
vocabulary vocabulario

W

wait (for) esperar
wake up despertar(se) (ie)
walk (*v.*) andar (*irreg.*), caminar
want querer (*irreg.*)
warm caliente; it is ____ hace calor;
   to be ____ tener calor (person)
waste (*v.*) gastar; ____ time perder
   (el) tiempo
watch reloj *m.*; (*v.*) mirar; ____
   television mirar la televisión
water (el) agua *f.*
way camino; manera, modo; by the
   ____ a propósito
wealth riqueza
wear (*v.*) llevar
weather tiempo; the ____ is good
   (bad) hace buen (mal) tiempo
wedding boda
Wednesday miércoles *m.*
week semana

well bien
what qué; lo que; ¡qué!; ___ is
  beautiful lo bello, lo hermoso
whatever cualquier cosa; lo que
when cuando
which que; el que, etc.; lo que; el
  cual, etc.; lo cual; ___ ? ¿qué?
  ¿cuál?; ___ one(s)? ¿cuál(-es)?
while mientras (que); rato; after a
  short ___ al poco rato
white blanco
who que, quien, el cual, el que
whose cuyo; ___ ? ¿de quién(-es)?
wife mujer *f.,* esposa
window ventana
wine vino
winter invierno
wish querer *(irreg.);* I ___   ¡ojalá! ...

with con; ___ me conmigo;
  ___ you *(fam.)* contigo
without sin (que)
woman mujer *f.*
work trabajar
world mundo
worse peor
worth valer *(irreg.);* to be ___ while
  valer la pena
would that . . . ¡ojalá! (que) ...
write escribir
writer escritor(-a)

Y

year año
yellow amarillo
yesterday ayer
young joven; ___ -er más joven;
  menor

Index